BYRNE'S
WONDERFUL WORLD OF
POOL
AND
BILLIARDS

ALSO BY ROBERT BYRNE

Byrne's Standard Book of Pool and Billiards

Byrne's Treasury of Trick Shots in Pool and Billiards

Byrne's Advanced Technique in Pool and Billiards

Byrne's Book of Great Pool Stories

BYRNE'S
WONDERFUL WORLD OF
POOL
AND
BILLIARDS

A Cornucopia of Instruction, Strategy, Anecdote, and Colorful Characters

ROBERT BYRNE

Harcourt Brace & Company
New York   San Diego   London

For Mike "The Amazing" Shamos

*Other sports and games
should be so lucky.*

Requests for permission to make copies of any part
of the work should be mailed to:
Permissions Department,
Harcourt Brace & Company,
6277 Sea Harbor Drive, Orlando, Florida 32887-6777.

Library of Congress Cataloging-in-Publication Data
Byrne, Robert, 1930–
Byrne's wonderful world of pool and billiards: a cornucopia of instruction,
strategy, anecdote, and colorful characters/Robert Byrne.—1st ed.
p.   cm.
Includes bibliographical references.
ISBN 0-15-100166-9 (hardcover).—
ISBN 0-15-600222-1 (A Harvest original pbk.)
1. Pool (Game). 2. Billiards.   I. Title.
GV891.B966   1996
794.7´3—dc20   96-22255

Text set in Bembo and ITC Grouch   Designed by Steve Lux Design

Printed in the United States of America
First edition   A C E D B

Permissions and acknowledgments appear on p. 260,
which constitutes a continuation of the copyright page.

Cover illustration: That's a young Willie Mosconi shooting a pool ball
off the mouth of old-time comic singer Jerry Colonna. A contemplative
Sang Lee chalks his cue while Jay Bozeman (left) and Welker Cochran
(right), former billiard greats, prepare to strike their cueballs.
At the lower left is Joe Davis, once the world's best in both
English billiards and snooker.

CONTENTS

PART ④
The Games People Play   149

PART ⑤
The Players and Their World   187

PART ⑥
The Books of the Game   249

"I always chalk up just before I would have miscued."
—New York Fatty, as quoted by Hal Mix

Introduction

The chapters in *Byrne's Advanced Technique in Pool and Billiards* were adapted from articles I wrote for *Billiards Digest* from its inception in 1978 to 1990. The present volume retrieves a few more pieces from that period but comprises mainly material published in the magazine between 1990 and the present.

This time I cast the net a little wider: the subject matter covers far more ground than any of my previous books. You'll find instruction on both pool and billiards, as well as profiles of some of the game's most colorful characters. There are selections on demographics, videotaping, collecting billiard memorabilia, alternative games, new books, and what a pool hall would be like in heaven. I've included a profile of old-time master Welker Cochran, with excerpts newly added from his handwritten letters, which first appeared in *The National Bowlers Journal and Billiard Review* in 1973. The essay on watching televised snooker by British newspaperman Oliver Pritchett appears for the first time in the United States. Some of the material—such as my reminiscence of "Minnesota Fats" and the pictorial essay on coping with sore losers—was written especially for this book. The world of pool and billiards is indeed wide as well as wonderful.

Mr. Pritchett is not the only guest author. There are also J. B. Priestley and Stephen Potter. *At Thurston's* and *How to Win Without Actually Cheating* are among my favorite pieces of writing about the game. My thanks to the copyright holders of those pieces for permission to reprint.

Much has changed in the six years since the publication of *Advanced Technique.* The explosive growth in the popularity of cue games around the world, which I mentioned in the introduction to that book, shows no sign of slowing. Ed Wright, publisher of *Cue Sports Journal,* estimates that in 1990 there were 15 pool halls in Northern California, the circulation area of his monthly tabloid. Five years ago there were 50. Today there are 150.

Magnificent upscale billiard rooms continue to open in major cities. In October of 1995, *Billiards Digest* ranked a dozen of the most impressive new establishments in its seventh annual architectural design issue. When I was a lad, it would have been unthinkable to suggest design awards for pool halls. Who would have sponsored the competition in those days? The makers of spittoons?

Pool is more popular than ever in advertising and show business. It's hard to get through a day without seeing the game depicted in some way in a magazine or on television.

Billiards Digest has changed. It has more color. There is more flash and glamour. It's thicker, too. The December 1990 edition—to pick a copy from my shelf at random—has 94 total pages; in December of 1995 the total is 128. Other months show similar growth.

I've changed in the last six years, too. Like *Billiards Digest,* I've gotten thicker. Glamour and flash are still missing, but I've grown more colorful, especially in the nose and eyes. I've been busy adding to my oeuvre. Two videos on trick shots were marketed by Premiere Home Video in 1993; *Byrne's Book of Great Pool Stories* was published by Harcourt Brace in 1995. In 1995 and 1996, Accu-Stats Video Productions released *The Best of Three-Cushion, I & II,* for which I supplied the narration. The biggest change for me came in June of 1995, when after forty-two years in California, I moved back to my old hometown in Iowa.

It was in 1990 that Accu-Stats added a second camera to its coverage of pool tournaments, greatly increasing the quality of its product. We take pool and billiard videos for granted now, but six years ago good ones were scarce. The growing library of good videotapes on cue games is a tremendous educational resource that wasn't available to earlier generations of students.

Even the terms *cue games* and *cue sports* are new. I'm not crazy about them, but I'm forced to use them for reasons of clarity. The trouble with *billiards* as a general term is that too many writers and organizations in the United States now use it as a synonym for *pool*. If billiards is pool, then what are carom games played on pocketless tables? The Professional Billiards Tour, the Camel Pro Billiards Series, the Women's Professional Billiard Association, all are concerned with pool, not billiards. The United States Billiard Association covers three-cushion. Unthinking writers sometimes produce tournament reports in which it is hard to tell which game was played.

One can understand the reluctance to use the clumsy and effete term *pocket billiards,* which was dreamed up by manufacturers before World War I in an effort to escape the negative connotations attached to the word *pool*. Wouldn't it be better to come right out and call pool *pool?* There's nothing to be ashamed of. Everybody should follow the lead of one hundred thousand league players who call themselves, proudly and plainly, the American Poolplayers Association—unless, of course, they are billiard players.

A significant change in recent years is the emergence of the Women's Professional Billiard Association (they play pool) into one of the world's most successful player groups. They do it right. They dress well, they behave like professionals, they attract television and sponsors, they present a unified front to promoters. After spending seventeen years as a kind of poor sister to the men's groups, they opted for independence in 1993 and came up with a tour paying $400,000 in prize money. Through a campaign of marketing and promotion that has been nothing short of brilliant, they pushed the total prize fund up to $1,000,000 for the 1996 calendar year. The men, divided into several bickering factions, look in amazement at lists of top ten money winners, half of which are now women. In 1995 Loree Jon Jones chalked up $98,000 in prize winnings, far more than anybody won on the men's tour. Talk about changes!

Someone once said that the life of a writer is partly looking back and being surprised at how much has been produced. I've been writing about the game for thirty years. If I had been, say, gardening instead, I'd have a colossal compost heap by now, which is what occurs to me when I look at my literary output. Never could I have imagined at the beginning that I would find so much to say about what is, after all, just a game. But what a game!—so many layers, such a long history, such an intriguing subculture, so many characters! I am in constant danger of sinking into it entirely and never seeing polite society again.

Assembling a collection of your own writing is like creating a Frankenstein's monster from salvaged parts. There is fat to cut through, vital organs to repair, gristle to discard, sutures to make. Always there is a feeling of dismay at the size of the undertaking. Now the job is finished. Nothing more to do but stand back and see if the villagers cry, "It's alive!"

My Wonderful World of Pool and Billiards

Once again, Robert Byrne fails to avoid publicity. The photo was taken by
Billiards Digest **editor Mike Panozzo at the 1988 Billiard Congress trade show in**
Louisville, Kentucky. It is Byrne's favorite photo because on the placard
he is listed first and Willie Mosconi last.

(Photograph by Mike Panozzo, reprinted courtesy of Mike Panozzo)

Another Golden Age Is upon Us

WHILE POOL AND BILLIARDS will almost certainly never again achieve the level of popularity they enjoyed during the so-called Golden Age of the game—from about 1890 to 1930—there are reasons for believing that the current boom is not just a flash in the pan. The surge of interest following the movie *The Hustler* in 1961 didn't last long; the current surge, sparked in 1986 by *The Color of Money,* is a bigger and different animal entirely. Why?

Consider these factors: (1) Immigration is rising; (2) Couples are getting married later; (3) Women are entering the game in a big way.

Sociology professor Ned Polsky, in his stimulating and insightful book, *Hustlers, Beats, and Others,* published in 1967, showed the relation between billiards and broad social trends. Immigration rose from less than three million in the decade of the 1870s, to more than eight million in the decade from 1901 to 1910, falling off to less than one million in the 1930s. The figures correlate well with the rise and fall of pool halls in this country. Immigrants, for reasons of language, economics, and discrimination, tend to marry later than the native-born. The more bachelors there are, the more business for pool halls. This was especially true in the old days, when pool halls served as all-male refuges for those who couldn't afford or didn't want to belong to private clubs.

Weddings were bad news for the owners of pool halls. Pool was overwhelmingly a man's game, and when a man got married he tended to hang up his cue. Wife, family, and mortgage required his full attention, and it was typical that he was lost to the game until he was divorced, widowed, fired, or retired.

The average groom in 1890 was 26.1 years old, a figure that steadily declined to 22.8 in 1950, when the game was in deep doldrums. (Brides average about three years younger than grooms, a figure that hasn't changed much in a hundred years.) As the marriage age declines, the reservoir of bachelors dries up, and billiard rooms suffer.

Professor Polsky, an avid player himself, was gloomy about the future of the game when he wrote his book thirty years ago. Immigration totaled less than three million in the previous decade, and the average American man was getting married when he was less than twenty-three years old, an all-time low. Further, the need for an all-male subculture was disappearing. Not only were there fewer bachelors than in the Golden Age, married men no longer expected to have weekly nights out with "the boys." Women weren't a significant presence in the game, and bar leagues were just beginning. Polsky saw no sign that the basic demographic and social trends would reverse themselves.

What do you say now, professor? The trends have, in fact, turned around. Immigration has jumped from less than three million in the decade of the 1950s to more than seven million in the 1980s, the highest total since the turn of the century. The average age at which a man gets married now has risen to 26.1, exactly what it was a hundred years ago, when the Golden Age was beginning to shine. Furthermore, when couples get married now, there's a chance they both have jobs and like to play pool after work. Then, there is divorce as a source of customers for pool halls. Since 1970, the divorce rate has tripled.

The arrival of women didn't result in the death of the public room. Quite the contrary. Instead of sending men into a panicked retreat, women in the game have given it a tremendous economic boost. One in three or four of all players now is female, and some estimate that the majority of *new* players are. Resisted and resented as perfumed invaders at first, women now are accepted in pool halls and on bar league teams as a matter of course.

Fifty and more years ago, men may have needed pool halls as an escape from their wives, their many children, and the stultifying propriety of small-town America. The situation now is strikingly different. Women are no longer housebound, they are having fewer children, and they are having them later. Women go everywhere that men do, and that includes into pool halls and bar leagues.

The pool hall in American society has undergone an amazing transformation in a few short years. Now it's a place to take a date or a spouse . . .

LEGAL IMMIGRATION TO THE UNITED STATES

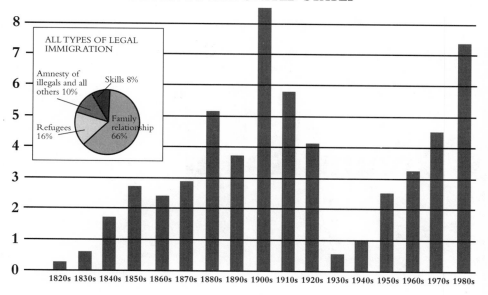

Immigration by decade in millions of immigrants

Data from U.S. Immigration and Naturalization Services

or to meet someone who might be interested in becoming one or the other. Room owners are well-advised to make sure their establishments are attractive to women. In some areas, they might also consider hiring someone who speaks Spanish, Vietnamese, or Korean.

A hundred years ago, the new arrivals in America were mainly European; now they are mainly Hispanic and Asian. The numbers are as impressive now as they were a century ago. In California, for example, there were three million immigrants in the last ten years, which is one-tenth the state's population. The newcomers are finding it harder to become assimilated than the earlier Caucasians, but their presence in billiard rooms is already noticeable in many areas of the country. Foreign-born players represent the difference between profit and loss in many rooms.

While the public billiard room is the most visible barometer of the game, especially the hundreds of upscale and even glamorous rooms that have opened in recent years, it is not the only one. More pool is played by far in taverns on coin-operated tables than in pool halls, and even more is played at home.

Why is the game booming? The answer lies in immigration and marriage statistics, the liberation of women, and the explosive growth in tavern pool. *The Color of Money* was merely the spark that started the fire. This time, the fire isn't as likely to die out.

My Dream Room

DECADES OF SPARE TIME spent knocking balls around with cues in public poolrooms has left me with strong feelings about what I like and don't like about them. Because new rooms continue to blossom at a breathtaking pace, I'll make my secret desires known in the hope of influencing a proprietor or two or three—especially if they are businessmen who have never had pool as a hobby or obsession.

The subject isn't trivial. A pool hall can fill a vital community function as a gathering and meeting place. It can broaden your horizons by enabling you to spend convivial hours with people different from yourself. A few years ago sociologist Ray Oldenburg wrote a book called *The Great Good Place,* in which he stresses the importance of "a third place." Work and home aren't enough in our segregated and homogenized society. To enrich and deepen life, you also need a place to go that isn't home and isn't work, a place to socialize with people of every class, type, age, and occupation.

In Europe there is the café, the trattoria, the taverna, and the pub. Nothing in America brings communities and neighborhoods together in quite the same way, except the billiard room. Where I usually play, my opponents include a tow-truck driver, an orchid grower, a restaurant owner, a mathematician, a college student, a shoe-store clerk, a retired teacher, a gas-station attendant, a rock musician, a computer programmer, and an American Indian who refinishes furniture. Where else could I get to know such a varied cross section of the local community? Not at a bar, where boozing and cruising are the main pursuits and where the patrons tend to be more of a type.

The wish list that follows is from the point of view of a player. Some of the suggestions will be dismissed by owners because they cost money. But they aren't *that* costly, especially when you consider the profit potential of a large and loyal clientele. It's easy to conjure up heavenly features without regard for cost, like a rack girl for every table, free lessons and practice time, new cloth once a month, etc., but what I have in mind are practical suggestions that pay dividends in the long run.

WHAT I LIKE IN A POOL HALL

1. Stuff on the walls: artwork, posters, announcements, memorabilia, snapshots, clippings, tournament results. In a new room, I always make a circuit of the walls and examine everything. I like to see evidence that the management is interested in the game and in communicating with its customers.

2. A comfortable place to sit and talk, spread a newspaper, or play a game of chess or checkers. That means some sort of cocktail tables or booths with *good lighting*. I've been in otherwise excellent rooms in which the only way to read a paper or magazine was to hold it under the light at a pool table.

3. Plenty of places for players to sit. You can't have too many stools. People won't play long if they have to stand between shots, or if they have to stand while waiting for a table. Players are more apt to quit when they're tired than when they're out of money. What if one member of a party doesn't want to play? Unless he or she has a comfortable seat, the party will soon be gone.

4. A good place to spectate. Ideal is an elevated bar area with cocktail tables and a railing. With that arrangement you can watch a game without being intrusive. A couple of rows of tiered theater seats is best, but not many rooms can afford the space.

5. Semiprivate tables. People like bowling not just because they can noisily knock things down. When you bowl, you have your own area with comfortable padded seats and a table to rest your elbows on. Nobody walks in front of you or bumps into you. No unwanted spectator can join your group. Why don't billiard rooms borrow the idea? Develop a floor plan that gives at least some tables a modicum

of privacy. In one corner, for example, set off a few tables with elevated padded benches, each with its own cocktail table. Or if the room hasn't the space for that, mark a few tables off from the rest of the room with planter boxes and provide extra chairs or stools. Those will be popular tables, I guarantee it, especially with groups, couples on dates, and shy beginners trying to learn the game.

6. No salt-lick talc dispensers! I hate those things. They encourage players to cover their hands, clothes, and tables with white powder. Small canisters of talc are a little better, especially if most of the holes are taped shut. Some daredevil owner should break new ground in customer service by providing damp and dry hand towels at each table along with a piece of Scotch-Brite. That would be a wonderful display of awareness of and concern for the players, from whom all profits flow. Keep the talcum at the desk for use on only the most stubborn cases of sweaty hands and sticky cues. Push the sale of silk gloves. Set out some of those large chalk cubes you see in European billiard clubs that are designed to be rubbed on fingers.

7. Carpeting. It's too tiring to stand on hardwood floors, linoleum, or tile no matter how beautiful it is.

8. Straight house cues with decent tips. Is that asking too much?

9. Unobtrusive music. Loud jukeboxes are for bars and dance halls. If you must have intrusive music, at least take the loudspeakers out of one area. Many rooms now ask arriving patrons if they want to play in the smoking or non-smoking section. How about adding a choice of noisy or peaceful?

10. A variety of games. I like a room that has at least one snooker and billiard table, even if they don't make as much money as the pool tables. A common story is that proprietors let the snooker and billiard tables run down, or they cover them with cheap cloth, which drives the players away. The tables are then replaced with pool tables because "nobody plays snooker or billiards." It's boring to have only pool.

11. An occasional freebie. Nothing makes a customer happier than to get a token of appreciation from the management once in a while, like a free drink or an hour of free play. There's a bagel diner across the road from Boca Billiards in Florida where the waiters and waitresses have the power to reward customers by picking up their checks. The place is always packed.

12. Under-the-table baskets. Put your coat, hat, purse, books, and cue case in a rolling bin or basket that fits under the table and you won't have to worry about them while you're playing. Okay, so they are a nuisance for the guy who has to vacuum the place.

13. Employees who are neatly dressed and friendly. I don't want to get my tray of balls from a surly slob. I want to deal with people who smile and pretend to be glad to see me.

14. House players. Several local players, maybe retirees, should be given free table time to encourage them to spend a lot of time in the room and be available to play with customers who don't like to practice alone. In exchange for table time, house players can do a little teaching.

15. Beads. For keeping score, there is simply no substitute for overhead strings of beads. Both players can watch what the other is doing when points are added to the string, and the score is easy to see for players and spectators alike. Does your interior designer feel that strings of beads are visual distractions? Tell him to take a hike.

16. A bridge at every table. It's aggravating to go on a scavenger hunt when you can't reach a shot.

17. Decent chalk. Giving players deeply worn chalk is too cheap for words.

18. Clean balls and brushed tables. Keep the cubes of chalk out of the ball trays, please!

19. Lots of events. Weekly handicap tournaments for local players, a regional tournament a couple of times a year so the regulars can see and play against top players, and an exhibition by a touring pro once a year or so. The house loses table time during tournaments, and somebody has to plan and run them, but they are the best way of building business.

20. Good cloth on the tables, clean rest rooms, smoke-free areas, waste-baskets, and lots of places to set down a drink. One reason drinks get spilled on tables is that there are so few other places to put them.

21. Informed desk people. Here's something that bugs me. A room puts on a tournament, and when I phone to get the standings or results, the person who answers doesn't know anything about it. Proprietors!

Chandeliers and formal clothing don't make a first-class billiard room. What it takes is good equipment, an attention to detail, and a consideration of the player's point of view.

Do something about this! Keep your desk people informed about what's going on.

22. House rules. The basic rules for every game played in a room should be in writing and posted on the wall. It seems obvious, but few rooms go to the trouble. To settle arguments over fine points, players can resort to the BCA rule book at the desk.

23. Books, magazines, and videotapes. In some rooms, there is no indication that the owners know or care about the larger world of pool and billiards. Because newspapers and television ignore the sport, it's up to room owners to show that pool is a major game worthy of serious interest. Pool magazines and books should be available at the desk. Tournament tapes should be available for both sale and rent, and should be played on in-house television monitors.

By all of these means and others, casual, once-in-a-while players can be converted into serious students of the game.

Return to Tinseltown

IT WAS DÉJÀ VU ALL OVER AGAIN, or did I say that before? There I was, back on a Hollywood sound stage shooting pool shots in front of fifteen technicians while three video cameras captured every miscue on tape. The set this time was decorated in Southwestern hues, rather like the lobby of the La Fonda Hotel in Santa Fe, New Mexico. Once again I was followed around by a woman with a powder puff whose only job was to make sure my nose didn't steal the show.

Speaking of noses, the day before shooting began I was standing behind the Hollywood Roosevelt Hotel, waiting for the parking lot's stunt driver to fetch my rent-a-heap, when a limo pulled up and deposited Dick Van Dyke practically in my lap. His nose, I was excited to see, was every bit as powerful and outstanding as my own. He was gone before I could compliment him on it. Van Dyke was in the neighborhood to be honored with a star on the famous Hollywood Sidewalk of Stars. During the televised unveiling ceremony, he noticed that his name in the concrete was misspelled! It was a bad omen.

In *Byrne's Advanced Technique* (1990), I described my experiences with Premiere Home Video in making *Byrne's Standard Video of Pool, Volumes I and II.* The few pool tapes on the market then were modest affairs, some of them hardly more than home movies featuring a top player explaining the basics to a fixed camera. While I intended to raise the standard if I could, I wasn't prepared for the production Premiere had in mind. I was blown away by the sound stage, the set, the big crew, the advance planning, the detailed script, the computer graphics, etc., etc.

My idea of how to make a profit is to keep expenses as close to zero as possible. Premiere's approach is to spend whatever is necessary to produce the best possible tapes. I remember being glad that none of my money was involved. The machine for adding computer graphics, for example, rents for five hundred dollars an hour.

The tapes were still selling well, and so it came to pass in early 1993 that Premiere wanted to crank up its cameras again. This time the goal was to create two tapes on trick shots, to be called Volumes III and IV.

But which trick shots, and how should the subject be approached? There are three hundred of the things in *Byrne's Treasury of Trick Shots,* and at least a hundred more have been invented in the fourteen years since that book came out. Mike Massey, Paul Gerni, Willie Jopling, Rick Wright, Larry Grindinger, Anton Riniti, and others come up with new shots and variations all the time. I have a stack of diagrams a foot high sent to me by readers of my books and articles. Now foreigners are getting into the act. Japanese players in particular have contributed some great stuff lately to the trick-shot field.

To cut the subject down to manageable size, I decided to stick to shots that depend more on a concept or secret information rather than on extraordinary skill, shots that any decent player can learn to make with a little coaching and practice. Clusters are avoided for the most part because precise ball placements are hard to show on television. I managed to find about eighty shots that are within reach of most players and still have good entertainment value. While a few popular classics are included, the emphasis is on new stuff never before seen on videotape.

As for a general approach to the subject, we adopted one main theme: trick shots are fun. Trick shots can be surprising, imaginative, educational, and funny. There's no end to the fun you can have at a pool table if you aren't trying to beat somebody in a game and if you free yourself from conventional rules.

Fortunately for me, the magicians of Tinseltown can make anybody look good. They have their own bag of tricks. When making a videotape about pool—Can we talk?—certain opportunities arise for, well, cheating. For example, if I tell the viewer a shot is easy and then it takes me four hours to make it, an editor can simply put the failures on the cutting-room floor. The performer can be made to appear as if he has skills of a semi-divine nature. Interestingly, playing a shot over and over till you get it right is easier to get away with when you are making a tape with a camcorder in your garage. It's a different story when fifteen technicians are on the payroll, a director is grinding his teeth and looking at his watch, and a producer is feeling a pool of red ink rising on his legs. Time is more than money; it's a whole hell of a *lot* of money. If you can't make a shot in two or three tries, you bum (I could imagine everyone thinking), hang up your cue and get a real job.

There are other, less obvious ways to cheat, and we succumbed on one occasion. While Jose Luis Mignone, the director of photography, fussed with the lights and director Chris Arnold positioned the three cameras, I practiced the next shot on the agenda, a novelty from Rick Wright shown at the upper left of Diagram 1. A wooden triangle is resting on three balls. As unlikely as it seems, it is possible to shoot the cueball under the triangle, pocket the ball nearest the pocket, and draw the cueball back to where it started before the triangle falls and traps it. (Hint: Use a set of well-used balls because the cueball will be a hair smaller than the others.)

After several successes in a row, I announced that I was ready. But with the camera rolling, I couldn't make it. Time after time the triangle fell and trapped the cueball. There were now four options: (1) I could be taken to the back lot and killed; (2) Because the shot is not difficult, Little Orphan Annie could be brought in to make it; (3) The shot could be omitted; (4) We could cheat. Because we were in Hollywood, the fourth option was selected and double-stick tape was applied to two of the balls. Was that such a terrible crime? I think not. Still, the moral ambiguity is troublesome.

One shot did have to be dropped in the interest of time, Kaczmarowski's Carom, so named after the man who sent it to me a couple of

Diagram 1

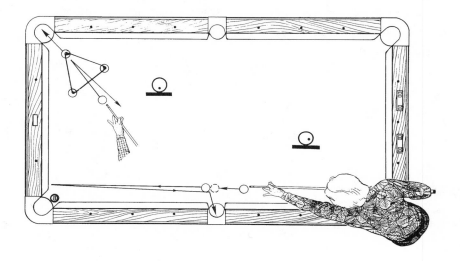

years ago. Refer to the bottom of Diagram 1. The game is eight-ball, and the corner pocket is blocked by the 8. What to do? Bank the 7 and kiss it off the cueball into the side pocket. The trick is to stop the cueball in place and use right spin to throw the 7 to the left on the rebound. It's not too tough on the tables back home, but it proved to be beyond me under hot lights and with new balls that were so clean they would hardly "throw" at all. Then, too, after a twelve-hour day I was a mere shell of my former self. Despite the heroic efforts of the powder-puff lady, I looked like one of the bad guys in *Night of the Living Dead*.

Director Chris Arnold deserved some sympathy for having to concern himself with such minutiae as double-stick tape and pool balls that were too clean, for he is used to painting on a somewhat larger canvas. His previous assignment, for example, was blowing up police cars in downtown Los Angeles for a preview of *The Last Action Hero*.

There was a final problem. If we stuck to our plan of featuring only shots that most players can learn if they're willing to work a little, it was hard to give the tapes socko climaxes. It was decided to conclude each one with a few monster stroke shots of the show-stopping variety. Pat Fleming of Accu-Stats Video Productions came to the rescue with some never-before-released footage of the Korean trick-shot master Cho Chung Sup. Wait till you see the close-up view of the mind-boggling eight-rail massé shot, which is also the favorite of another Korean exhibition player, Kim Suk Yong. See Diagram 100.

Before leaving Hollywood I saw another celebrity, this one of the female configuration. In a restaurant on the last night, Ann Miller, yesterday's tap-dancing star of the stage and screen, walked right by my table! She looked great for my age! There was such a bounce in her step and smile on her face that she buoyed the spirits of everybody in the place.

It was a good omen.

The Pleasures of Collecting

TWENTY YEARS AGO AT A NEWSSTAND, I leafed through a magazine-style guide to the hobby of collecting. It was organized alphabetically, giving a few paragraphs on each subject about the most popular items collectors seek and the kinds of prices they pay. The listing under "Billiards" was laughably scanty, mentioning a few early poolroom items like drink trays and clocks and stating that there was very little to collect relating to the game. The remarks were infused with such ignorance and were so richly erroneous that I wish I had bought the magazine and had it bronzed.

Collecting billiard memorabilia—or billiardiana—has become something of an underground rage. A lot of players and fans of cue games keep whatever they happen across, and there are hundreds who aggressively seek rare items. There is so much billiard-related material to collect that it's common to specialize. Some people collect cues and aspire to have the handiwork of every cuemaker, living or dead, famous or obscure. There are postcard collectors—one in Sacramento, California, has gathered three thousand that relate in some way to billiards, and until he reached that total, nobody knew that the postcard universe was so big. (Reproductions of some fifty rare billiard postcards, most in full color, can be found in *The Billiard Encyclopedia* [1994, second ed. 1996] by Stein and Rubino.)

There are collections of billiard toys, antique cue chalk, billiard-room tokens and souvenirs, magazine articles and advertisements, ivory balls, fine art (Van Gogh and Gauguin come to mind), etchings and engravings by artists whose work appeared in periodicals of the last century, hand-colored lithographs published by Currier & Ives, newspaper clippings, photographs of players, trick shots, wall art, cue racks, ball trays, time clocks, scorekeeping devices, tables (there is more than one warehouse full of antique tables), maces, matchbooks, autographs, and Lord knows what all.

There are collectors who pursue everything that relates to a famous player or a given period or a given game, like balkline. Balkline was the special interest of the late Clem Trainer, who during the course of a long life unearthed the particulars of every championship 18.2 balkline tournament or match ever held. In 1971, Trainer printed one hundred numbered copies of a fifty-six-page booklet titled *History of the 18.2 Balkline Game of Billiards in the United States, 1896–1934,* which is now itself a collectible item. (I have numbers twenty-three and sixty-five.) One of Trainer's triumphs was to provide the data for and persuade the *New York Times* to run a sixteen-column-inch obituary of Jake Schaefer, Jr., the greatest balkliner of them all, when Schaefer died at the age of eight-one. (Attention collectors of billiard obituaries! The *NYT* piece appeared on Tuesday, December 2, 1975.)

Then there are books. Even if the field is limited to the English language, nobody knows how many books there are, which is part of the fun. You might find among your grandfather's effects a self-published book by somebody or other than nobody knew existed. There is even a book *about* billiard books, a useful work entitled *Billiards, Bowling, Table Tennis, Pinball and Video Games: A Bibliographic Guide,* compiled in 1984 by Robert R. Craven and published by the Greenwood Press of Westport, Connecticut. Craven gives the essential details of 15 English-language books on billiards published before 1800, 121 published between 1800 and 1899, 173 between 1900 and 1939, 60 between 1940 and 1969, and 77 between 1970 and 1982. That's a total of 446 books, though some might more accurately be called booklets rather than books.

Craven lists 127 books in foreign languages. There have been at least twenty books a year published around the world since 1983—that's 240 more titles—bringing the total to 813. The Billiard Archive in Pittsburgh, the curator of which is Mike Shamos, has that many and a few more. The Craven bibliography is still available from Greenwood Press, but for the punitive price of $49.50, up from $29.95 six years ago. That's a lot for a 164-page book, only 49 of which are devoted to billiards. But it's essential if you're a serious book collector. (You can phone Greenwood at 213-226-3571.)

When I profiled Shamos for *Billiards Digest* in 1988 (an article that was included in *Byrne's Advanced Technique* [1990]), his archive contained 600 books, 600 pieces of art, 1,000 photos, and thousands of newspaper clippings. Since then he has added substantially to every category. It is the archive, indexed and accessible, that enables Shamos to enrich his "Chronicles" feature in *Billiards Digest* with so much specific detail and to include so many beautiful photographs of old-time art and artifacts.

The Billiard Archive, while in many ways the most complete, is not the only major repository of billiard memorabilia. Two I have visited are the Norman Clare Museum at Thurston's in Liverpool, England, the other is the Heinrich Weingartner Museum in Vienna, Austria. Serious collectors I have corresponded with include Roger Lee in England (emphasis: snooker and English billiards), Victor Maduro in Panama (emphasis: Latin America), Valeriano Parera Sans in Spain (carom games), and Cees Sprangers in the Netherlands (carom games). Their collections combined would be worth a snug fortune.

Fortunes—that's what people are interested in. How much are various books, prints, and mementos worth? Depends on their condition. Depends on how much the buyer is willing to pay. Because billiard collectors lack good information (but see below), prices vary all over the lot. Two extensive private collections that I know about sold in recent years for $50,000 each. Individual items are anybody's guess. I picked up six different editions of *Modern Billiards* over a twenty-year period for prices ranging from ten to twenty dollars. When I realized that I needed only two more editions to complete the set of eight, I was glad to pay seventy-five dollars for number seven. No telling what I might pay for the last one, but I'd probably have to hide the figure from my wife.

I've been collecting billiard-related material for over thirty years, and while I have a few choice items, there are many others that I lack and covet. As author of a book on trick shots, it is fitting and just that I should own a copy of François Mingaud's 1827 work on the subject, but I don't. A guy offered me a copy once for $1,500. I told him I agreed with him completely, that I would rather have $1,500 than the book. I own photocopied pages of Joe Hood's 1908 *Trick and Fancy Pool Shots Exposed*, but I'd like a copy of the actual book, which is very scarce. I'm intrigued by a book that no collector I know owns: *Bullock's Billiard Manual and Handbook of Reference,* published by Thomas R. Bullock in 1884 in Providence, Rhode Island. (Obituary fans! Bullock's death notice appeared in the *Providence Journal* on May 11, 1926.) To save Rhode Island collectors some trouble, I can report that the Providence Public Library does not have a copy. Try the Library of Congress, which lists Bullock among its 240-odd billiard titles.

When I started my collection in the early 1960s, it was still possible to wander through secondhand bookstores and pay five or ten dollars for Cochran's *Scientific Billiards* (1942), *Daly's Billiard Book* (1913), one of the editions of *Modern Billiards* published between 1881 and 1912, and first editions of Hoppe's *Thirty Years of Billiards* (1925) and *Billiards As It Should Be Played* (1941). Those were the good old days. The books have become valuable, and alert booksellers know it. To find such titles now, you have to deal with specialists in old books, attend antiquarian book fairs, haunt antique shops, advertise in trade journals, or find another collector willing to part with an extra copy for cash or trade.

Despite the growing number of billiard collectors here and abroad, billiard memorabilia hasn't come to the attention of collectors in general, not even sports collectors. Go to a library and consult the many reference books on collecting and you won't even find an index listing for billiards. What that means is that you can still acquire some excellent material without paying exorbitant prices. (There are, however, splendid books on collecting beer cans and Pez dispensers.)

Collecting billiardiana—Roger Lee suggests the term memorabilliard—appears ready to emerge from the underground. New Deco, a dealer in Florida, organized, with the help of Mike Shamos, the first auction of billiard historical items at the 1995 Billiard Congress trade show in Las Vegas. About half the items offered were sold, and New Deco got four hundred phone calls in the following several months. Brad Morris of New Deco will mail a catalog of available items—in exchange for a modest fee—to anybody who will phone 800-543-3326. The catalog will serve as the basis of telephone auctions to be held several times a year. After a year or two of auctions, it will be possible to put together a reliable price list. With a price list based on recent transactions, buyers and sellers for the first time in history will be able to negotiate with some degree of confidence. And for the first time, buyers and sellers will at least be able to *find* each other without going to a lot of trouble and expense.

Additional evidence that billiard collecting is emerging from the shadows is that professional auction houses such as Christie's and Butterfield's in New York have recently offered billiard-related lots.

This could become bigger than Pez dispensers!

I got most of my best stuff by being in the right place at the right time, which happens if you hang around with your eyes open and your hand out for thirty or forty years. Danny McGoorty gave me a couple of rare items just before he died in 1969. Welker Cochran's sister Altavene gave me a shoe box full of letters and clippings documenting the career of her famous brother.

Twenty-five years ago I visited a pool hall in Long Beach, California, The Mecca, owned by Frank Alvarez and his wife. I carefully examined the old photos and tournament records that were posted on the walls. After Frank died, his wife packed a cardboard box full of "old junk" and *delivered* it to me, saying she was glad to put it in the hands of an interested party. In the box I found many items from the estate of Charlie Peterson, which Mrs. Alvarez had rescued just before they were to be thrown in the trash, including silent films of Charlie shooting trick shots as well as tournament and match statistics from the 1920s and 30s in both pool and billiards.

Those are my greatest coups. Most of what I have was acquired for very little money. I've told as many people as possible, especially some billiard friends I've made overseas, about my interest in tournament posters and programs, and every so often something interesting arrives in the mail.

Just starting a collection? Tell your friends and relations about your interests, make yourself known to local booksellers and antique dealers, and save everything you get in the mail. No telling what might be worth money in the year 2026.

In 1995 I moved from California to Iowa. Packing up my billiard collection required three dozen cartons, not counting framed posters. I used a tape recorder to describe each item as I laid it away. When I typed it up later, I had thirty-two pages of single-spaced entries. My wife thinks I am crazy, and perhaps I am, because the bulk of the stuff I have refused to throw away over the years is probably—no, is certainly—worthless.

I enjoy my trash pile, despite the worthlessness of most of it. I spend a lot of time looking at it, pawing through it, and thinking about filling gaps in it that only I can see. It is much more interesting than other things I could have amassed, like toasters, balls of string, or beer cans.

When senility finally has me in its clammy embrace, just put me among my papers to putter and I'll be happy as a . . . well, as a clam.

How to Win Without Actually Cheating

Forty years ago, Stephen Potter (1900–1969) was known throughout the civilized world for his books on how to achieve undeserved success. Writing in a mock-academic style complete with footnotes, absurd charts, and references to nonexistent earlier researchers, he outlined the rules for driving the competition mad with psychological tricks, or "ploys." Presented here are excerpts from his main work, Gamesmanship, the Art of Winning Without Actually Cheating. *A later book was* Lifemanship, the Art of Getting Away With It Without Being an Absolute Plonk, *followed by* One-upmanship, *designed to lead the reader—called "the gamesman"—to an exalted state called Gameslifemastery. The books were published as one volume in 1962 by Holt, Rinehart and Winston under the title* Three-upmanship.

Potter's rules for rattling tennis players and golfers can, of course, be adapted to cue games, or any game. Where he mentions billiards, he means what we in America call English billiards, a game played with three balls on a snooker table that combines cannons (caroms), potting (pocketing), and in-offs (deliberate scratches off an object ball).

Potter's books are out of print in the United States but are available in most libraries. Follow his sneaky suggestions if you lack the skill to win fair and square . . . and kiss your friends good-bye.

WHAT IS GAMESMANSHIP? Most difficult of questions to answer briefly. "The Art of Winning Games Without Actually Cheating"—that is my personal working definition. What is the object? There have been five hundred books written on the subject of games. Not one on the art of win-ning. . . .

Let us start with a few simple exercises for beginners, and let us begin with the pre-game, for much of the most important gamesmanship play takes place before the game has started. Yet if mistakes are made, there is plenty of time to recover.

[A fundamental] axiom of gamesmanship is worded as follows: THE FIRST MUSCLE STIFFENED (in his opponent by the gamesman) IS THE FIRST POINT GAINED. Let us consider some of the processes of Defeat by Tension.

The standard method is known as the "flurry."

The "flurry" is for use when changing in the locker-room before a rackets match, perhaps, or leaving home in your opponent's car for, say, a game of lawn tennis. The object is to create a state of anxiety, to build up an atmosphere of muddled fluster.

Supposing, for instance, that your opponent has a small car. He kindly comes along to pick you up before the game. Your procedure should be as follows: (1) Be late in answering the bell. (2) Don't have your things ready. Appearing at last, (3) call *in an anxious or "rattled" voice* to wife (who need not, of course, be there at all) some taut last-minute questions about din-ner. Walk down path and (4) realize that you have forgotten shoes. Return with shoes; then just before getting into car pause (5) *a certain length of time* (see any threepenny edition of *Bohn's Tables*) and wonder (i) whether [your] racket is at the club, or (ii) whether you have left it "in the bathroom at the top of the house."

Like the first hint of paralysis, a scarcely observable fixing of your opponent's expression should now be visible. Now is the time to redouble the attack. Map-play can be brought to bear. On the journey let it be known that you "think you know a better way," *which should turn out, when followed, to be incorrect and should if possible lead to a blind alley.*

Meanwhile, time is getting on. Opponent's tension should have increased. Psychological tendency, if not temporal necessity, will cause him to drive faster, and—behold!—now the gamesman can widen his field and bring in carmanship by suggesting, with the minutest stiffening of the legs at corners, an unconscious tendency to put on the brakes, indicating an unexpressed desire to tell his opponent that he is not driving very well and cornering rather too fast. . . .

The famous "Second Rule" of gamesmanship is formulated as follows:

IF THE OPPONENT WEARS, OR ATTEMPTS TO WEAR, CLOTHES CORRECT AND SUITABLE FOR THE GAME, BY AS MUCH AS HIS CLOTHES SUCCEED IN THIS FUNCTION, BY SO MUCH SHOULD THE GAMESMAN'S CLOTHES FAIL.

Corollary: Conversely, if the opponent wears the wrong clothes, the gamesman should wear the right.

"If you can't volley, wear velvet socks," as we Old Gamesmen used to say. The good-looking young athlete, perfectly dressed, is made to feel a fool if his bad shot is returned by a man who looks as if he has never been on a tennis court before. His good clothes become a handicap by virtue of their very suitability. . . .

But the average gamesman must beware, at this point, of counter-gamesmanship. He may find himself up against an experienced hand, such as J. K. C. Dalziel, who, when going out to golf, used to keep two changes of clothes . . . in his car, one correct and the other incorrect. . . .

SOME BASIC PLAYS

"How to Win Games Without Being Able to Play Them." Reduced to the simplest terms, that is the formula, and the student must not at first try flights too far away from this basic thought. . . .

The use of sportsmanship is, of course, important. In general, with the athletic but stupid player, . . . who is going to take it out on you, by God, if he suspects you of being unsporting, extreme sportingness is the thing, and the instant waiving of any rule which works in your favor is the procedure.

On the other hand, playing against the introverted crusty cynical type, remember that sportingness will be wasted on him. There must be no unsportingness on your part, of course; but a keen knowledge of little-known rules and penalties will cause him to feel he is being beaten at his own game. . . .

When questioned about the etiquette of gamesmanship—so important for the young player—I talk about Fidgets. If your adversary is edgy and put off by the mannerisms of his opponent, it is unsporting, and therefore not gamesmanship, to go in, e.g., for a loud noseblow, say, at billiards, or to chalk your cue squeakingly, when he is either making or considering a shot.

On the other hand, a basic play, in perfect order, can be achieved by, say, whistling fidgetingly *while playing yourself.* I once converted two down into two up when playing golf against P. Beard, known also as the leader of an orchestra, by constantly whistling a phrase from the Dorabella Variation with one note—always the same note—wrong.[1]

---

[1]It may be worth recalling that Elgar himself, when playing croquet against fellow musicians, made use of the horn *motiv* from the *Ring*. He would whistle this correctly except for the second note, substituting for A some inappropriate variant, often a slightly flattened D sharp, *sliding* up to it, from the opening note of the phrase. A voice from the past, indeed. Yet have any of our modern experts in the music ploy really improved on this, devised before Gamesmanship was formulated or even described?

A good general attack can be made by talking to your opponent about his job, in the character of the kind of man who always tries to know more about your own profession than you know yourself. . . .

A bigger subject which may be introduced here revolves around the huge question of nice chapmanship and its uses. (I refuse to use the hideous neologism "nicemanship," which I see much in evidence lately.)

Here is the general principle: that Being a Nice Chap *in certain circumstances* is valuable when playing against . . . players who are genuinely nice. A train of thought can be started in their minds to the effect that "it would be rather a rotten trick to beat old G. by too much." Thereby that fatal "letting up" is inaugurated which can be the undoing of so many fine players. . . .

So much for some of the principal ploys.[2] Now for some common technical phrases.

The word *counterpoint,* now used exclusively in music, originally stood for Number Three of the General Principles of Gamesmanship: PLAY AGAINST YOUR OPPONENT'S TEMPO. This is one of the oldest gambits and is now almost entirely used in the form "My Slow to Your Fast." At billiards or snooker, or golf especially, against a player who makes a great deal of wanting to get on with the game, the technique is (1) to agree (Jeffreys always adds here "as long as we don't hurry on the shot"); and (2) to hold things up by fifteen to twenty disguised pauses. Tees for golf were introduced by Samuel in 1933 for this use. The technique is to tee the ball, frame up for the shot, and then at the last moment stop, pretend to push the peg a little farther in or pull it a little farther out, and then start all over again. At the next hole vary this with Samuel's "Golden Perfecto" tee, made in such a way that the ball, after sitting still in the cup for two to three seconds, rolls off. . . .

NOTE: *Do not attempt to irritate your opponent by spending too long looking for your lost ball.* This is unsporting. But good gamesmanship which is also very good sportsmanship can be practiced if the gamesman makes a great and irritatingly prolonged parade of spending extra time looking for his *opponent's* ball.

At billiards, the custom of arranging to be summoned to the telephone on fake calls so as to break your opponent's concentration is out of date now and interesting only as a reminder of the days when couriers were paid to gallop up to the old billiard halls for the same purpose. In snooker, the usual practice is to walk quickly up to the table, squat half down on the

---

[2]Sub-plays, or individual maneuvers of a gambit, are usually referred to as "ploys." It is not known why this is.

haunches to look at sight-lines, move to the other end of the table to look at sight-lines of balls that may come into play later on in the run you are supposed to be planning. Decide on the shot. Frame up for it, and then at the last moment see some obvious shot you had "missed" and which your opponent and everybody else will have noticed before you moved to the table, and which they knew is the shot you are going to play in the end anyhow.[3]

Jack Rivers Opening

Perhaps the most difficult type for the gamesman to beat is the man who indulges in pure play. He gets down to it, he gets on with it, he plays each shot according to its merits, and his own powers, without a trace of exhibitionism and no by-play whatever. . . .

My only counter to this, which some have praised, is to invent, early in the game or before it has started, an imaginary character called "Jack Rivers." I speak of his charm, his good looks, his fine war record, and his talent for games—and, "by the way, he is a first-class pianist as well." Then, a little later: "I like Jack Rivers's game," I say. "He doesn't care a damn whether he wins or loses so long as he has a good match."

Some such rubbish as this, although at first it may not be effective, often wears down the most successfully cautious opponent *if the method is given time to soak in.* . . . If he has been hearing about Jack Rivers for thirty minutes he will begin to think: "Well, perhaps I am being a bit of a stick-in-the-mud." He feels an irrational desire to play up to what appears to be your ideal of a good fellow. . . . Soon he is throwing away point after point by adopting a happy-go-lucky, hit-or-miss style that doesn't suit his game in the least.

WINMANSHIP

The assiduous student of gamesmanship has little time for the minutiae of the game itself—little opportunity for learning how to play the shots, for instance. His skill in stroke-making may indeed be almost nonexistent. So that the gamesman who finds himself winning in the early stages of the match is sometimes at a loss. . . . This seems to . . . be the place to set down a few words of friendly advice to the winning gamesman, to help him keep

---

[3]Gamesman Frith-Morteroy, who rarely lost, spent much of his spare time reading medical books on the subject of minor cardiac weaknesses.

his head; to assist him to maintain his advantage, and rub his opponent's face in the dirt.

Very often the opponent will show signs, just as he is beginning to lose, of being irritated by distractions. At golf, "somebody moved." At billiards, "somebody talked." Take the opportunity to make him feel that he is not really a player at all by talking along these lines:

"Somebody yelling, did you say? Do you know, I didn't notice it. I'm a fool at games. Don't seem to be able to be aware of anything when I'm playing the shot. I remember when Joyce Wethered was putting, eighteenth green—semifinal. An express train went by within fifteen feet of her nose. 'How did you manage to sink that putt—with the train . . . ?' 'What train?' she said."

Always tell the same story to the same man. (See "Story, constant repetition of.")

When to Give Advice

In my own view (but compare Motherwell) there is only one correct time when the gamesman can give advice, and that is when the gamesman has achieved a *useful* though not necessarily a *winning* lead. [In billiards, for example:]

Gamesman: Look . . . may I say something?

Layman: What?

Gamesman: Take it easy.

Layman: What do you mean?

Gamesman: I mean—you know how to make the strokes but you're stretching yourself . . . all the time. Look. Walk up to the ball. Look at the line. And make your stroke. Comfortable. Easy. It's as simple as that.

In other words, the advice *must be vague,* to make certain it is not helpful. . . . If properly managed, the mere giving of advice is sufficient to place the gamesman in a practically invincible position.

Practice Shots

The best shot to practice with cue and ivories is undoubtedly the Imitation Fluke. In billiards, play for an in-off the top red left of a kind which will give color to your apology that you meant to pot the red top right. A. Boult (the snooker player, not the conductor) demonstrates a shot in which

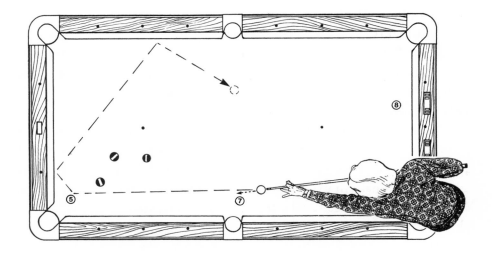

Diagram 2: The Imitation Fluke as applied to a game of eight-ball: The correct shot is to cut the 5-ball into the corner and bring the cueball to the middle section of the table, from where it is easy to make the 7-ball in the side and get position on the 8-ball. In an effort to "gaslight" his opponent (that is, drive him crazy the way Charles Boyer drove Ingrid Bergman crazy in the classic film *Gaslight*), the gamesman announces his intention to cut the 7-ball in the side, and aims as if trying to do so. On the last stroke, he shifts his aim slightly and cuts the 5-ball in the corner. As the cueball comes to rest in the center of the table as intended, "chalk the cue ostentatiously while apologizing," as Potter explains.

he pots the black while apparently framing up to hit a ball of inferior scoring value.

A good tip, says Boult, is to chalk the cue ostentatiously while apologizing after making the shot. . . .

Breaking the Flow

Straight now to the underlying principle of winning the losing game. What is the chief danger from the opponent who is getting the better of you? Over and above the advantage in the score comes the fact that he is in the *winning vein*. He is playing at his best. Yet this is but one end of a balance. It is your job to turn the winning vein into a *losing streak*.

There is only one rule: BREAK THE FLOW. This act . . . may bear directly on the game itself (*Primary Hamper*) or the net may be cast wider, in a direction apparently far removed from the main target, in an attempt to entangle the character, or even to bring forces to bear from your knowledge of the private life and intimate circumstances of your opponent (*Secondary Hamper*). . . . It is worth remembering that some of the earliest tentative ploys in what Toynbee calls, in an amusing essay, the Paleogamesman period, were directed to the essential *breaking of the flow*. They consisted of such naive devices as tying up a shoelace in a prolonged manner; ... the extended noseblow, with subsequent mopping up not only of the nose and surrounding surfaces, but of imaginary sweat from the forehead and neck as well; leaving your driver on the tee and going back for it, etc., etc.

My own name has been associated—against my will—with an attempt to bring the Primary Hamper up to date. The essence of the modern approach is the making of the pause *as if for the sake of your opponent's game*. ...

In a billiard room, your opponent has made a run of eight and looks as if he may be going to make eight more. If two or more people are present, they are likely not to be especially interested in the game, and quietly talking, perhaps. Or moving teacups. Or glasses. Simulate annoyance, *on your opponent's behalf,* with the onlookers. An occasional irritated glance will prepare the way, then stop your opponent and say:

Gamesman (quietly): Are they bothering you?

Layman: Who?

Gamesman: Compton and Peters.

Layman: It's all right.

Or say to the whisperers, half, but only half, jokingly: "Hi, I say. This is a billiard room, you know. Dead silence, please!"

This should not only put an end to your opponent's run. It may cause him, if young, to be genuinely embarrassed.

Further [improvements] are (*a*) the removal of an imaginary hair from opponent's ball when he is shooting; (*b*) licking a finger to pick up a speck of dust, etc. ....

The Secondary Hamper is still in the early stages of development. ... The object is to bring to bear *private life*—your own or your opponent's. The whole ploy is based, of course, on the proved fact that in certain circumstances and at certain times, such a simple remark as "We're very lucky with our new son-in-law" may have a profound effect on the game.

(NOTE: This section is for *advanced students only*. All others move straight to Chapter VII. Students who have made no progress at all should go back to the beginning.)

Simpson's Statue

I have been asked to give an exact explanation of a phrase used by many young gamesmen who do not, I fancy, properly know the meaning of the term, much less its origin. I refer to the phrase "Simpson's Statue," a simple gambit often used in croquet or snooker. . . . R. Simpson had the idea of standing in the "wrong place" while his opponent was playing his shot—in the line of the putt in golf (or the pot in billiards). . . . Having elicited a remonstrance, Simpson then proceeded, before every subsequent shot, not only in that game but in all future matches against the same opponent, to remember that he was in the wrong position more or less at the last moment, leap into the correct position with exaggerated agility, and stand rigidly still with his head bowed. (See drawing below.) Simpson . . . sometimes increased the irritating effect by [facetiously resting the cue head] downward on his boot. . . . To make [the ploy] effective, repeat it again and again. . . .

Snooker Player's Drivel

I strongly recommend Rushington's one-and-sixpenny brochure on *Snooker-Talk Without Tears.* This booklet contains full vocabularies of the drivelly facetious language that has been found to be equally suitable to billiards and snooker, including a phonetic representation of such sounds as the imitation of the drawing of a cork, for use whenever the opponent's ball goes into the pocket. This is a most useful ploy against good billiard players of the older generation, who believe in correct manners and meticulous etiquette in the billiard room. I often saw Rushington at work in the good old days before the war. His masterpiece, I always thought, was never to say "five," "eight," etc., after scoring five, or eight, etc., but always "five skins," "eight skins," etc. . . .

In my pamphlet for the British Council I listed eighteen ways of saying "Bad luck." I do not believe there are more.

Simpson's Statue, The Billiard Position

How to Cope with Sore Losers

LOSING BUILDS CHARACTER, THEY SAY. It toughens you and teaches you how to handle reverses in the real world. Learn from your defeats, give your opponent credit, and vow to do better next time.

What nonsense! Losing is embarrassing and expensive, that's what it is. Losing is frustrating, unfair, and infuriating. Who among us has not sympathized with chessmaster Aron Nimzovitch (1886–1935), who jumped on a table during a tournament and shouted, "Why must I lose to this idiot?"

If it happens too often, losing leads to self-loathing, despair, and frightening eruptions of bile. I've heard of extreme cases where players got so sick and tired of losing at pool that they sank to bowling.

Some players are known for boiling over when they lose. Especially to you. Especially when you miscue and slop in the winning ball. Two games in a row.

Unopposed by anyone familiar with the rudiments of poolroom psychology, this out-of-control sore loser was able to completely triangulate his opponent.

Under certain circumstances and against certain people, playing pool is hazardous to your health. A friend of mine in Northern California wandered into a bar and got into a game of eight-ball with a large stranger. The bet was five dollars. Five minutes into the game, he was faced with nothing but sell-out shots, so he played a deliberate safety. His opponent responded by punching him in the nose and knocking him to the floor. No words were exchanged. Safeties, you see, were not permitted under house rules.

What should you do if your opponent blows his cork? Assuming you want to avoid violence, there are a number of possible moves you can make to cool him down and ease his cork back into its receptacle. Picking the one that suits the character of your assailant and the speed of his approach is seldom easy, yet peace and war can hang in the balance.

Because you must act quickly, it's wise to plan a course of action well in advance of the crisis—when you notice your opponent's ears reddening, for example, or when he no longer smiles when making physical threats. Don't wait until he is advancing on you with fists clenched, spittle flying, and a piece of sports gear raised aloft. With foresight, you can suavely defuse the bomb by taking steps you have already rehearsed in your mind.

With the help of various dead artists from the last century, I have assembled seventeen possible methods of coping with a sore loser. Memorize them for safety's sake.

If it becomes apparent in a given situation that you have chosen the wrong response, don't complain to me. There isn't time.

THINGS TO DO IF THREATENED BY A SORE LOSER

Make sure he's really sore.

Offer him the comfort of the Bible.

Fake a coronary.

Hide.

Adopt a disguise.

Make a muscle.

Pray.

Tell him you're sorry.

Threaten to tell everybody you beat him.

Expel him from the room.

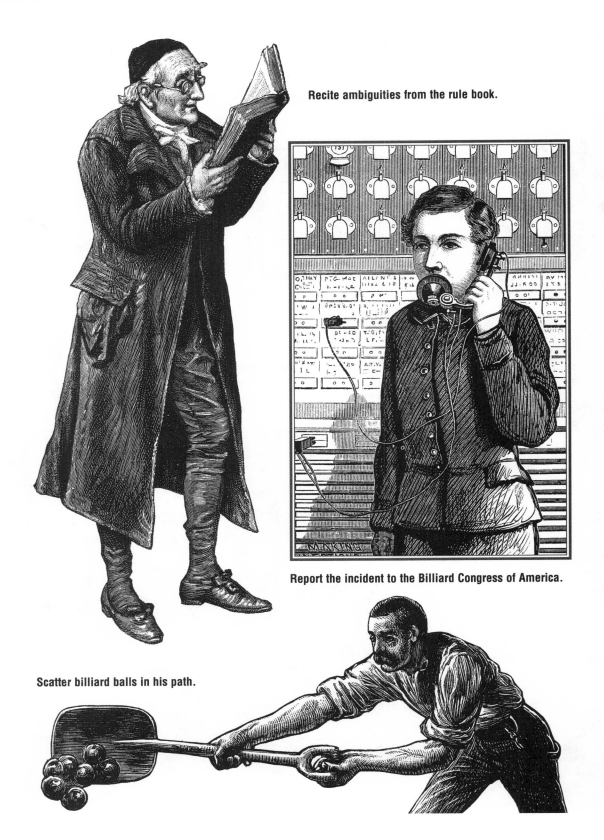

Recite ambiguities from the rule book.

Report the incident to the Billiard Congress of America.

Scatter billiard balls in his path.

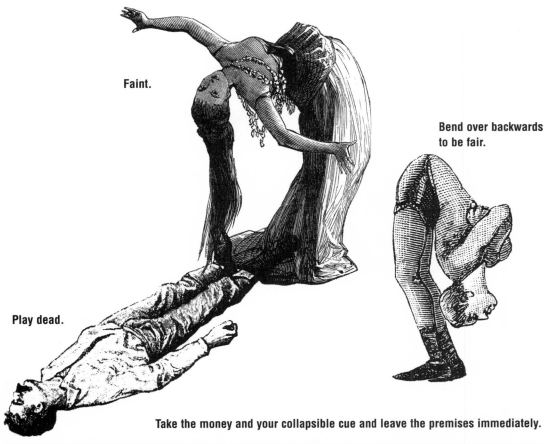

Faint.

Bend over backwards to be fair.

Play dead.

Take the money and your collapsible cue and leave the premises immediately.

How to Improve Your Pool Game

Champions come in assorted sizes. Italian giant Primo Carnera, heavyweight boxing champion in 1933, takes a pool lesson from mighty mite Kinrey Matsuyama, perennial billiard king of Japan. At the right is swimming champion Eleanor Holm.

(Courtesy of the Billiard Archive)

The Crucial Fundamentals

WHY DON'T YOU WIN more often than you do? Maybe you need glasses, or new glasses. Maybe you've reached the limits of your hand-eye coordination and should put more stress on shot selection, thinking ahead, and defense. Maybe you don't play as much as the people who beat you; maybe when you do play you are too casual and miss the lessons that are there to be learned.

The key to improvement often lies in better fundamentals, the ABCs of the game you haven't thought much about since you first picked up a cue. Do you *really* want to improve? Then you might have to pay the price of unlearning bad habits—not easy when you've reinforced them for years.

The following suggestions have been stripped of qualifiers. There's no need to write and tell me that so-and-so plays great and violates these and other rules. Talent and dedication can overcome any number of handicaps. I know so-and-so and his odd style very well, having lost to him many times.

COACHING

It doesn't make sense to spend hundreds of dollars in table time and not five cents on instruction. There are books and tapes on the market that will pay for themselves many times over. If you can find the right teacher, you will *really* benefit, because it is impossible to see yourself as others see you.

A teacher, or even a friend, can sometimes spot flaws in your mechanics you are utterly unaware of and show you how to correct them.

STANCE

Position your dominant eye directly over the cue. Keep the bridge arm straight. Your feet and torso should be at roughly a 45-degree angle to the line of aim. After playing for a few hours, does a muscle anywhere in your legs, arms, or neck feel sore? If yes, you need a better-balanced, more comfortable stance.

Is your elbow directly over the cue? It should be, but it's hard to tell on your own.

I have advised in the past that the forearm should point straight down at the floor when the tip is at the cueball, but I have lately noticed that the forearms of a lot of good players are straight down when the tip is about halfway between the cueball and the bridge hand.

Are long shots a weakness? Try bending closer to the cue when great aiming accuracy is required. It takes energy to stoop low and straighten up over and over, and some players stand too erect out of laziness, including your author. Snooker champions, who play a game requiring extreme accuracy, bend so low their chins ride the cue.

GRIP

Light but firm. No white knuckles. The wrist should be in line with your forearm, not curled in or cocked out. The wrist can be loose or not so loose.

Never let the thumb rest on top of the cue, for that restricts the stroke. The thumb should circle the cue and touch the forefinger. The middle joints of the fingers should be at the bottom of the cue. Whether the fourth and fifth fingers touch the cue or not while aiming is immaterial, but they should draw away at the rear of the backstroke.

When breaking in eight-ball or nine-ball, move the grip closer to the rear of the cue and use a longer bridge; power can thereby be increased by using a longer backswing, but accuracy is reduced.

BRIDGE

Some beginners have trouble forming a looped bridge with the forefinger over the top of the cue, but it's the only way to go when power or spin are required. For the majority of shots in pool, however, an open or V bridge is okay. Rest the heel of your hand on the cloth for maximum stability.

Does the cue cling to your skin? Clean the shaft with a damp cloth or caress it with a scouring pad, very fine sandpaper, or one of the newly available superfine abrasive papers. Washing your hands is a good idea. Talcum powder is a last resort. A stylish new option: three-fingered nylon gloves.

How far away from the cueball you should place your bridge hand varies among top players from six to fourteen inches. Shorten the bridge and hold the cue snugly when drawing or spinning the cueball; lengthen it when aiming accuracy is paramount.

If you have to make your bridge on the rail or are shooting over an interfering ball, give extra attention to hitting the cueball in the center to keep it from curving.

AIMING

Notice that good players almost never have to readjust their bridge hands once they plant them on the table: they get it right the first time by correctly choosing the cueball path before going into the aiming crouch.

Once your cue is in place, fine-tune the aim when the tip is at the ball and the cue is motionless. Use the warm-up strokes to prepare for pulling the trigger and for getting a feel for how hard you have to hit the ball.

There are two main aiming methods, neither of which is used by top players, who rely instead on the judgment and feel that come from thousands of carefully observed repetitions. The best-known method is to imagine a "ghost ball," which is the cueball at the moment of contact with the object ball. If you've allowed correctly for throw and positioned the ghost ball correctly, then all you have to do is shoot through the center of it to make the shot.

The second method involves drawing imaginary lines through the cueball and the object ball. Twice in 1994, once in a billiard newspaper column and once in a book, the system was described incorrectly, with both lines starting from the target pocket. That way the line of aim is wrong for cut shots of every angle. Only the line through the object ball should start from the pocket. The line through the cueball must be parallel to the first one. The system is explained in Diagram 3, on page 25 of my *Standard Book,* and on pages 71–73 of Willie Mosconi's "blue book" (1965 and later editions). See Diagram 3 on the following page.

On long, thin cut shots, some players aim for a point half a ball-width away from the object ball. Another idea is to imagine the path the edge of the cueball must take to the object ball.

Long straight-in shots are an excellent test of skill. Practice them with the object ball halfway from the cueball to the pocket, the toughest position. Use no sidespin. Follow straight through toward the middle of the object ball. Keep the cue on line until the end of the stroke—one way to ensure that is to let the tip come to rest on a preselected point on the cloth. Only with good mechanics can you make long, straight shots consistently.

STROKE

A book could be written on stroke; variations that work are endless. Should you hesitate at the back of the last warm-up stroke? Some good players do, some don't. Should the last backstroke be shorter than the previous ones? Some, but not most, players would say yes. Should the final backstroke be slower than the others, as though you are stretching a bowstring? Adopt the style that works best for you.

At the front of your forestroke, the tip should stop about a quarter-inch from the ball so when you pull the trigger you won't have to lunge beyond your warm-up limits.

Three factors influence the cueball during the millisecond the tip is in contact with it: the angle of inclination of the cue, the speed of the cue at

Diagram 3: Aiming method: Imagine line AB from the pocket through the center of the object ball. Where it emerges from the cueball is point Y. Imagine line CD through the center of the cueball and parallel to AB. Where CD intersects the cueball is point X. To pocket the ball, drive point X into point Y by aiming the cueball parallel to line XY, as shown.

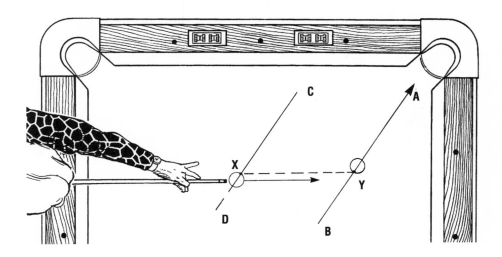

impact, and how far off center the cueball is struck. Unimportant in a technical sense are length of follow-through, tightness of grip, looseness of wrist, the twist of the cue and the acceleration (defined as the rate of change of velocity) of the cue at impact.

A very long follow-through is nothing more than an affectation, a check stroke is a waste of energy (unless it is needed to avoid a foul). The harder you hit the cueball, the longer it takes to bring the cue to a stop. As a general rule, the follow-through should be roughly the same length as the backswing.

The elbow should be a hinge frozen in space during the warm-up strokes and during the hit. Never let it drop before the hit.

Teachers differ on whether or not the student should keep the cue level during the follow-through, which requires dropping the elbow after the hit, or letting the tip dip naturally to the cloth. It seems to me that the effort to keep the cue level by dropping the elbow is wasted because the cueball is long gone by then and no longer cares what you do. When shooting hard, of course, you don't want the tip to hit the cloth, and so the elbow must come down.

Should you take a lot of warm-up strokes, just a few, or should the number vary with the difficulty of the shot? Whatever works. There are many roads to Rome; the problem lies in finding the one that suits your horse and carriage best.

So far we've touched on coaching, stance, grip, bridge, aiming, and stroke. Now let's consider lagging for break, breaking, sidespin, curve, draw, and follow . . . and take a further look at stroke.

LAGGING

Put the cueball as far forward as possible, the shorter the distance the better. Hit the cueball seven-tenths of its diameter above the cloth (a little below halfway from the center to the top). The reason is that the cueball will start out immediately with natural roll. Hitting it lower creates an initial slipping between the ball and the cloth and a slight frictional drag that must be allowed for. The seven-tenths hit eliminates the need to make an allowance. It's probably better to try to impart just enough speed to bring the cueball back to touch the near rail rather than to stop short of it, because a ball rebounding straight back from a rail loses a lot of its speed— up to 40 percent on some tables.

Because a good lag shot requires delicate estimation of a rather slow speed, a big free-flowing stroke isn't needed. Shorten your bridge to four to six inches and move your grip hand a few inches forward from its normal position. Since you don't have to find a precise line of aim or apply English, try watching only the tip of the cue during the warm-up strokes.

BREAKING

Once you've won the lag you must shift into a completely different gear and go for maximum power. Lengthen your bridge to eight to ten inches to allow for a long backswing and move your normal grip a few inches to the rear. When you finish your warm-up strokes and decide to pull the trigger, try to time it so that the cue reaches maximum speed at the moment of contact with the cueball. No matter how much cue speed you can generate, the most important single factor in spreading the balls is getting a dead solid hit on the apex ball of the rack, so concentrate most of your attention on achieving that. In addition, a square hit lessens the chances of scratching.

It's best if the cueball comes to rest near the center of the table, which requires a slight draw. If the cueball rockets back off the pack, you're hitting it too low. Using an off-center hit involves a trade-off, for any energy

Diagram 4: Two shots you have to be able to make to call yourself a player: at the top, pocket the ball and draw back the length of the table and stop within a foot of the end rail. At the bottom, pocket the ball and use follow to send the cueball to within a foot of the end rail. If you can't make these shots at least half the time, you need a teacher right now.

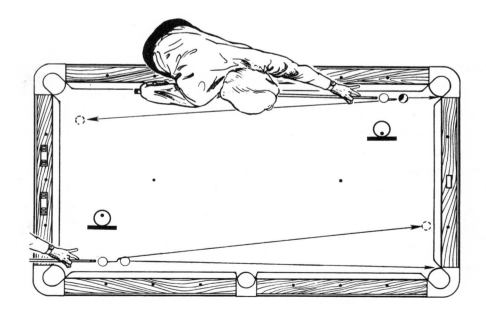

that goes into spinning the cueball takes energy away from linear speed.

Keep the cue level, but make sure you don't risk smashing your knuckles on the edge of the table. An elevated cue makes the cueball leave the cloth; it seems to me that getting the cueball airborne wastes energy that could go into speed, and also increases the chances of sending the cueball off the table. Still, some pros seem to like a little hop on the cueball.

For full-rack, open-break games like eight-ball, put the cueball as far forward as possible and at the center of the table to minimize the distance the cueball must travel. For nine-ball, it is widely felt that it is best to break from the side of the table—from there a ball often goes in the diagonally opposite corner pocket, and the 1-ball often goes in the side.

While it's widely believed that the breaker has an advantage in nine-ball, the facts aren't convincing. Pat Fleming of Accu-Stats Video Productions has covered tournaments in which the breaker won less often than the second player. Sometimes no ball drops, sometimes a ball drops and there is no second shot, sometimes a ball drops and the breaker fails to run out, and 10 percent of the time, the cueball goes in on the break.

Many nine-ball players rack the balls in a numerical pattern designed to make a run-out more difficult for their opponent. For example, you can put the 2-ball in the fourth row because the two balls in that row tend to stay at the foot of the table while the 1-ball usually stops near the center or the head of the table—thus if a ball drops, it may not be easy for the breaker to get from the 1-ball to the 2-ball.

It makes sense to break with a cue other than your regular cue to prolong the life of the tip. Your break cue should be stiff, not whippy, should have a thin, hard tip, and should be an ounce or two lighter than your regular cue.

STROKE

Most fundamentals are simply a matter of knowledge. All the student has to do is get some information into his or her head. When it comes to stroke, though, the teacher as well as the student can easily become frustrated. A good stroke is dependent on whatever hand-eye coordination the student brings to the table. If you aren't coordinated enough to groove your warm-up strokes and deliver the cue into the ball at the point in-tended and along the correct line—with a certain rhythm and feel for the proper speed—then learning how to play pool or billiards well is going to be a long, hard struggle. Talent can't be taught. Touch and feel can't be taught. The ability to come up with ingenious solutions to problems can't be taught. If you have talent, it's up to you to develop it through your own efforts. A teacher can help you avoid wasting time in blind alleys, especially at the beginning of your quest for pool prowess, and give you a lot of useful information, but you are the one who will have to do the work.

The bad news when it comes to developing a smooth, consistent, and accurate stroke is that it requires inborn ability. The good news is that there are many kinds of stroke that work; chances are there is one that's good for you. Study top players live or on tape and try the various nuances.

In teaching somebody how to stroke the ball, or if you are trying to improve your own stroke, it seems obvious that you should move the cue back and forth along the exact line of aim, and I have recommended that in previous writings. The trouble is, many top players display all kinds of curves and waggles. A new product on the market can be used to prove the point. It's a small laser that clamps on to the cue like a telescopic sight on a rifle. Focus the vertical red line so it crosses both the cueball and the object ball and you'll find out how crooked your stroke is. Even top players are surprised at how hard it is to keep the red line from wandering all over the place.

What counts, of course, is where the cue is at the moment of impact—if it gets there along a slightly curved path it doesn't matter. Having said that, it still seems best to try to make your stroke perfectly straight. Practice by stroking toward a mirror on the table, or into the mouth of a pop bottle, or along a laser's red line. If no paraphernalia is handy, simply pick out a spot on the cloth beyond the cueball and send the cuetip to it on your follow-through.

SIDESPIN

Use sidespin when you want to affect the way the cueball bounces off a rail. It has little or no effect in changing the way the cueball caroms off another ball. To alter the cueball's path off a ball, use high or low, not side. Sidespin causes a lot of missed shots because it changes the direction in which the cueball leaves the tip (a phenomenon called squirt or deflection), throwing the object ball slightly off line and increasing the chances of a miscue. It's safer to stay on the cueball's vertical axis. If you must use sidespin, don't try to hit the cueball farther off center than halfway to the edge.

CURVE

If you want the cueball to curve, you must elevate the cue and use sidespin. If the cue is perfectly level, the cueball path will not bend, even with maximum English.

DRAW

To get lively draw action, make sure your tip is groomed and chalked, your bridge is snug, your hit on the cueball is low, and you use enough speed. To make sure you get a low hit on the cueball, it helps to let the tip go forward through the cueball to the cloth. How low is low? The upper part of the tip should contact the cueball at a point halfway from the middle to the bottom. George Onoda found an easy way to practice draw shots—use a striped ball as the cueball and orient it so the stripe is horizontal. Because the stripe is half the width of a ball, you can see exactly where to hit: the bottom edge of the stripe. Any lower and you'll miscue. See Onoda's excellent article on draw shots in *Billiards Digest,* August 1991, pages 27–28.

FOLLOW

For maximum effect, hit the cueball halfway from the middle to the top and no higher. Use a striped ball with the stripe horizontal to help you get used to the halfway point. If you are hitting the cueball at the upper edge of the stripe, the length of the follow will depend entirely on the speed of the cue at impact.

STOP

Some students have an unrealistic idea of what the cueball can be made to do, and they are disappointed when they can't achieve the impossible. For example, only if a shot is straight in can you draw the cueball straight back,

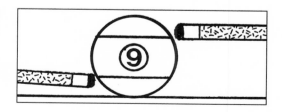

Diagram 5: Lively action results from hitting the cueball at the maximum off-center point, which is halfway from the center to the edge. To get used to how high and low that is, use a striped ball for a cueball and hit the edge of the stripe, as shown.

follow straight forward, or stop it dead in its tracks. To stop the cueball on straight-in shots requires backspin that wears off just as the cueball reaches the object ball. On short shots, a hit only slightly below center will suffice; on long shots, maximum low is required as well as considerable speed. It pays to practice stop shots at all distances. Strive to kill the cueball completely without the slightest movement after hitting the object ball.

> "Before you can conquer the three rebellious ivory balls and make them do your bidding, you must first conquer yourself. I have found billiards to be more than a game; I have found it to be a philosophy of self-control."
>
> —Willie Hoppe
> *Thirty Years of Billiards*, 1925

Finding the
Line of Aim

TRYING TO TEACH A BEGINNER how to aim a cut shot can be frustrating because some of them have only the vaguest idea of what they have to do. First, you have to explain that the cueball must contact the object ball at a point opposite the target. Then you have to explain that they can't aim at the contact point; instead they have to aim at a point in space, the point that represents the center of the cueball at the moment of contact.

Teachers for years have been devising aiming aids—gimmicks made of plastic or paper—to make the idea clear. All that is really needed to do the job is an index card with an arrow, a notch, and an ink spot, but that hasn't stopped manufacturers and inventors who hope to find a market for a prefabricated gadget.

The earliest aiming aid I'm familiar with is a folding paper arm that accompanied a 1911 book called *The Practical Science of Billiards and Its "Pointers,"* published in London by Charles Maximillian Western. The 154-page book is a mathematical treatment of the game and the "device" was intended to help the student find the right line of aim on cut shots.

About twenty years ago a plastic gadget was marketed carrying the name of the late, great Harold Worst of Michigan, a world-class player of both pool and three-cushion. It consisted of a short, flat plastic arm joined with a grommet to a longer arm, allowing the arms to pivot freely. A hole was punched in the short arm so a ball would stay in place when the apparatus was placed on the table.

The idea was that a cueball rolled down the long arm (kept on line by raised ridges on each edge) would strike the object ball at the same point no matter what angle was formed by the arms. The beginner could therefore see where the cueball had to be aimed for various cuts. I've often wondered how many were manufactured and if any were sold.

When I saw the Worst aiming tool, it occurred to me that the same thing could be accomplished with a small card. Put a notch in the middle of the short side so it can be slipped under an object ball and held in place without moving the ball. Make an ink spot exactly one ball-width away from the notch, with an arrow pointing at the notch. Once the arrow is pointed in the right direction, it remains only to aim the cueball at the ink spot from any angle to make the correct hit. (Friction and throw are ignored, of course, because we are dealing with abject beginners.)

In 1986 in Denver, a man named Peter Harth handed me an index card with the same markings on it. He called it Peter's Pointer. Great minds follow similar ruts.

In 1988 a neatly printed card called Pool Target with an accompanying folder was put on the market by a company in Atlanta called Gladiators. The aiming idea was the same, but Pool Target also had some sighting lines to help the neophyte determine the size of the pocket opening as seen from the given ball position.

The ultimate gadget along these lines is the Aim Trainer, made available in 1994 by a company with the hard-to-forget name of Elephant

Diagram 6: An aiming aid, Byrne version. (Not actual size.) Slide the card under an object ball, centering the resting point in the notch. Aim the arrow at the pocket. Because the spot in the card is exactly two ball-widths away from the notch, the spot is the correct aiming point, no matter where the cueball is, save for the throw effect.

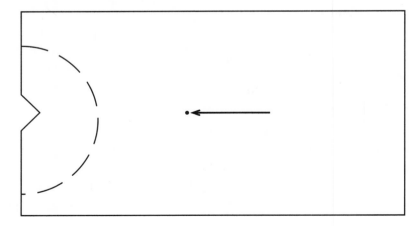

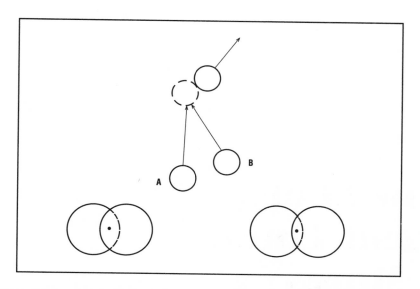

Diagram 7: Another way of visualizing the aiming line. The circles at the left represent a cue-ball hitting an object ball rather full (Shot A, in the center drawing). The circles at the right represent a thin hit (Shot B, center). In both cases (in *all* cases), the contact point is exactly the middle of the intersecting arcs, as shown by the dot.

Balls, which comes with a detailed booklet on mastering cut shots. For information, call 800–840–8833.

Another teaching idea that might be useful for some students was sent to me in 1988 by Paul Hahn of University City, Missouri. The diagrams in some books, including mine, often show two overlapping circles that represent a table-level view of the cueball hitting an object ball. Such circles show roughly how much ball to hit for cuts of various angles. But where in the diagram is the contact point? Hahn's helpful observation is that the contact point between two spheres is always exactly halfway between the intersecting arcs, as shown in Diagram 7. Obvious, once you think of it.

Happy teaching!

Throw Shots, Tangent Lines, and More

YOU WOULD THINK that after five hundred years, the human race would have learned everything there is to know about the game of billiards, but such is not the case. There are countless areas for fruitful argument.

Mr. X claims to have made the 9-ball on the break six times in a row in the same pocket while practicing on his table at home. I'll call him, and other gurus of pool I feel are on a darkling plain, by letters of the alphabet because my quarrel is not with them personally. Mr. X, in fact, is a prince of a fellow and a fine player who has made many contributions to the game during his long career. But which is more likely, that he made the 9-ball six times in a row or that his memory has tricked him? A hoax is another possibility.

According to records compiled by Accu-Stats, in nine-ball tournaments the 9 goes about once in every thirty-five breaks, which is less often than most people think. In some major tournaments, the 9 has dropped only once in fifty breaks. Let's say that Mr. X has such a strong stroke that he makes it once in every thirty tries.

If the chances of doing something are 1 in 30, then doing it twice in a row is a 1 in 900 proposition. Six successes in a row face odds of 1 times 30 to the sixth power, which is roughly 729,000,000. If Mr. X broke the balls a thousand times a day, he'd need two thousand years to break that many times. Never mind his additional claim that he made the 9 *in the same pocket* every time. Two thousand years is long enough to wait, and I have already decided not to do it.

Mr. Y, a top pro player, writes that on a draw shot the cueball advances beyond the contact point before going back, which goes to prove that you don't need to know physics to be a top pro player. He points out that the object ball is not nailed down and is not a brick wall (true) and that the distance the cueball advances beyond the contact point before coming back depends on speed of stroke (slightly true).

For all practical purposes, when a cueball hits an object ball full in the face, it stops dead after advancing only the tiny distance equal to the amount it is compressed by the collision, which is about a tenth of an inch on a maximum strength stroke. All of its linear force—less the energy lost by compressing the two balls—is transferred to the object ball. What the cueball does after it stops depends on whether it has topspin or backspin. With no spin it stays put: the stop shot. With topspin it moves forward, but from a standing start after the collision.

It's easy to measure the tiny distance the cueball advances at the instant of a full hit before topspin or backspin take effect. Freeze a cueball against an object ball and put a cigarette or a straw between them on the cloth at right angles so that it is about a tenth of an inch from touching the cueball. See Diagram 8. Now back the cueball off six inches or so and shoot a draw shot full into the object ball. Shoot as hard as you can and see if the cigarette moves before the cueball comes back.

If you have the parlor toy that features a row of steel balls hanging from two horizontal rods and touching each other, there is another proof. Remove all the balls except two adjacent ones. Raise one and drop it against the other. The dropped ball will stop dead on impact. The other will rise to the same height from which the first was dropped . . . less a small amount due to the less-than-perfect elasticity of the balls.

There *is* a class of pool and billiard shots called the jump draw, in which the cueball advances beyond the object ball before coming back. For that

Diagram 8

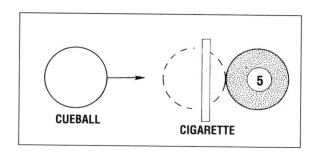

CUEBALL   CIGARETTE

to happen, the cueball must be struck a downward blow to make it leave the cloth. A spectacular example of the jump draw is the so-called "over-and-under" trick shot, in which the cueball hits an object ball, jumps over a rake resting on the rails, and draws back under it to pocket another ball. (See pages 9 and 259 of *Byrne's Treasury of Trick Shots in Pool and Billiards*.)

Mr. Y goes on to imply that on a cut shot with draw, the cueball deflects at an angle greater than 90 degrees (false), and travels in a straight line before the draw takes effect (also false).

On a cut shot, the paths taken by the object ball and a sliding cueball always form an angle of 90 degrees. (Sometimes a degree or two can be lost to the throw effect.) If there is draw or follow on the cueball, it caroms off the object ball along the right-angle line and *immediately* begins to curve away from it, unless it has left the cloth because of jump action. The curve is a parabola. Shoot softly with follow or draw and the curve is sharp; shoot hard and the curve is flat; but the path is always curved until the spin wears off. See Diagram 9. The curves are traced in slow motion in *Byrne's Standard Video of Pool and Billiards*.

Mr. Z, our final target, gives misleading advice to students regarding the throw effect when two object balls are frozen. If the two frozen balls and the cueball are in the same line and you want to throw the second object ball to the right, then Mr. Z correctly states that the first ball must be hit on the left side. He muddies the water when he recommends outside (left in the position described) English as well. No English of any sort will work. Hitting the first ball on the side opposite the desired throw is

Diagram 9

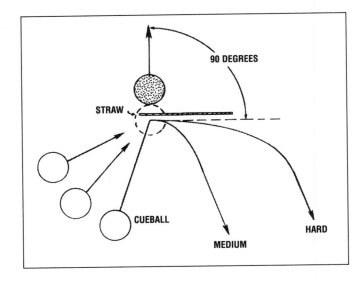

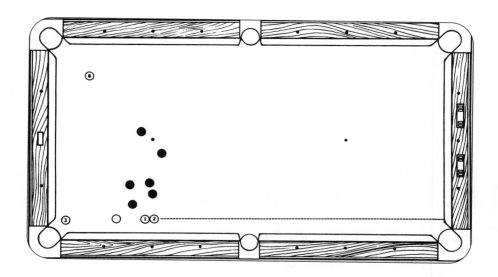

Diagram 10

all you need. On full hits, in fact, left English works against what you are trying to achieve, which brings me to a little-known nuance.

In Diagram 10, the cueball is on the same line as two frozen object balls. It is necessary to throw the second ball to the right to pocket it, which normally requires a left-side hit on the first ball. But that will send the cueball to the left, which might put you out of position. The good news is that the combination can be made with a full hit, which keeps the cueball close to the rail. Use heavy right English, just the opposite of what you would apply if throwing a single ball to the right.

The Right-Angle Rule and the Half-Ball Hit

WHAT'S YOUR ANGLE? Everybody's got an angle. Pool and billiard players, if they are national class, have two angles in particular: the right angle and the half-ball angle. When I say they "have" them, I mean they understand them on an intuitive level, if not on the level of mathematics and physics. Their understanding enables them to control the cueball on certain shots down to a gnat's eyelash.

THE RIGHT-ANGLE RULE

When a cueball glances off an object ball, the initial angle formed by the paths of the two balls is 90 degrees. Call it *the right-angle rule*. The rule is precise when the balls weigh the same, there is no friction between them, and they are perfectly elastic . . . conditions more often found in physics textbooks than on pool tables.

The right-angle rule is illustrated in Diagram 11. At the instant of contact between the two balls, the object ball (shaded) starts moving along the line of centers while the cueball moves along a line perpendicular to it. In theory, only if the paths of the two balls form a right angle can the laws of conservation of kinetic energy and momentum be satisfied.

Imagining the right angle is very helpful in position play because it enables the shooter to predict with considerable accuracy the path the cueball will take off the object ball.

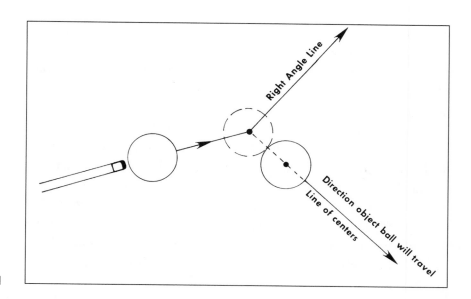

Diagram 11

Now for the exceptions. One results from the less-than-perfect elasticity of the balls. When balls collide, they are compressed. (The size of the circular areas on the balls that touch each other is surprisingly big. To see it, put a piece of carbon paper against a ball and drive a cueball into it.) Energy is lost when the balls are compressed and then return to their spherical shape, and the energy loss shows up in the paths taken by the balls after the collision; the angle formed is less than 90 degrees. The difference is almost undetectable for thin hits; for almost full hits it can be seen and demonstrated easily.

The other major factor that affects the right-angle rule is friction between the balls, which can cause the object ball to take a direction not quite opposite the point of contact, as in the throw effect. In other words, ball-to-ball friction can make the object ball move on a path that diverges from the line of centers.

Keep in mind that unless the cueball slides into the object ball without topspin or backspin, the right-angle rule holds only for an instant after the collision. Topspin, or natural forward roll, and backspin will cause the cueball to curve away from the right angle path it takes initially. (For diagrams of the curves, see pages 56 and 71 of *Byrne's Standard Book of Pool and Billiards;* to see the curves traced in slow motion at various speeds, see Vol. II of *Byrne's Standard Video of Pool and Billiards;* for the mathematics of ball collisions, see the articles in the *American Journal of Physics*—September 1988 [Wallace and Schroeder] and May 1989 [Onoda].)

I have written more than once that sidespin has no significant effect on the angle the cueball takes off an object ball. Sidespin is used mainly to influence the rebound angle off a cushion. Sidespin, however, does alter the right-angle rule because of the throw effect.

In Diagram 12, the player is faced with cutting the ball marked A into the side. If the cueball slides into the object ball with no spin of any kind and drives it into the center of the pocket, the cueball will travel in a straight line at right angles to the end rail, striking at about point E.

If, however, inside English (right in this example) is applied to the cueball, then a thinner hit can be used because the object ball will be thrown a little to the left of the line of centers. In the diagram, line AC shows the line of centers at the instant of contact, line AB is the path taken by the object ball. The cueball will still carom off the ball at right angles to the line of centers, but because the line of centers is now aimed at C rather than B, the cueball will strike the end rail near D. (Sidespin only, no follow or draw.)

By the same reasoning, if left sidespin is put on the cueball, a fuller hit can be made on the object ball. In that case, the object ball will be thrown a little to the right and the cueball will hit the end rail near point F.

With outside English, the angle formed by the two ball paths is slightly greater than 90 degrees; with inside English it is slightly less. In all cases, the cueball caroms off the object ball along a path perpendicular to the line of centers.

Diagram 12

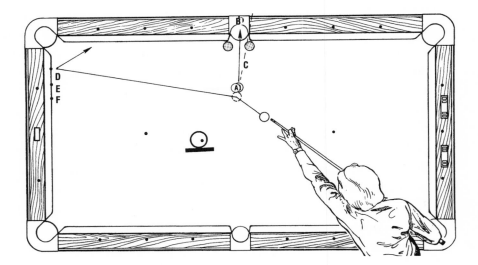

Students should be reminded that using sidespin makes aiming more difficult. Don't use it unless you decide the positional rewards outweigh the increased chance of missing the shot.

If you want to test the influence of sidespin on the right-angle rule, bracket the side pocket with two balls, as shown in Diagram 12, leaving a space just wide enough for a ball to enter. This eliminates "cheating" the pocket. Discard any trial in which the object ball touches one of the guard balls.

THE HALF-BALL HIT

If you send the cueball into another ball so that it is rolling naturally (no slippage between the ball and the cloth), the cueball will be deflected the maximum amount with a half-ball hit. To get what is defined as a half-ball hit, aim the cueball at the edge of the object ball. At the moment of contact, the cueball deflects along a line at right angles to the line of centers, bends forward in a parabolic curve, and resumes moving in a straight line. During the final straight segment of the path, the cueball is once again rolling naturally without slipping on the cloth.

The reason the half-ball hit is so important is not just that it results in the greatest possible deflection, but that it is resistant to error. Hit slightly more or less than half a ball, and the cueball deflects at close to the same angle. (For a full discussion of the half-ball hit, see *Byrne's Advanced Technique in Pool and Billiards,* pages 45–47.)

The carom angle for a half-ball hit and a naturally rolling ball is 34 degrees. A surprising fact emerges from the equations. The angle of deflection is the same no matter what the speed. This seems to violate common sense, for all players know that the harder you shoot the cueball, the farther it bounces off to one side when it hits another ball. What counts, though, is how you measure the angle.

In Diagram 13, the cueball is aimed at point B so that its path grazes the edge of the object ball: the so-called half-ball hit. Point A is the center of the cueball at the instant of contact with the object ball. With medium speed, the cueball leaves A along the right-angle line, bends forward to point E, then rolls straight to the rail at C. The angle of deflection must be measured by projecting line CE backward until it intersects the aiming line at G. Angle BGC is 34 degrees.

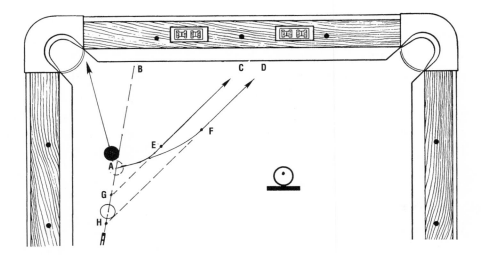

Diagram 13

If you shoot hard, the cueball curves from A to F before it straightens out and goes to the rail at D. Project the DF line back to the point H. The angle BHD will also be 34 degrees. The relevant mathematical proof is given in the previously cited articles in the *American Journal of Physics.*

While I am indebted to Bob Jewett and Dr. George Onoda for helping me understand these technical concepts, responsibility for errors and misapprehension is mine alone.

Three-Shot Planning

FUELING THE POOL BOOM are hordes of beginners. Survey the scene in any of the new upscale rooms, especially on a busy weekend night, and you'll be struck by the number of players who can hardly make a ball. You can sense the absence of serious players by the number of happy faces, by the whoops of joy and dismay during games, and by the loudness of the juke-box. You'd rather watch a grim money match between two predatory pool pros? You'll have to go someplace else.

Beginners seem to have more fun, maybe because their games are full of surprises, amazing flukes, grotesque miscues, and last-second reversals of fortune. With beginners, every shot is an adventure and every game in doubt until the final scratch. Yet some of the laughter is born of embarrassment. Not knowing what you are doing is only amusing for a little while, then you want to find out what you're doing wrong.

One thing you might be doing wrong, if you're new to the game, is not looking far enough ahead. Making the shot at hand and getting position on the next ball isn't enough; you must get the right angle on the second ball so you can get to the third. Tables are run three shots at a time. The good news is that great skill is often not required, only a way of thinking. The skill required is often a very minimal ability to draw and follow and estimate speed.

Good players plan three shots ahead without thinking about it. They

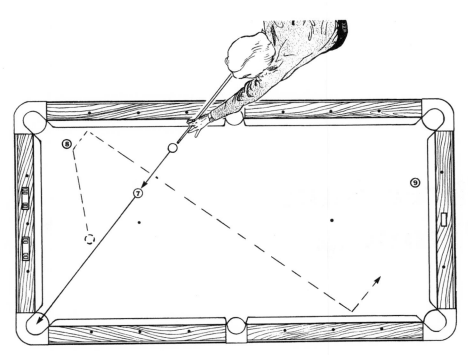

Diagram 14

can solve the problems in this section at a glance. If you are in that category, you can either skip to the next section or use what follows as a teaching aid. Those beginners out there who fill today's new world of pool need to be told about three-ball planning. It's a gift that keeps on giving.

In Diagram 14, the game is nine-ball and the 7 is straight in. If you have the ability to make such a shot, you can easily run out by getting an angle on the 8. A stop shot is the worst thing you can do, for then you will need a long draw (what the British call "a deep screw") from the 8 to get up the table for the 9. Avoid getting straight in on the 8 by drawing back or following forward a foot or so. Easiest is to let the cueball follow the 7 so the 8 can be cut in as indicated by the dashed lines to get position on the 9. You think this is obvious? Then you haven't done much teaching.

In Diagram 15, the 8-ball is at the other end of the table and not shown. The problem is to make the 6 and 7 and get to the other end for the 8, then back down for the 9. Following to point B won't work because the 9 blocks the path used in the previous diagram. Better to draw the cueball to the vicinity of point A, giving you a cut shot on the 7 and an easy way to send the cueball into the top cushion and down to the other end.

In Diagram 16, the 9-ball is at the opposite end and not shown. You

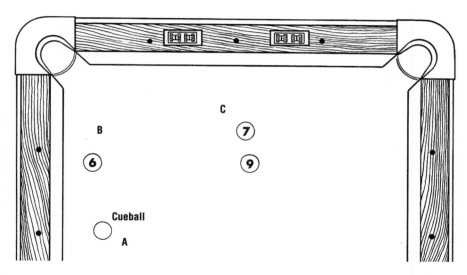

Diagram 15

must find a way to make the 7 and get a good angle on the 8—not just a little angle, a good angle. Because the 7 is so easy to make, you should be able to play precise position. Some might like to use follow and send the cueball two rails to point B. I prefer a short draw as shown, leaving the cueball on the rail and close to the 8. Cutting the 8 in from there sends the cueball to the other end without effort. Seemingly simple shots like this are well worth practicing to develop the needed precision.

Diagram 16

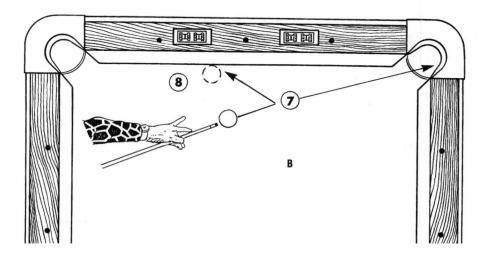

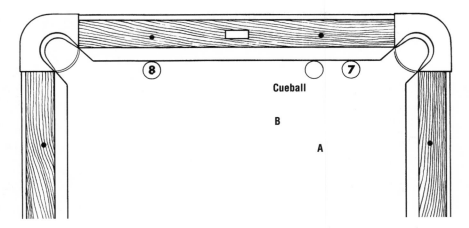

Diagram 17

The position in Diagram 17 is instructive. Again, the 9-ball is off the diagram at the other end of the table. With the cueball frozen to the rail along with the 7 and 8, what can be done?

Top players will have no problem; neophytes will scratch their heads. To make the 7 and get an angle on the 8, cheat the pocket. Aim a hair off dead straight and let the 7 come off the rail slightly on its way to the hole. With only a few inches to go, there is plenty of room for error. Follow on the cueball will send it one rail to point A, draw will pull it back to B. The technique is easy to employ if the balls are close together and close to the pocket. Increase either distance to a foot or more and the margin of error narrows to near zero.

Diagram 18

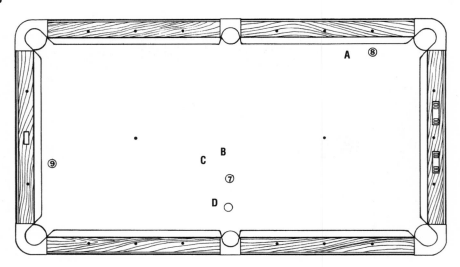

You have ball in hand and are faced with the layout in Diagram 18. Can you run out? One solution is to place the cueball at D and shoot softly, leaving yourself a zigzag pattern similar to the one in Diagram 14. Better is try to send the cueball to point A, close to the 8. Straight in, or nearly so, and you have a draw shot easy to reach for a right-handed player and easy to execute because the cueball is close to the 8. What's the most reliable way to make the 7 and send the cueball to the rail near point A? One way is to place the cueball at C and shoot a cut shot, sending the cueball off the end rail near the top score marker. Another is to draw back from B. I prefer the follow shot from D on the grounds that the length of travel of the cueball is much easier to judge accurately with follow than with draw.

Another ball-in-hand problem is given in Diagram 19. The problem is to make the 7 and get up table for the 8. One possibility is to place the cueball at A and cut the 7 along the rail. Easier, and less often thought of by pre-intermediate players, is to place the cueball extremely close to the 7, as shown. No problem from there to cut the 7 with a soft stroke and send the cueball the length of the table. The idea can be used even if the 7 is frozen to the rail, provided it's close to the pocket.

Diagram 19

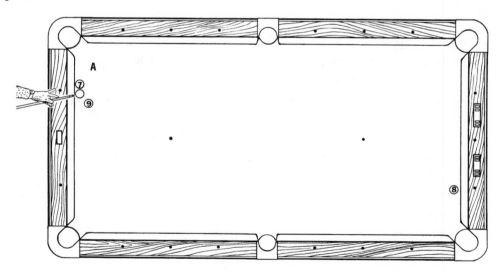

Double-Duty Defense

NINE-BALL IS CONSIDERED A SHOTMAKER'S GAME, but even players who are half blind are tough to beat if they take full advantage of defensive possibilities. Today's sermonette is aimed at those who don't have the uncanny accuracy of the top professionals. The glad tidings are that you can win a lot of games by using your head.

First, get rid of the notion that you must try to make every open shot, or that there is something "chicken" about playing safe when a run-out is possible. Even if you have been left an easy shot, it might be too hard to get the necessary position on the next ball, or there may be a cluster down the line that can't easily be broken up if you pocket the first ball. It may be that a run-out would be more likely if you had a different angle on the first ball.

When you come to the table, always look to see if there is an easy safety play. If there is, it might be good to take advantage of it. It's not so much that you should look for ways to win on three successive fouls—though that is a worthy goal—but rather that you should take the opportunity to improve your overall chances of winning the game. If you think a given layout gives you a two-thirds chance of running the table, a good safety might result in a 90 percent chance of a run-out on your next turn.

The ball-in-hand-anywhere rule is usually a ticket to a run-out for a good player, even if there is a cluster that must be separated, but there are plenty of situations when the freedom to place the cueball anywhere should be used for defensive purposes.

A couple of observations for beginners: if the object ball is close to a second ball, then there is usually an easy safety play. You can hit the object ball softly and let the cueball roll against the second ball, or you can shoot a stop shot and drive the object ball around to the other side of the second ball. These obvious moves hardly merit discussion.

When faced with a difficult or impossible safety yourself, there are several well-known maneuvers. One is to deliberately pocket the wrong ball so that it is spotted behind a ball already on the spot, thus creating a cluster that your opponent must find a way to break up if he is to run out. Another is to drive a ball against another so that they create a cluster. When the 9-ball is hanging in a pocket and you can't hit the lowest-numbered ball, sink the 9 and respot it—anything is better than leaving it for your opponent to make with a simple ball-in-hand combination or carom. At least make him run the balls.

So much for the refresher course. Now for the post-graduate studies.

Consider the position in Diagram 20. It's easy to make the 6-ball, but almost impossible to make it and get correct position on the 7, which is at the other end of the table. A young hotshot might play position for a length-of-the-table bank on the 7 or a thin cut, but a mature player such as yourself—more interested in winning the game than showing off—will play a safety.

Diagram 20

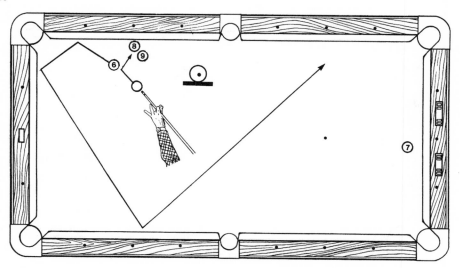

Hit the 6 full, stop the cueball, and bank the 6 around the table so that it comes to rest on the other side of the 8 and 9. If you have the freedom to do so, hit the 6 a little to one side so that the cueball drifts to the right and snuggles against the 8 or 9. A danger in shots like this is that you will accidentally pocket the 6, thus snookering yourself instead of your opponent. Guard against that by all means.

The trouble is, even if you hook your opponent so well that he fouls and gives you ball in hand, you will have a hard time getting out because of the problem cluster. The key to the position is to send the cueball into the 8 and 9 with just enough speed to separate them. Now you've put your opponent in great jeopardy, for unless he manages to escape from your hook and leave you safe, the way is clear for a run-out.

In spreading a cluster of only two or three balls, by the way, keep in mind that only a slight nudge is needed. There is no need to lose control of the cueball.

In Diagram 21 a safety is called for because there is no good way to make the 1 and get decent position on the 2. Even if you succeed, the 7-8 problem cluster remains. Here's a perfect place for double-duty defense. Drive the 1-ball down the table as indicated and at the same time try to put the cueball behind the 8-ball. Use enough force to break the 7 and 8 apart. The point is that unless you spread the 7 and 8, a hook won't hurt your opponent enough.

It's important to realize that your position is improved by this play even if you don't get the hook, provided you move the 7 or 8 a few inches. Your

Diagram 21

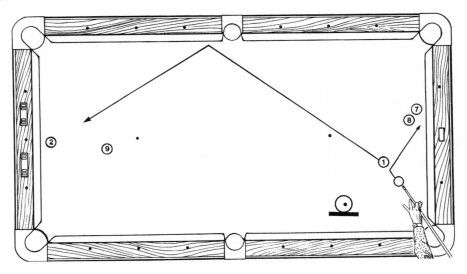

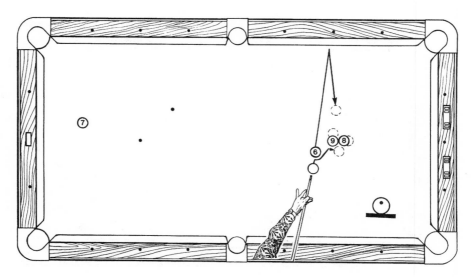

Diagram 22

opponent faces a tough shot in a position where you can run out if he makes a mistake.

What would you do if the balls are as shown in Diagram 22 and you have cueball in hand? There are lots of ways to make the 6 and get position on the 7, but that won't help much as long as the 9 is on the spot with the 8 frozen to it. One good idea is to set up a straight-in shot for the 6 in the side, draw back slightly, and play a safety on the 8, leaving the cueball against the 9. I ask you to consider something sneakier. The move shown in the diagram greatly improves your winning chances. Place the cueball so that you can shoot a soft follow, leaving the balls as indicated. Now your opponent is in serious trouble; he will have a hard time even *hitting* the 6 much less leaving you safe. By bumping the cueball into the cluster you've cleared the path to victory.

One last example (Diagram 23). Assume once again that you have cueball in hand. Because of the 8-9 cluster, it doesn't help a lot to run the 5, 6, and 7. Playing a safety similar to the one in the first diagram is okay, but your opponent isn't left in much danger because the 8-9 cluster protects him against your running out on your next turn. The double-duty idea is a good choice here. Place the cueball as shown, hit it thin, and try to send the cueball into the 8 and 9, which is a big target. If you succeed in eliminating the problem cluster and hooking your opponent, you will have a tremendous advantage. If you create a problem cluster out of the 5 and 6, your opponent will likely separate them again when banking for the 5.

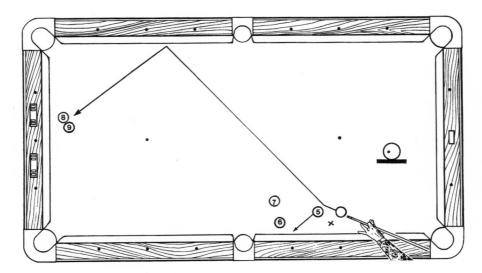

Diagram 23

Because of the ball-in-hand-anywhere rule, safety play can be a devastating weapon. Yet when is the last time you saw somebody practicing safeties? The ability to judge banking angles and cueball speed is essential in playing position and in playing safe as well. Fortunately, players who aren't blessed with extraordinary hand-eye coordination, who don't have time to practice for hours every day, and who forgot to spend their childhoods in pool halls, can win a lot of games by cleverness alone.

New and
Unusual Shots

IN BYRNE'S TREASURY OF TRICK SHOTS are some 300 examples of ingenuity on pool and billiard tables, some of them going back hundreds of years. Since the book was published in 1982, I've accumulated a thick file folder of additional brainstorms. A few of them are my own; some are contributions from such renowned specialists as Willie Jopling; but most are from amateur players who worked out something interesting while practicing at home and wanted to share it with somebody.

Most trick shots are variations of a few dozen basic themes; it's hard to come up with anything that is genuinely new. However, the Drawbridge Shot, sent to me by a Southern Californian player named "Chef Anton" Riniti, is unlike anything I've ever seen. It's a bit touchy to set up, but once you get it right you will be rewarded with an amusing three-dimensional stunt that will make you the talk of the town.

The shot is seen from above in Diagram 24. Needed are two cues and a plastic triangle with a lip. The shot is based on the idea of counterbalancing a ball on top of the triangle with the weight of the cues and a couple of balls. When the balls on the cues are removed, the weight of the upper ball is enough to make the triangle lever downward so that the ball is deposited on the cues after which it rolls into the side pocket. The moment the ball is off the triangle, the triangle flips back up.

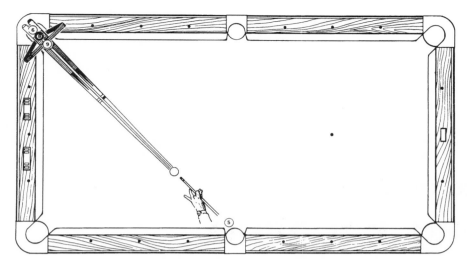

Diagram 24

Stick a corner of the triangle into a corner pocket as shown in the first photo. Place two cues through the triangle, rest the butts on the corner of the table, and aim them at the side pocket. Rest two balls (you might need three) near the ends of the cues and keep them in place with a paper match. The weight of the cues and the two balls enables the triangle to support the 9-ball. Take care to keep the upper side of the triangle square with the cues, and position the 9-ball so that it is directly above the track formed by the cues. Position a ball on the lip of the side pocket; the cue-

The weight of two balls and two cues is enough to keep the 9-ball elevated on the lip of a triangle.

ball goes on the ferrules of the cues, and is kept from rolling off with another paper match. See photo.

Here's the action: Shoot the cueball lightly up the cues. When it strikes the two-ball combination, the far ball is sent off the table and into a wastebasket (unless your touch is good enough to hit the combo so lightly that only the paper match is dislodged). The cueball and the remaining ball(s) roll through the triangle toward the side pocket, where the cueball knocks in the lipped ball, clearing the way for the following ball. With the weight off the cues, the 9-ball is lowered to the cues and runs downhill and into the side pocket while the audience explodes in wild applause.

The second stunt is laid out in Diagram 25. It was sent to me by Bob Barney of El Cajon, California, and was inspired by some of the penny wrapper shots in my trick shot book. As you can see, it's a combination of the famous Miller Lite shot and the almost-as-famous railroad shot. Barney suggests presenting it as an 8-ball shot, using the 8-ball as the cueball. Set it up as given in the diagram and you can make the seven low spot balls in numerical order, followed by the 8-ball. What makes it possible is the placement of the 6-ball atop a penny wrapper. The 2-ball takes out the wrapper and drops the 6-ball to the table. After the 8-ball has gone three rails and turned the corner at the top of the cues, the cueball will roll downhill, knock in the 6-ball, and get out of the way for the 7-ball and 8-ball. (Other ball paths omitted for simplicity.)

Diagram 25

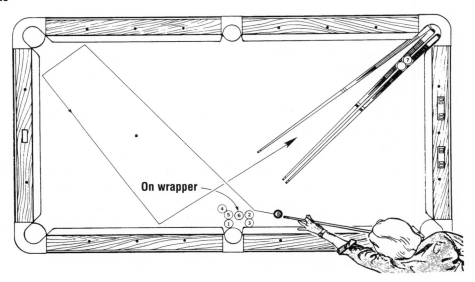

On wrapper

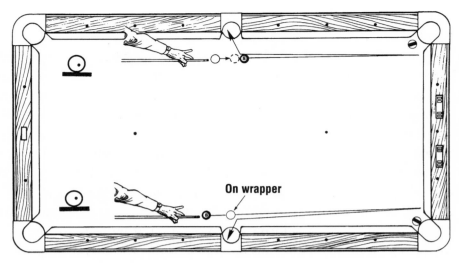

Diagram 26

On wrapper

The shot in Diagram 26, top, was invented by Martin Kaczmarowski of O'Fallon, Illinois. The challenge is to make the 8-ball in the side pocket. This would stump most players, but once you know what to do the shot is much easier than the correct spelling of its inventor's name. Shoot a stop shot with a touch of right English so that the 8-ball comes back close to the rail and kisses in off the waiting cueball. (See also page 15.)

Once you can make that, you should have no trouble with the shot on the bottom of the diagram. Put the cueball atop a coin wrapper and use the 8-ball as the cueball. Shoot the 8-ball under the cueball, taking out the coin wrapper, and watch the 8 carom into the side off the cueball. I invented this shot. I have no idea why.

It's not easy to come up with a trick shot that is both interesting and easy. One such is the coin wrapper overlap shot, which I invented in the spring of 1981. I've seen it performed by many professional players since then (usually without credit to the inventor, but I hate to whine). It's diagrammed in *Byrne's Treasury of Trick Shots,* 1982, and demonstrated in *Byrne's Standard Video of Trick Shots, Vol. III,* 1993.

The side view inset in Diagram 27 shows how to place two balls atop coin wrappers cut to different lengths. When you shoot a cueball under the balls, they fall, strike each other, and depart in opposite directions. In the center of the diagram is a nice variation by the Georgia trick shot inventor Rick Wright, author of *Trick Shot Wizardry in Pocket Billiards,* 1983. Send the 6-ball under the elevated balls and draw back to pocket the 7-ball. Only slightly harder than my original version and a lot showier.

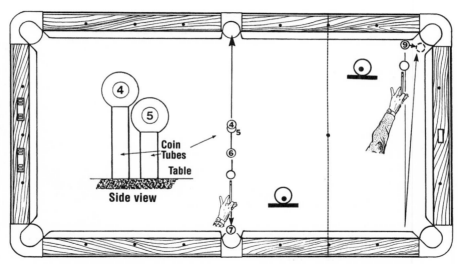

Diagram 27

On the right side of Diagram 27 is a shot dreamed up one morning when Mike Massey and Paul Gerni were having breakfast in Columbus, Ohio, during some now-forgotten tournament. Maybe one of them still has the original paper napkin. Hit the 9-ball with a touch of left English, which will nudge it in front of the pocket. The cueball kicks back to the near rail and, thanks to a touch of retained English, returns to pocket the relocated 9-ball. High marks for concept, even higher marks for difficulty. To have any chance at all, the cueball must not be struck above center.

For something really easy, I direct you to my trick shot video again and the cap-pistol shot, which is more like a gunshot than a pool shot. Go to a toy store and buy a roll of caps for a cap pistol. Tear off a couple and tape or paste them to the side of a pool ball. When the time is right, pull the ball from a pocket, conceal the caps with your thumb, and set up a combination with the gunpowder at the contact point. Tell the onlookers you have developed explosive power in your stroke, or something equally absurd. "Watch closely!" Smack the combo smartly with the cueball. The resulting blast is startling, to say the least.

At one exhibition, I made a woman standing near the table jump a foot in the air. That's my personal best, but I think fourteen inches is possible.

Back to Georgia: "Fast Larry" Grindinger, whose right arm is one of the biggest cannons in the game, suggests the two-stroke trifle in Diagram 28 for those of us with only normal abilities. First shoot the black ball slowly toward the corner pocket; while it's still rolling fire the cueball along the indicated four-rail path, timing it so that the cueball gives the black ball

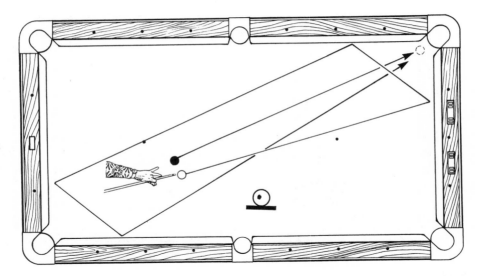

Diagram 28

a friendly bump into the pocket at the last instant. The two balls can also be struck in reverse order. It looks best if the black ball has to be redirected into the pocket by the late-arriving cueball.

When Jeff Olney sent me the two shots in Diagram 29 he was in the Navy and stationed at Pearl Harbor. At the top is an electrifying time shot . . . when it goes. The cueball and the 3-ball are touching and frozen to the rail. The 4-ball blocks the 3-ball's path to the corner pocket. With your cue parallel to the rail use right-hand English and shoot straight ahead. If you are lucky, the 3-ball will rebound off the end rail and—hotly pursued by the cueball—get rammed into the corner pocket by a second collision.

Jeff says one time in three is possible with practice, and adds that with a hard stroke "it really looks good." Readers who have closely studied my previous writings will know why the 3-ball diverges from the rail when right spin is applied to the cueball.

At the bottom of Diagram 29 is another shot that Jeff Olney first called to my attention. It's a beautiful thing, almost an optical illusion, especially if you've never seen it before. Let's say you're playing nine-ball and the last two balls come to rest as shown. What should you do? Shoot at the 9-ball as if the 8-ball weren't there. It's a time shot, you see; both the cueball and the 9-ball are bumped off line by the cueball's initial contact with the 8-ball. It is fanciful, of course, to imagine that the precise position will ever come up in a game, but it's a nice exhibition or challenge shot. You'll have to experiment to find exactly where to spot the balls.

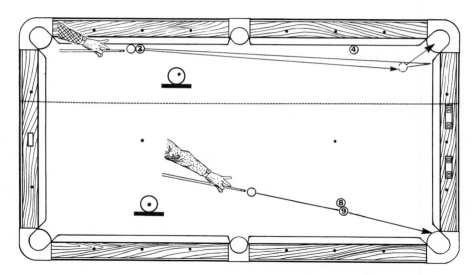

Diagram 29

In Diagram 30 is a flashy crowd-pleaser from Rick Wright. Everybody loves the railroad shot, so why not use two tracks at once? In the diagram, the two-ball combinations are aimed into the rails to compensate for throw. By shooting the cueball at the opposite side pocket, the 1-ball and the 2-ball are sent up the tracks, around the corners, and back down into the side pockets. It's interesting to watch the progress of the balls, because they never arrive at the side at exactly the same time.

Diagram 30

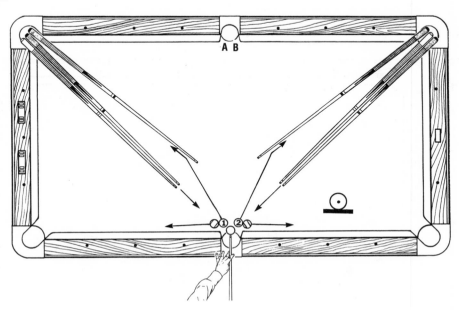

It is possible to influence the speed of the two railroad balls, which might be of interest to those who enjoy cheating their friends. All you have to do is alter the alignment of your cue toward one ball or the other. To make the 1 beat the 2 into the side pocket, aim at point A. To make the 2 beat the 1, aim at point B. Place your bets accordingly.

Publication of the shot in Diagram 31 might so encourage Brent Johnson that I might get into trouble with Canadian authorities for contributing to the delinquency of a minor. Brent, a resident of Brantford, Ontario, is a teenager and would rather play pool than just about anything else. (Brent! Stay in school!) In the diagram, imagine that the shooter must hit the 8-ball and finds every good banking path blocked by his opponent's balls. The solution is a six-rail bank. Brent claims that he made the shot in a game in 1993. "People went crazy and my opponent almost fainted."

I still think he should stay in school.

First it was a song, "The Night the Lights Went Out in Georgia," then it was a 1981 movie starring Dennis Quaid and Kristy McNichol, then it was a 1995 trick shot, and finally it was seen on *America's Funniest Home Videos*.

Larry Grindinger and Rick Wright, both from the Atlanta area, had an idea for a two-man jump shot so difficult it might take them the rest of their lives to make it. But if they made it and captured it on videotape they would have proof that they were part of a miracle. They would qualify for that special corner of heaven with people who have made holes-in-one

Diagram 31

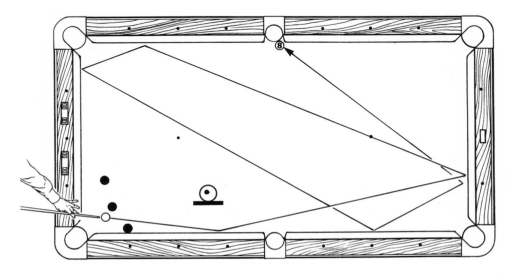

with pop bottles, have been struck by lightning and lived, and have made the 9-ball on the break six times in a row.

The concept was simple. They would elevate their cues and shoot jump shots toward each other from diagonally opposite corners of a pool table. The cueballs would collide squarely in the middle (they could see it in their minds) about a foot above the cloth and rebound straight back toward the starting points to pocket balls hanging in the jaws. To dress up the stunt, two triangles were placed on edge for the balls to jump through. Diagram 32 shows the idea.

They turned on the camera and started shooting, rewinding the tape after each failure. Finally they enjoyed success of an unexpected and disastrous sort. The balls met exactly on line but at slightly different elevations. The higher ball caromed straight up into the overhead fluorescent tubes; the lower one was driven into the cloth and bounced vertically into the lights inches behind the first one. The balls hit the light fixture like smart bombs, creating a splendid shower of glass, hardware, and smoke. The explosion is hilarious, especially in slow motion, and is like watching the fall of a dynamited building. The reaction of the gunners is pretty funny, too. They are speechless, and their body language suggests that visions of berserk proprietors are dancing in their heads.

Ah, but who had the last laugh? A copy of the videotape was sent to *America's Funniest Home Videos* in Los Angeles, and within a week ABC phoned with the news that the clip had been selected to air on the show

Diagram 32

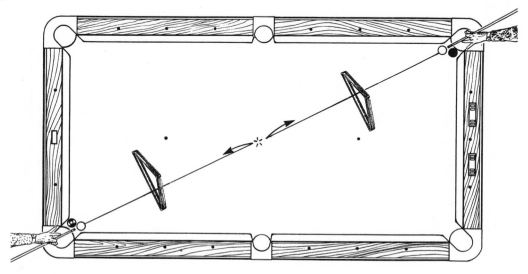

on October 1, 1995. If the studio audience were to be enchanted enough, Grindinger and Wright would win the weekly prize of $10,000 and have a chance at the grand prize of $100,000. Sad to report, they were eliminated by a large lady jumping around a backyard barbecue because a bug was in her slacks. The good news is that the shot is on the second pool highlights tape available from Accu-Stats Video Productions.

What I have dubbed "The Night the Lights Went Out in Georgia" is an elaboration of an earlier two-player theme. The first incarnation appears in a 1948 Pete Smith specialty that ran as a short subject in movie theaters. Willie Mosconi and Jimmy Caras shoot cueballs toward each other from opposite corners, but only Caras elevates his cue. His cueball jumps over Mosconi's as they pass at the center of the table. The action is so fast that the balls seem to melt through one another in an optical illusion.

Thirty years later, Paul Gerni and Jim Rempe, experimenting in Davenport, Iowa, came up with another version. Both cues are level. The cueballs meet and rebound straight back into the corner pockets. For a diagram, turn to page 115 of *Byrne's Treasury of Trick Shots in Pool and Billiards* (1982).

Anthony Thomas writes to say that while vacationing in Arizona a couple of years ago he wandered into the Rack and Q, a room in Tempe, where he saw a young man named Scott perform a series of stunning trick shots. One that particularly impressed him is shown in Diagram 33. Jump over the ring of balls, pocket the 1-ball, jump out of the ring, and pocket two more balls. Scott made it on the second try. (Scott who, Tony? Get the details next time.)

Diagram 33

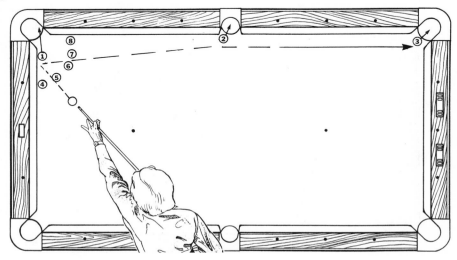

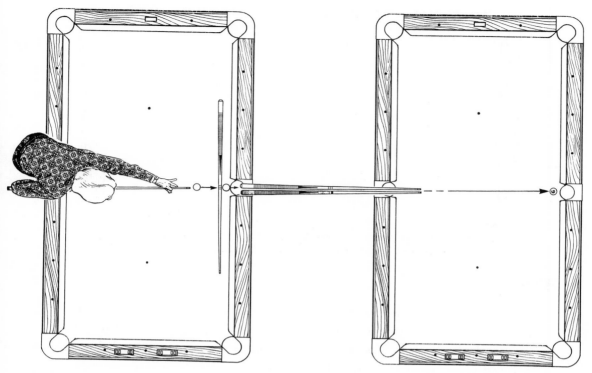

Diagram 34

Another correspondent who likes trick shots more than last names is Joe Kane of Phoenix, Arizona. He spent a week a while back in Vista, California. Every day he visited a room called Green Felt Downs, and every day Joey, an eight-year-old boy, asked him to show him a trick shot. Kane "never did get his last name." On the last day, Joey had a shot to demonstrate, one he claimed he had invented himself. Let's call it "Joey's Shot." Diagram 34 is based on the sketch Kane sent me. Shoot straight at the ball on the lip of the side pocket. The cue will bump it in and cause the cueball to jump onto the two side-by-side cues, which are held in position by coins on the rails. The cueball rolls across the cues and crosses the adjoining table to pocket the 9-ball. Not bad for a third grader. Imagine the contributions he will make in junior high school.

My final example of mailbag madness comes from Joe Savorin of Memphis, Tennessee, who presents it as a challenge. To see if you can solve the problem yourself, cover Diagram 36 with your hand and look only at Diagram 35. The game is one-pocket and your pocket is labeled "your pocket." There are three balls left and you need all three to win. Can you run out from the given position? Think about it, then read on.

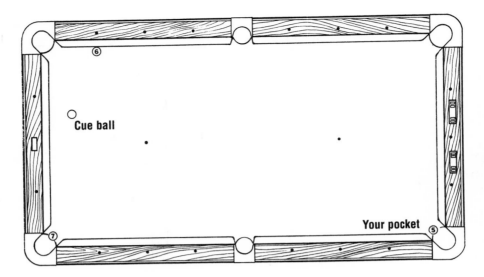

Diagram 35

The first step of the solution is given upside down in Diagram 36. Make the 5-ball by banking the 6-ball into it, at the same time making the 7-ball with the cueball. Not too tough if you secretly practice for half an hour and if you have, say, three chances. The 6-ball stops in front of your pocket while the 7-ball is respotted. Now it's easy to make the 6-ball and send the cueball along the dashed path for position on the 7-ball.

While I'm opposed to gambling in general and swindling friends in particular, I can see that a lot of money can be made with this shot. I will lay two-to-one odds that nobody will share any winnings with me.

Diagram 36

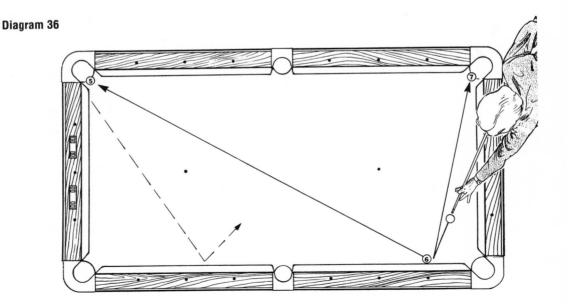

Finger Pool

MIKE MASSEY HAS A PILE-DRIVER STROKE, and when he gives an exhibition he demonstrates a variety of impressive power shots. The real cheering and whistling begins when he puts his cue aside and spins the cueball onto the table with a flick of his fingers. His "limbo" shot (Diagram 37, top) is a classic, and if he tried to end his show without it, a riot would ensue.

Much more spin can be imparted with a twist of the fingers than with a blow from a cue, and it is nothing short of amazing to see what a ball can be made to do. Finger pool—or hand billiards—goes back hundreds of years, and displays of it once were common in trick shot shows. In the October 1992 *Billiards Digest,* Mike Shamos reviewed its long history and its colorful practitioners. Here I'll present a dozen contemporary examples of this specialized art form and challenge you to try to make them.

While Massey is the best-known finger flipper in this country, he isn't the only one. There's also Rives Smith of Houston, Texas. The calluses on his right hand aren't from working in the garden. Carl "Cueball Kelly" Zingale, who died in 1986 at the age of ninety, had a large repertory of finger shots and often entertained at tournaments when he wasn't refereeing. South America, especially Argentina, has produced some formidable finger

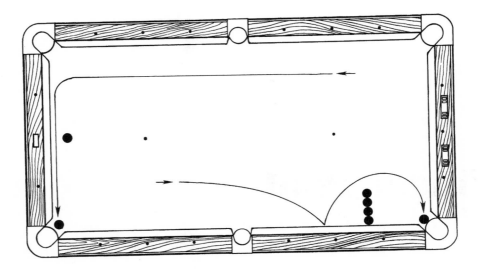

Diagram 37

spinners . . . Juan Navarra, for one. In Europe there is Spain's Valeriano Perera Sans, whose 1990 book (in Spanish) *Billar—Mis Jugadas Favoritas* contains a lengthy section with photos and drawings aimed at enabling the reader to learn the art. See also chapter 15 in my book on trick shots.

Looking at Diagram 37, it doesn't seem possible that a ball thrown down the table can make a left-hand turn that sharp and go behind the first object ball. In December of 1993, in the stunning new Chalkers billiard room in San Francisco, I saw Mike Massey send the cueball on that path and go through a space just a hair wider than a ball. I spilled my drink. Also in the diagram is a Massey stunt that always gets good audience reaction—curving a cueball around a line of up to four balls.

Diagram 38, left, is a shot that both Massey and Rives Smith do. Throw the ball past the side pocket and make it curve back to pocket a ball in the corner. At the right is one of Smith's concoctions.

Two more Smith shots are shown in Diagram 39. At the left, the backspin doesn't take until after the cueball has rebounded from the first rail. At the right, the cueball curves all the way around an object ball without touching it and without touching any rails.

Smith can make the spectacular around–the–table shot in Diagram 40 which is the same pattern used for one of the massé shots in the European "artistic billiards" competitions. Mike Massey claims to be able to make almost all of the seventy-five artistic shots with his hand alone. (The jump draw shots are almost impossible without a cue.)

Spain's Perera Sans has a lot of shots in his bag of tricks in which the

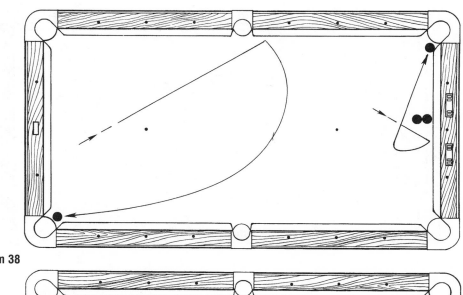

Diagram 38

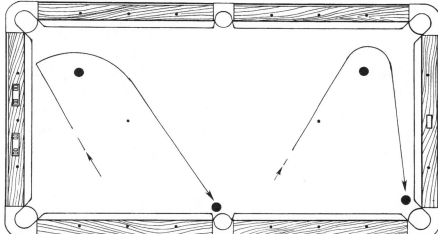

Diagram 39

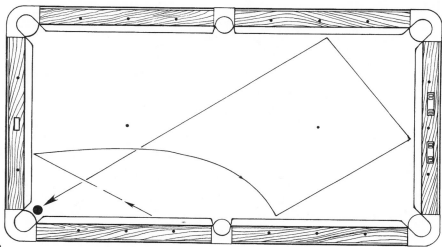

Diagram 40

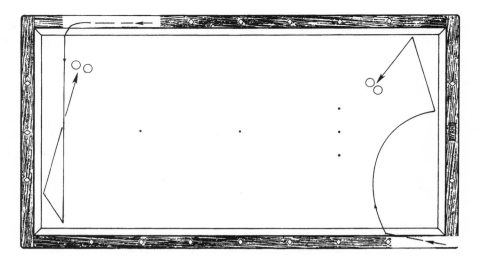

Diagram 41

cueball begins on the wood of the rail. At the left of Diagram 41 the cueball is thrown toward the corner on the wood, then crosses the table and
returns to make a billiard on the two object balls. At the right, the ball is
thrown away from the corner along the wood; after it falls to the bed of
the table it returns to the right end rail and spins out of the corner to the
object balls. I've seen him do it, but only on videotape. Next time I'm in
Spain, I'm heading to Barcelona to see him do it in person.

Strategy and Tactics in Three-Cushion Billiards

Legends in their own lifetimes, straight pool master Willie Mosconi and billiard wizard Willie Hoppe pose in Chicago with their trophies after the 1951 tournaments at Navy Pier. Both players were adept in each other's specialty—Mosconi, in fact, finished fourth in the 1947 world three-cushion tournament.

(Courtesy of the Billiard Archive)

Handling Tough Leaves

MOST AMERICAN THREE-CUSHION PLAYERS emphasize defense, overemphasize it in the opinion of foreign experts. When you play billiards in the United States, you get used to seeing the cueball at one end of the table and the object balls at the other. Knowing how to handle tough leaves is essential, especially since the rule permitting deliberate safeties (not trying to score) is a thing of the past.

Often there is no way to turn the tables on an opponent who has left you safe—that is, leaving him a tough shot in return. You must do your best to score, even though the chances of doing so are slim. If there is more than one way the shot can be attempted, it becomes a matter of picking the best one. The better the player, the more options will be seen. The wealth of experience and knowledge that a champion carries with him to the table enables him to assess the percentages on alternate shots more accurately than lesser players as well as to see more shots. He can check the applicability of a tremendous number of patterns he has learned over the years. There is no substitute for experience, talent, and imagination, but I can help you learn patterns.

This section deals with just one class of "safe" leaves. The cueball is near one corner and the object balls are at the other end of the table along the same long rail. To save space in Diagrams 43 and 44, the empty part of the table has been omitted. In each case the cueball is at the left, and the rail shown is the long rail. The positions are hard to evaluate presented on partial diagrams at such a small scale, so set them up on a table. What is the best shot? My recommendations will be discussed with the aid of Diagram 42.

Shot 1 Aiming at E for a three-cushion natural bank or at F for a five-cushion bank are poor choices because approaching the object balls diagonally provides a small chance of scoring. Better is the up-and-down bank using left English. Hit the end rail at A, the other end rail at B, and the side rail around C or K.

Shot 2 When the cueball is closer to the object balls, another option can be considered. With low left it might be possible to double the end rail off the red (A-F-A). The same pattern recommended in the previous shot can also be tried, though the backward angle off the first rail is more severe. A third option, and the one I would play, is to aim away from the object balls and double the long rail (D-G-D).

Shot 3 This stumps most players. All sorts of remote possibilities are tried here, but the best choice is a cross-table off the white with left English, slightly below center (ball-K-F-A). The shot can be made even when there is only a quarter-inch of space between the rail and the white ball; all you need is enough room to drive the white past the red.

Shot 4 Depending on the exact position of the balls, it might be best to play a cross-table shot as in the previous diagram, but as shown there is a possibility of a kiss as the object ball rebounds off the end rail. Some players might try a left-handed, natural four-rail bank, shooting the cueball into E. Another pattern to be considered is one almost always overlooked by beginners, the left-handed two-rails-first shot, hitting the first rail near G, the second rail near C, then the white ball, then the third rail.

Diagram 42

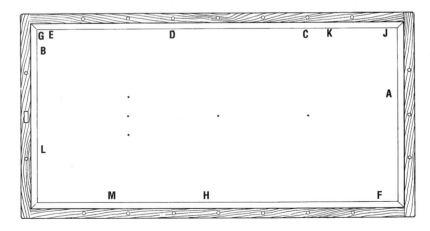

Shot 5 With the cueball frozen, the pattern suggested in the previous diagram is ruled out. With the white ball positioned as shown, the up-and-down bank favored in Shot 1 can be tried, getting a fourth rail after hitting the white ball. A pattern to think about in positions like this is the "outside umbrella," which calls for hitting two rails first. Here the cueball is sent along the path H, A, red ball, K, white ball. Bill Maloney, owner of Corner Pocket Billiards in Fort Lauderdale, Florida, has a good feel for this pattern. He made one on me twenty years ago that I still can't get out of my mind, even though I've seen several psychiatrists.

Shot 6 It might be possible to make a ticky here off either ball. There are several feasible banks as well. In the given position, though, there is a special shot that is almost a cinch. Shoot the cueball with slight running English, or just follow, into the long rail at J. The cueball comes off the end rail and into the red ball rather full, snapping sharply into the side rail again

Diagram 43

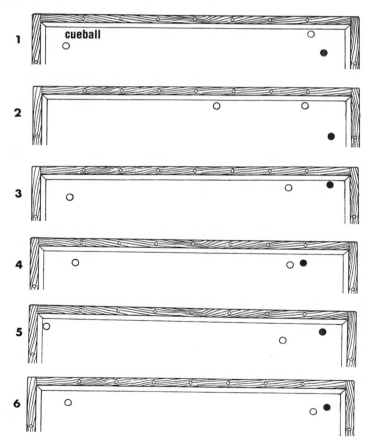

near J and back to the white ball. The sharpness of the rebound angle off the third rail will surprise you if you are unfamiliar with the action.

Shot 7 Not much room for argument here. The best shot is the five- or six-rail-first pattern beginning with F, hitting the red before the white.

Shot 8 If the object balls were closer to the corner you could play a standard five-rail bank starting at F. A fairly good choice here would be to play a five-rail bank short, hitting the sixth rail at K, then both balls. But there are two other patterns to weigh in positions like this that often are better than the running English banks. One is a reverse English bank. Shoot into H with maximum right spin, which carries the cueball to a point just above H, then into the end rail behind the red. Slow speed. When familiarizing yourself with a strange table it pays to try this pattern to see what the returns are, as it can occasionally be used to get out of trouble. For a variation, see the Yousri shot on page 144 of *Byrne's Advanced Technique in Pool and Billiards*. The second pattern to consider in positions of this type is a hold-up up-and-down. Shoot the cueball into J on the long rail with slight hold-up English. The cueball returns to about D, then G, then—with luck—the balls.

Shot 9 A very common position. The only shot worth considering is thin off the left side of the white, sending the cueball to K, L, and M. There is nothing tricky about it. All you have to be able to do is hit a ball thin that is ten feet away. Don't use follow, and only enough speed to suit the thinness of the hit. This is one of those shots that often enables a top player to "turn the tables" on a safety player—they die near the red while bringing the opponent's cueball to the opposite end. I hate the shot. There is no rule that says I have to like it.

Shot 10 You could try the up-and-down bank advocated in Shot 1 here, but that wouldn't work if the object balls were another foot from the corner. With the balls as shown, you can't get long enough with a five-rail bank, and trying to hit a sixth rail to the left of J doesn't look good because of the way the two balls are tilted. Give some consideration to a shot beginners never think of. Turn away from the object balls and shoot a left-handed double-the-rail, hitting the first rail at E. Good accuracy is attainable with practice, especially when the cueball is close to the first rail.

Shot 11 This is easy. Best is a six-rail bank starting at F and ending near K.

Shot 12 A tough one to conclude. Various kinds of banks commend themselves, but imagine how happy you will be making the four-rail time shot that begins by hitting the left side of the white and ends by scoring the point in the vicinity of J. The red is banked once across the table.

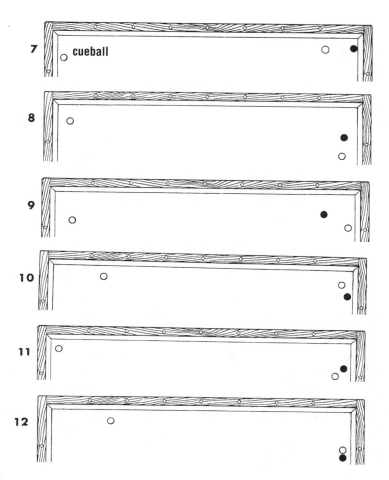

Diagram 44

These twelve shots by no means exhaust the possibilities of positions along the side rail. Part of the charm of the game is that it is, in fact, inexhaustible. It's up to you to decide which options best suit the circumstances.

One of the nice things about three-cushion billiards is that knowledge is just as important as talent. The more you play, especially if you play good players, the more you learn. Many older players without the eyesight and steadiness of hand they once possessed can still play top-class billiards because of the tremendous stock of tricks, stratagems, and special shots they have acquired over the years.

Let's test your knowledge of shot selection in five tough diagonal positions. In each case the cueball is at the upper left of the diagram and the object balls are at the lower right. Experienced tournament players won't learn any options they haven't seen before, but more than a few will be reminded of a shot or two they may have forgotten about or underrated.

I'll say a word about each position first without giving away what I feel is the best shot. The "answers" given at the end of this section refer to the letters in Diagram 50.

Shot 1, Diagram 45 Rail-first behind the white—the so-called "ticky" must always be considered, but here the white is too close to the rail and the red is too far to the left. Even if you could get behind the white, the red might get kissed away. A five-rail bank, hitting the first rail near F, is often the best bet in positions like this, but here there is another good possibility. The inexperienced never think of it.

Shot 2, Diagram 46 Here the red makes the solution suggested for the previous shot a poor choice. A cross-table off the white can be tried, as can a five-rail-first bank. See anything else?

Shot 3, Diagram 47 The cross-table off the right side of the white and the four-railer off the left side both appear to have kisses in them. Driving the cueball into M for a three-rail bank and into F for a five-rail bank are not bad, but there is a special shot for this particular position that has a better chance of success.

Shot 4, Diagram 48 As in the last diagram, the cross-table and the four-railer off the white look kissy and the previous solution is impossible. Everything is tough here. What would you do?

Shot 5, Diagram 49 Many players confronted with this layout would try the two-rail-first shot beginning with M. It's hard to keep the cueball close enough to the rail, though, after hitting the red. One way to counteract the tendency of the cueball to spring away from the third rail on patterns like this is to approach the second rail at a steeper angle. Here that would mean hitting the first rail about a diamond away from the corner, spinning the cueball toward the hole behind the red with right English. There is another shot, though, for this situation that I think is better.

THE ANSWERS

Shot 1 There is a four- or five-rail shot that has a good chance of scoring. Go into the corner two rails first (H and J) with right English and send the cueball through the hole behind the red for two or three more rails. It looks like s how-off shot, but is often the best choice.

Shot 2 The same pattern suggested for the previous shot can be tried here, but the hole behind the red is uncomfortably small. If a five-rail bank is chosen, it would probably be best to come in short, catching a sixth rail just before the white at about K. There is another shot that is not bad and

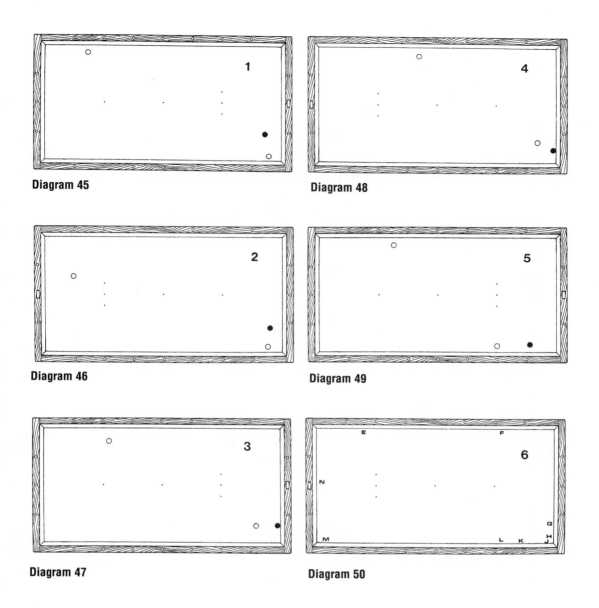

Diagram 45

Diagram 46

Diagram 47

Diagram 48

Diagram 49

Diagram 50

for some reason is often overlooked. Try a three-rail bank, aiming the cue-ball at E, from which it will go to H and J, then off the white and into the red. Not so tough. Any billiard player ought to have good judgment in banking a ball one rail into a corner or a little to either side of it.

Shot 3 I think the best shot here is the "smash through" into the red, more commonly called a force follow. Hit the red square in the face with high right. Properly stroked, the red ball will be banked through the hold and the cueball will follow to catch the end rail twice before spinning off the side rail into the white. Great power is not needed. Concentrate on hitting the cueball high and the red ball squarely.

Shot 4 Try hitting the rail first just to the left of the red ball with right spin. The idea is to go around the table after hitting the red as thinly as possible rail-first, continuing to L, N, and E. Not a high-percentage shot, but what else is there? Keep the rail-first option in mind when the first ball is frozen or close to it.

Shot 5 When the problem is keeping the cueball on the rail, try going rail-first behind the red with high right (hitting the rail at K) then two or three more rails. The shot is a form of "hold-up" ticky. Follow tends to keep the cue ball on the rail from this angle. It is a stroke shot rather than a precision shot. Danny McGoorty once told me that Ray Kilgore, who was world professional champion in 1953, developed uncanny accuracy on this shot by practicing it over and over. If Ray "St. Paul" Kilgore practiced this shot, you and I should, too.

The Either-Ball Shot
and Other Subtleties

THERE IS A TYPE OF SHOT IN three-cushion billiards that requires a soft stroke and very little English, yet is just as much fun to make as the big power-draws and follows. The reason is the sheer ingenuity of the shot. After two rails first, the cueball can hit either of the object balls before catching the third rail and the other ball. The position for such a shot doesn't arise often, but it's a shame to overlook it when it does.

The shot in its purest form is Shot 1 in Diagram 51. The cueball is directly opposite a gap in the two object balls, which are positioned as shown. If the gap is just a hair wider than a ball, shoot straight into that gap with no English, sending the cueball on a double bank across the table. The charm of the shot lies not only in that you don't have to know which object ball will be struck first, but that you rely on your own *in*ability to put absolutely no spin on the cueball. The cueball will return off the second rail a hair off perpendicular, and will not pass through the gap cleanly again; instead, it will touch one of the balls lightly, then the rail, then the other ball. If your opponent is unfamiliar with the idea, he'll put you down as brilliant. Willie Hoppe sometimes included the shot in his exhibition program, setting it up across the length rather than the width of the table.

Under game conditions, what we might call the "cross-table, either-ball" shot rarely appears with such heavenly symmetry. It is more likely that the cueball will not be directly opposite the gap, as seen in Shot 2 in the diagram. Here it is necessary to hit the first rail outside the two balls with

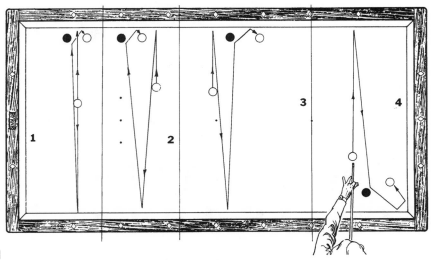

Diagram 51

just enough sidespin to send the cueball back across the table toward the gap. As before, either ball can be struck first.

When the space between the object balls is too great for the either-ball feature, as shown in Shot 3, then you must make a definite choice as to which ball to hit before the third rail. That makes it more difficult, and for that reason even more satisfying when you make it. The idea in Shot 3 can be used when the object balls are much more widely separated than shown.

Another cross-table idea good players watch for is Shot 4. Here you use a soft stroke and just enough English to bank the cueball across the table and off the side of the red. In the position as diagrammed there are other shots to consider. But it is easy to think of situations (for example, when the cueball is almost frozen to the left side of the red) when this pattern offers the best chance of scoring. See also Diagram 59, center.

Diagrams 52 and 53 illustrate a subtlety in double-the-rail shots that many players seem unaware of. In Diagram 52, a thin hit is needed on the first ball. It is best, therefore, to contact the first rail as close to the corner as practicable, so that the cueball approaches the first ball at the flattest possible angle. In Diagram 53, a thin hit on the first ball would result in a miss, as the cueball would go through the hole. Not only is a full hit needed here, but the cueball must approach the first ball at a bit of an angle. Aim the cueball at the first rail a diamond or two away from the corner, and use more English than in the previous shot in order to bring the cueball into the third rail and off the first ball at the most favorable angle.

When the angle of approach to the first ball is not important, there is a general rule to consider on double-the-rail shots: *hit the first rail close to*

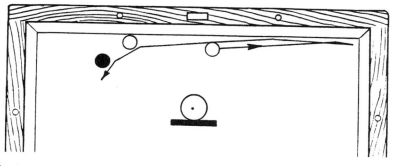

Diagram 52

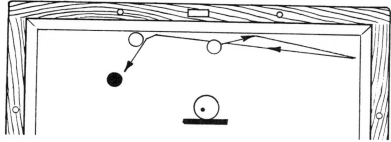

Diagram 53

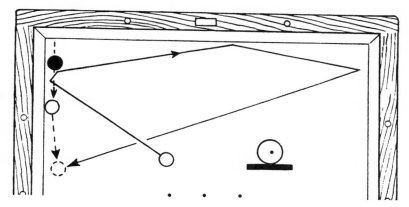

Diagram 54

the corner to minimize the amount of sidespin required. But be sure you get back to the third rail! There's no way to score if you don't.

I present the shot in Diagram 54 as a novelty and a possible exhibition shot, not a recommendation. Miguel Campos of Villajoyosa, Spain, thought of it during a game and made it. As you can see, it is a rail-first time shot in which the red ball banks off the end rail and bumps the white ball into a more favorable position. Senor Campos is only a .500 player, so if he can make it, you can, too.

Evaluating
Bank Shots

PHOTOCOPY THIS SECTION and put it in the file marked "What every three-cushion player should know." What follows is second nature to advanced players, but if you average below .500, you might profit from looking at bank shots in the manner described here.

Bank shots are no picnic, even the "easy" ones. Miscalculate the speed, the spin, or the direction even a little, and your inning might be over. Many top players shy away from banks. One old-timer told me that Willie Hoppe and Welker Cochran played very few banks. "They always seemed to find some damned way to go off a ball," is how he put it.

United States Champion Sang Chun Lee makes no secret of his distaste for banks—and the various systems for planning them—and avoids them whenever possible. Even Junichi Komori of Japan, one of the best bankers in the world, shoots them only when nothing better can be found.

But what is "better"? When presented with a ball-first or rails-first choice, how do you decide?

Consider this: A single ball in the center of the table presents a bigger target for the cueball than the most favorable arrangement of two balls, A single ball is, in effect, two ball-widths because you can score on it thin on the left edge or thin on the right edge. On a bank shot, the widest target two balls offer is less than two diameters.

In Diagram 55, the player is preparing to bank three rails around the table. The object balls are in the best possible position; they are one

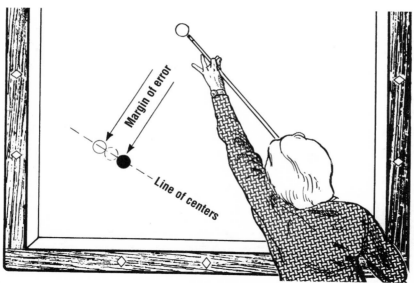

Diagram 55

ball-width apart and their line of centers is at right angles to the cueball's line of approach. At first glance it appears that the margin of error is two balls wide, but it is slightly less than that because the cueball can hit one of the balls almost full and curve forward without hitting the other ball.

When evaluating the difficulty of a bank shot, then, watch for positions in which you can hit up to half of either ball first and still score. That's a big target. When the balls are less than one ball-width apart, or if the line of centers is not at right angles to the cueball's approach path, the size of the target shrinks.

If the object balls are a ball-width apart and the line of centers is tilted off the perpendicular, the width of the target drops by half, for now only one of the balls can be hit first. At the left side of Diagram 56, it is clear that the white ball must be hit first to score the point. The margin of error is one ball-width because the cueball can hit the white ball thick or thin.

At the right side of the diagram, the object balls are frozen. Many players don't like banking into balls that close together even when the angle of approach is ideal, as shown, because the target seems so small. In fact, the margin of error is one ball-width, the same as the other position in the diagram.

There are special positions that present a big target to the banker, even though the object balls are more than a ball-width apart and aren't lined up to be perpendicular to the cueball's line of approach. At the left of

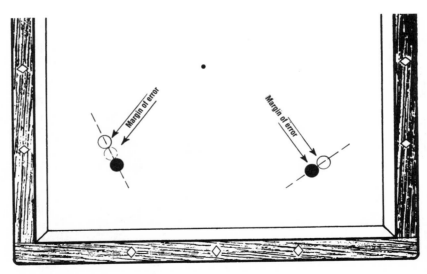

Diagram 56

Diagram 57, the cueball can miss the white ball and still score by going two more rails off the red. At the right, missing the white ball on the way in is okay because the cueball will hit the red and carom off the rail into the white. In both cases the margin of error is two balls' diameters, which is as wide as it ever gets.

Sometimes you have a choice of bank shots, as in Diagram 58. Which one is best? For the moment, ignore the balls in the upper right corner. At the lower left corner, the player can go the long way around the table, three or five rails first, marked Plan A. The other possibility is Plan B, the short way. I like Plan B because the cueball can hit either ball first to score.

Diagram 57

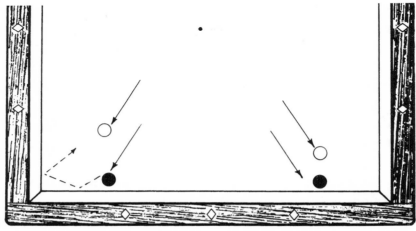

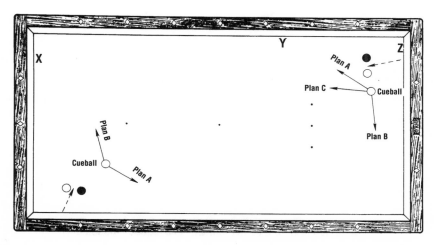

Diagram 58

The target presented to the cueball is therefore almost twice as wide as in Plan A.

In the upper right of Diagram 58, there are more choices. In Plan A, three rails first, the white must be hit first. Going longer, four rails first, also requires hitting the white first. Plan B, the short-angle bank, requires hitting the red first off the third rail. Plan C, contacting the rails at X, Y, and Z, permits the cue ball to approach the balls at close to right angles to their line of centers, which means that either ball can be hit first, greatly enlarging the target.

Diagram 59 shows a good cross-table off the white if you can reach it. But the double-the-rail shot (lower right) is an excellent alternative

Diagram 59

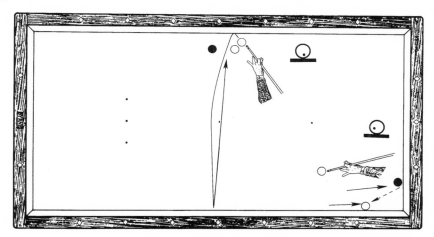

because the cue ball can score off either ball. The margin of error is two balls wide.

The cross-table shot in the center of Diagram 59 is one I made during a pastime game. By banking between the two object balls and using back-spin to curve the cueball as shown, the point can be scored off either object ball, getting a third rail just before the count.

> "It is humiliating to reflect that eminence cannot be attained even in the art of knocking about three ivory balls with a stick without the devotion of a lifetime, [though] not the slightest mental effort is required. Neither chess nor whist can be played, even moderately well, by an arrant fool; but a billiard table can be found in every well-conducted lunatic asylum in the kingdom."
>
> —From the *London Saturday Review*,
> quoted by Dudly Kavanagh in
> *The Billiard World*, 1869

Missing on
the Pro Side

A GUY RAISES HIS ARM and says to his doctor, "It hurts when I do this," to which the doctor replies, "So stop doing it." I think of that Henny Youngman joke whenever I hear a three-cushion player say something along the lines of "I always come in short on that shot."

If you're always short, you're lucky, because all you have to do is play the shot longer and you'll never miss again.

Some shots are apt to be missed more often one way than another. If you recognize the positions and make the appropriate adjustments, you can raise your scoring average. Top players know how shots are usually missed, and they allow for it in their aiming. When they fail to score because of overcompensation, it's called "missing on the professional side."

Consider the position in Diagram 60. The shot is almost never missed by hitting the first ball too thin. It's much more likely that the player will hit too much white ball and hit the red after two rails or come in short, near A. Next time you are faced with such a shot, make sure neither of those things happens. Force yourself to use no sidespin and hit the white so thin that if you miss the second ball it will be on the professional side.

Another example is the very common shot in Diagram 61. I'll bet that when you miss the shot, it's usually because you hit the first ball too thick, which makes the cueball go short, hitting the fifth rail near A or worse. So stop doing it! Fight off the natural tendency to hit too much of the first ball. Use a below-center hit on the cueball and avoid sidespin.

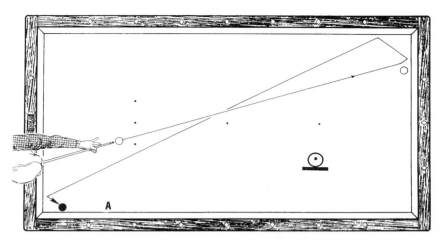

Diagram 60

I think one reason players so often hit too much ball when a feather-thin hit is required is that they fear the embarrassment of missing the ball entirely. Take the risk; it's worth it.

At the left of Diagram 62 is another thin-hit position. It's almost impossible to miss the shot by hitting the first ball too thin, so all you have to do is concentrate on not hitting the first ball too thick. Use no English and soak your head if you miss the shot long. If you miss by coming out of the corner short, good—that's the professional side.

At the right of Diagram 62 is a double-the-rail shot that is an absolute cinch if you stroke it with authority and with plenty of sidespin, hitting the first rail close to the corner. The common way to miss is to underdo it, bringing the cueball back too close to the end rail. It's difficult to double

Diagram 61

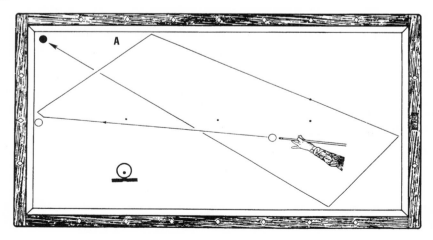

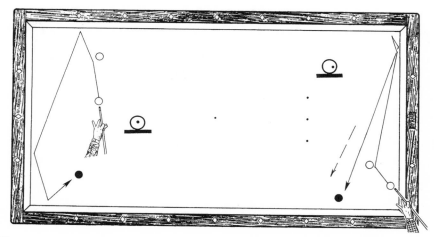

Diagram 62

the rail and overdo it, missing it as indicated by the dashed line. So all you have to do is avoid underdoing it.

The shot on the left side of Diagram 63 requires draw to curve the cueball into a short path. The first ball can be hit even thinner than indicated by the dashed arrow. When the shot is missed, it's almost always on the long side. Aim to either make it or miss it on the short side and your success rate will improve.

At the right side of Diagram 63 is a shot that is hard to miss long. Players usually miss it short, contacting the second rail too close to the corner. Don't do that! Hit it plenty long and you have a better chance of scoring. There is a self-correcting element in positions like this. The more of the first ball you hit, the farther away from the corner the cueball will

Diagram 63

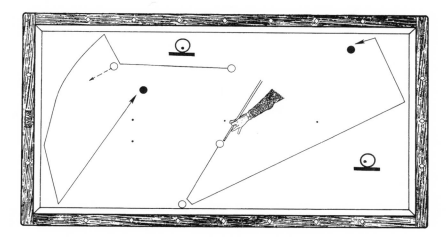

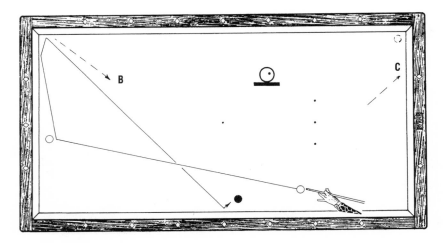

Diagram 64

contact the second rail, but because it will be going more slowly, the sidespin will have more effect. This approach is helpful on many so-called "spin shots."

Study the position given in Diagram 64. The red ball is lying off the third rail at diamond 4. If you use high right on the cueball, hit plenty of the white ball, and use strong speed, the cueball tends to hit the middle of the third rail as shown. It's hard without using overpowering topspin to hit the third rail short of diamond 4. Try it and see. It's much more likely that you will miss the shot long, as shown by the dashed line B.

The pattern in Diagram 64 is also a good choice if the red ball is big in the upper right corner. It's easy to miss the shot long, as indicated by the dashed line C, and hard to miss it short. So make sure you don't miss it long.

Kilgore's Opposite 3 System

FORTY YEARS AGO, a student of three-cushion billiards in Los Angeles named Manuel Baukens interviewed Ray Kilgore, who won the world three-cushion title in Chicago in 1953. Baukens compiled a 113-page manuscript describing what he learned from Kilgore and other Los Angeles players of the time.

Kilgore detailed a banking system called "Opposite 3" that he used frequently in his games. It's especially accurate on four- and five-rail bank shots and when the two object balls are close to the fourth rail. The system depends on estimating with accuracy where you want the cueball to hit on the fourth rail, which is often obvious at a glance.

Here's the key to the system. A cueball with slight running English that is directed at the point on the nose of the cushion opposite the third diamond will travel around the table and hit a point on the fourth rail symmetrical to the origin of the cueball.

Check Diagram 65. The solid line shows the path from one corner three rails to the adjacent corner. (In the better-known Corner 5 system, you shoot through the third diamond on the rail to reach the corner, but you need more English than in the Opposite 3 system.) Note that the cueball is directed at a point on the cushion opposite the third diamond. The dashed line shows the path from point C around the table to point D on

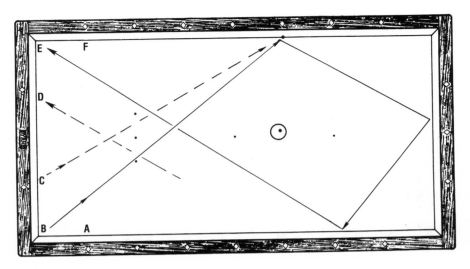

Diagram 65

the fourth rail. Points C and D are the same distance from the corners—that is, BC equals DE.

In the same way, a cueball starting at A and shot toward the point opposite the third diamond will go to F on the fourth rail. F is directly opposite A. If you've never tried it, you'll be surprised at how accurate the geometry is.

Anytime the cueball and object balls are on such symmetrical paths, you have an easy shot. To make the system practical, though, you need a way of adjusting when the balls aren't in ideal positions. When the cueball is starting from the end rail, a simple parallel works well. Consider the layout in Diagram 66. Let's say you have decided to play four rails first. The point you have to hit on the fourth rail—determined by estimation—is C. *If the cueball were at point B,* exactly as far from corner A as C is from corner D, you could aim the cueball at the point opposite diamond 3 on the first rail (dashed line) and make the shot with regularity. To make it from the given position, shoot the cueball in a line parallel to the dashed line.

Now for an example on the long rail. In Diagram 67, the shot can be made four rails as shown by the dashed line. The point that must be hit on the fourth rail is E. Directly across the table at the same position on the rail is B. If the cueball was on the rail at B, all you would have to do is aim at D (the point on the nose of the cushion opposite diamond 3) with running English, and the cueball would bank around the table to point E. If the cueball was at point A instead, Kilgore used a "half count" method to

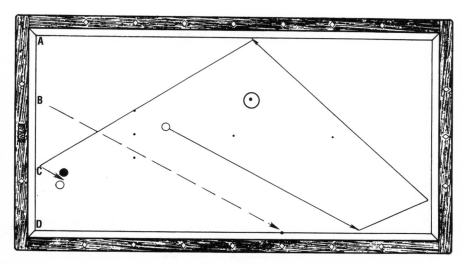

Diagram 66

find an aiming point on the first rail. The cueball is 1.5 diamonds down the rail from the ideal point B. Half of 1.5 is .75; therefore, aim three-fourths of a diamond away from D, a point marked C. Stated another way, CD is half as long as AB. That works well when the cueball is on the rail and the origin point is fixed, but when it is a foot or two or three from the rail, the calculations get too fussy to use because each time you pick a trial point on the first rail, the origin of the cueball changes. I suggest using a distant point.

Diagram 67

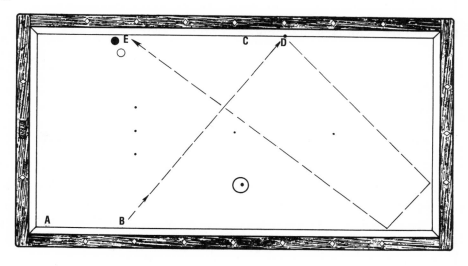

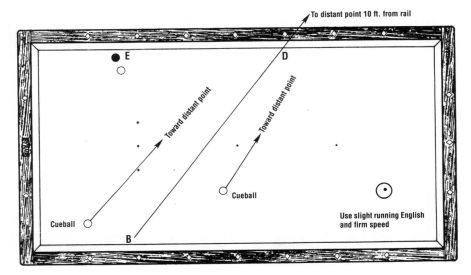

Diagram 68

In Diagram 68, the balls are in the same position as in Diagram 67. E is the desired fourth-rail contact point, B is the ideal starting point, and D is the point opposite 3 that would send a ball from B three rails to E. Extend the line BD about ten feet beyond the rail to a point on another table, on a wall, or on the floor. Aim at the distant point from wherever the cueball is and you'll hit point E or come awfully close to it. What could be simpler than that? Quick and easy and remarkably accurate.

The "Distant Point—Opposite 3" system in five steps:

1. Pick a point on the fourth rail the cueball must hit to score.

2. Find the symmetrically opposite point.

3. Imagine a line from the symmetrical point to the cushion opposite diamond 3.

4. Extend the line to a distant point.

5. Send the cueball toward the distant point with running English.

Tables, cloth, and strokes differ, so you'll have to determine how much speed and spin to use to maximize the accuracy of the system on your equipment. You'll also have to find, through practice, what adjustments have to be made in speed and spin when the angle into the first rail is outside the broad normal rage. I predict that you are going to be very pleased with the Opposite 3 system if you've never tried it before.

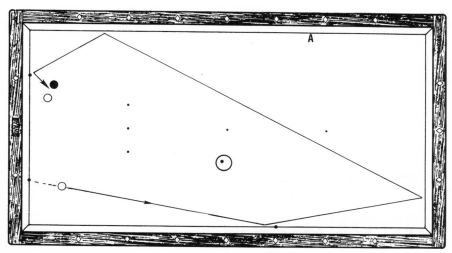

Diagram 69

A final thought from Kilgore. He was convinced that the "long" angles were the most predictable. In Diagram 69, for example, he would not play a three-rail bank by aiming at point A on the first rail. Instead, he would go the "long" way, using high running English and a firm stroke, claiming he could make the shot ten times in ten tries using the Opposite 3 method. In the diagram, the cueball is conveniently starting from the ideal point (symmetrically opposite the desired fourth-rail point), so the cueball is sent directly at the cushion opposite the third diamond. If the cueball is to one side or the other of the given position, parallel over it to using the cue as a guide or find a distant point for aiming.

Surprising Shots
from Spain

EVER SINCE WATCHING AVELINO RICO of Madrid upset Raymond
Ceulemans and Torbjörn Blomdahl in Las Vegas to win the 1986 world
three-cushion championship, I've wanted to check out the scene in Spain.
Spain, and neighboring Portugal as well, has master players in every form
of the carom game, especially in three-cushion and artistic (stroke) billiards. Early in 1989 I had the chance and settled for several months on
the east coast—the Costa Blanca—between Valencia and Alicante, where
people are friendly, Americans are nearly nonexistent, and the billiards are
plentiful . . . if you know where to look.

In Spain, as in the rest of Europe, there are pool tables in many bars
and clubs, but they almost always are the small coin-operated kind. Carom
games on pocketless tables are the overwhelming choice. There are public
rooms in some big cities, but most of the action takes place in private
clubs, and I do mean private, for rarely are they listed in the phone books.
Equipment suppliers and repairers are listed, though, in the Yellow Pages.
Wherever you are in Europe, a call to an equipment supplier will lead you
to the clubs. You may need a translator, because directions are hard to follow unless you speak the language. In the clubs, you'll find a pleasant and
congenial atmosphere, excellent tables, cloth, and lighting, and a willing-
ness to let you play a few times if you are just visiting.

After diligent sleuthing, I found a place to play twenty minutes from

Byrne's Spanish Dictionary for Billiards

Corta/larga—short/long

Efecto—spin, or ball action

Falta un pelo—missed by a hair

Promedia—average (points/inning)

Muy bien—very well done

Buena bola—nice shot

Bonita carambola—beautiful shot

Mucha bola—too much ball

Bola que juega—cueball

Demasiado fino—too thin

Blanco—white ball

Punto—spot ball, or point

Remache—kiss back

Mala suerta—bad luck

Que suerte!—what luck!

Quien gano?—who won?

Cuero—leather tip

Taco—cue

Fuerte—strong

Despacio—slow

Partida—match

Jugador—player

Ganador—winner

Perder—to miss

Serie—run

Fallo—miscue

Retor—draw

Defensa—defense

Posicion—position

Tico—chalk

Fino—thin

Bandes—cushion

Bien—well done

Entrada—inning

my rented apartment in the town of Villajoyosa on the shore of the Mediterranean. Club Billar Villajoyosa has four fine, old-style heated carom tables and two small bar-pool tables, all of which are kept in perfect condition. The club has 120 members, each one of whom pays $9.00 a month dues. Table rental is $2.60 an hour. (In the provincial capital of Alicante, twenty-five miles south, dues at the main club are $22.00 a month and table time is free.)

Because Spain has produced many world-class performers in artistic billiards (Domingo and Nadal come to mind), it isn't surprising that Spaniards have a special fondness for stroke shots. The president and champion of Club Billar Villajoyosa is a city tax man named Kiko Tono, a solid three-cushion player with many stroke shots in his repertoire, two of which are diagrammed here.

The shot in Diagram 70 is a difficult position. If I had been at the table, I might have tried a short angle off the left side of the red, using draw and no sidespin. Kiko Tono's solution, an idea I don't recall ever seeing, was better because the second ball becomes big. He went off the left side of the

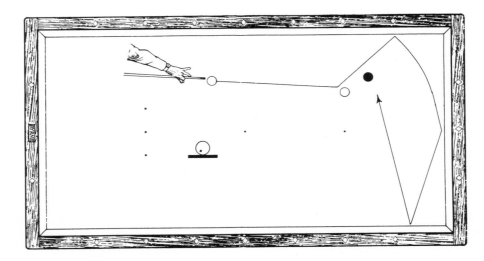

Diagram 70

white ball with draw and a touch of hold–up English, going around behind the red. The draw brings the cueball short off the third rail, and the reverse sidespin brings it almost straight across the table where it can hit the white directly or off a fourth rail.

Another shot he made against me is shown in Diagram 71. With high left follow and plenty of speed, the cueball follows almost straight after the red, but takes a different path off the first rail because of the left sidespin. On good Granito cloth (made in Spain and used all over the world along with Belgium's Simonis), there is enough speed left for the cueball to go through the hole and double the rail.

Diagram 71

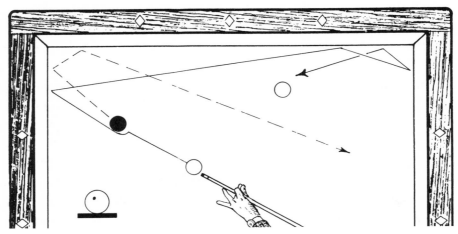

There is another club member in Villajoyosa (the name means "City of Jewels") who is so entranced with stroke shots that he can barely play an ordinary game. Miguel Campos is his name, and you can almost see the pain on his face when he has to play a shot that doesn't involving a curving cueball. He carries in his pocket a sheaf of papers on which are drawings of shots of his own invention, most of which require a King Kong stroke. One of his creations that isn't too hard is given in Diagram 72.

Both object balls are frozen to the rail. Using high follow with no sidespin, kiss back off the first ball. The red ball stays in place. Properly executed, the cueball will follow the diagrammed path.

If you find yourself in a billiard room or club in a Spanish-speaking country, get somebody's attention and say, "*Quiere usted jugar tres bandes?*" It means, "Do you want to play three-cushion?" If he says "*Si,*" chances are you will have all you can handle, and I don't care how good you are.

Some of the world's greatest exhibition players are Spanish-speaking, and they are especially strong in "finger billiards," in which the cueball is spun onto the table by hand for massé-like effects.

The shot shown in Diagram 73 can be used in an exhibition program and is also a very practical solution to a difficult position. What else is there? Most players can bank the cueball one rail and hit the side of the first ball. According to Joe Plazonja, a world traveler who collects billiard brainstorms, it's a favorite shot in Buenos Aires. The only American I know who tries patterns like this is Carlos Hallon, who grew up in Ecuador.

Diagram 72

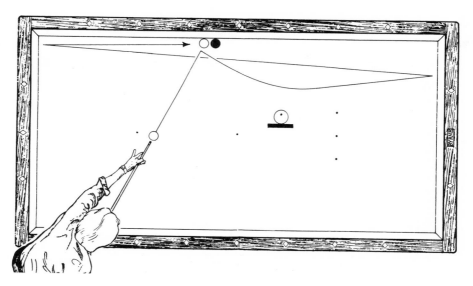

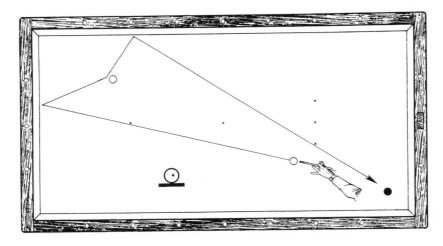

Diagram 73

The next three shots are from a 1990 book by Valeriano Perera Sans of Tarrasa, Spain (near Barcelona). My thanks to Victor Maduro of the Republic of Panama for sending me photocopies of several interesting pages.

Diagram 74 shows a very nice time shot: twice across with the cueball, a short bump for the white. Hit the red very thin and it shouldn't move into an interfering position. The shot is quite a bit easier if the three balls are moved off the rail a few inches. I like time shots of this type—they're crowd-pleasers and many of them aren't particularly hard. A few should be added to the program of artistic billiards, which at present is confined to difficult stroke shots. Now that the artistic tournaments no longer use

Diagram 74

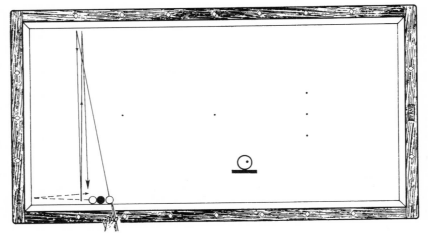

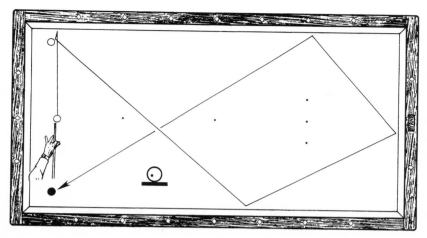

Diagram 75

ivory balls, which are especially good for force-follow shots, the organizers should be receptive to examples of finesse rather than power.

Another practical shot is given in Diagram 75—rail first with left English, then the ball, then three more rails. The only other shot I would consider in the exact position shown is two rails first into the corner behind the white, then back to the left end rail. Both shots have built-in defense because the white ball will likely end up at the right end of the table.

Diagram 76 takes some explaining. It is an imaginative novelty shot that brings out the possibilities of finger billiards, at which Señor Parera Sans is an expert. He credits the concept to Pedro Nadal. In the diagram,

Diagram 76

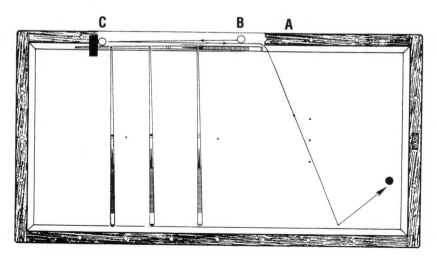

I have masked part of the wood grain of the rail to make it easier to follow the path of the cueball. Four cues are required along with a wooden ball box. Place one cue on top of the rail rubber as shown at the top of the drawing. Hold it in place by resting it on a ball box and three cues, positioned as shown. One ball is placed against the box and the rail cue, marked C. The red ball is on the table near the nameplate.

Now for a *carambola con los manos!* Stand at A and toss the cueball so it lands at B and travels down the rail to hit the ball at C. Thanks to the backspin imparted to the cueball by the way it is snapped from the fingers, it slows down as it travels from B to C, and once it hits the white ball, which is supported by the box, it scoots back toward B, hugging the cue; it falls off the rubber and travels across the width of the table to score. Maybe Mike Massey, who puts on a very entertaining finger-billiard show, can add this, or a version of it, to his act, though it won't work as diagrammed on a pool table because the side pocket would get in the way.

If you can't flip a ball onto the table with enough spin, the shot can also be done with a massé stroke . . . but not by me. I report miracles; I don't perform them.

"Let the king prohibit gambling and betting, for these are vices that destroy kingdoms."

—The Code of Manu, circa A.D. 100

Fifteen Examples of Master Play

RULES MAKERS IN THE VARIOUS CUE GAMES around the world can't agree on how to treat a cueball that is frozen to an object ball. In snooker, you can shoot away from the frozen ball and it counts as a hit. In pool, you must move the object ball to which you are frozen for the shot to count as a hit. In three-cushion billiards, the player has the choice of shooting away from the ball to which the cueball is frozen or spotting both balls.

And if the two balls aren't quite touching? That's the case the referees dread. It's a foul if the cueball hits the object ball twice, or the cue tip hits the cueball twice. In many positions the action is too fast for the eye to follow, but an experienced player or referee can deduce what happened by the sound of the hit and by the action of the balls.

In pool, if there is a slight space between the balls and the player shoots straight ahead, it is a foul if the two balls go down the table at close to the same speed . . . a foul that is often ignored. (In a legal follow shot, the cueball hesitates after hitting the object ball, then gradually picks up forward motion as the topspin grabs the cloth.) That's an easy call. The tough call is the cut shot.

Check the shot at the right side of Diagram 77. The cueball is a half-inch from the red ball and the player is aiming for a rather full hit with right English. People shoot this all the time and nobody thinks a thing about it, but it is almost always a foul. American three-cushion star Allen Gilbert tells me that on the international level referees will call it every time; when the

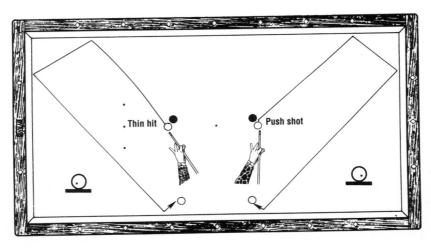

Diagram 77

balls are close together, you simply are not allowed to use a full hit with outside English. If you don't think such a shot is a foul, try it a couple of times, then set it up again at the same angle but with four or five inches separating the balls. You will hear a different sound and see a slightly different behavior of the balls.

The only legal way to handle the position is given at the left side of Diagram 77. You must go for a thin hit and use an elevated cue with sidespin to bend the cueball path into the correct scoring line.

In Diagram 78, what would you shoot? Smashing through the white ball and doubling the rail is tough because it's hard to keep the cueball on the rail as it comes back. Drawing back off the left side of the white and going around the table is possible, but not appetizing. There might be a hold-up ticky off the red. The easiest shot may well be the one shown. No sidespin is necessary.

You can see world champion Blomdahl make this shot and Shot 2 in Diagram 82 on *The Best of Three-Cushion,* a 1995 videotape available from Accu-Stats.

Diagram 79 shows a nice time shot: The red banks one rail and knocks the white into the vicinity of the upper left corner. It's not a high percentage shot, but it may well be the easiest option available. I was shown the idea by Bay Area player Pete Harley, who said he learned it from Eddie Alvarez.

The time shot in Diagram 80 is not flashy enough for an exhibition, but it is practical under game conditions. I know because I made it a couple of years ago during a tournament in San Francisco. The two object balls are frozen, thus presenting a very small target for any of several

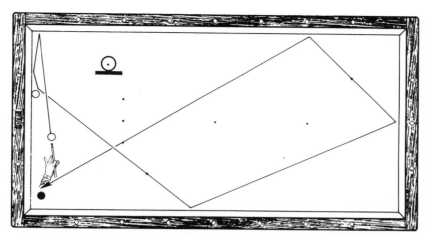

Diagram 78

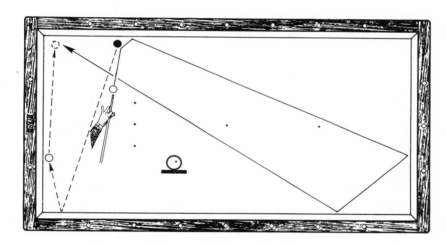

Diagram 79

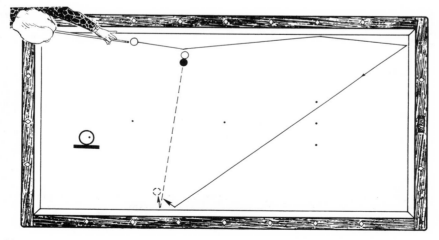

Diagram 80

possible bank and double-the-rail shots. (Making a shot like this in a game compensates for any number of defeats.)

In Diagram 81 is a shot that is flashy enough for an exhibition. The idea is to aim for roughly half the white ball using left English and try for a kiss that will send the cueball through the hole for a double-the-rail count. To learn it, set up the balls the same way every time and use the same speed. The shot was sent to me by Victor Maduro of Panama, who credits it to Guillermo "Mimo" Martinez, the man immortalized on page 231 of *Byrne's Treasury of Trick Shots in Pool and Billiards* for what I called The Panamanian Bag Shot.

The next few shots might look tough, but they are eminently usable in practical play. The problems posed by positions in the diagrams come up frequently. You'll escape from many a trap, if you can remember the solutions shown. Great skill isn't necessary.

Shot 1 in Diagram 82 (to the left of the vertical dashed line) is presented as a puzzle. The answer will be given by means of the letters, which are scrambled to give you a chance to figure it out for yourself. The cueball is indicated by the curved arrow. What shots would you consider trying? In the next paragraph you'll find out what United States Champion Sang Lee did in the 1991 national tournament. Read no more until you guess.

One possibility in positions of this type is twice across, using all side rails. Shoot the cueball into C with low left, bring it back to G, over to B, and back to the two object balls. That idea is out of the question here

Diagram 81

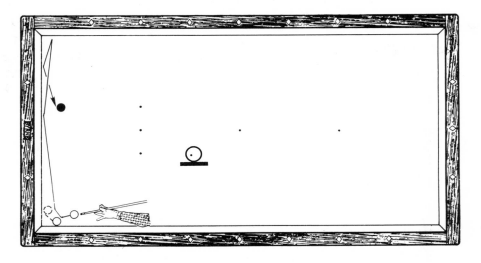

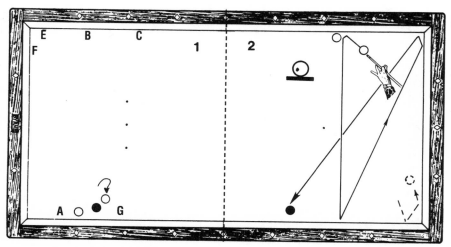

Diagram 82

because the red ball makes it impossible to deliver a proper stroke. Sometimes the same pattern can be executed by going below the balls (E to A to B and back). Sang Lee's beautiful answer to the problem: no spin, four rails first, and only medium speed. He sent the cue ball to B, then to A, over to the end rail at F, the side rail at E, and back to the balls. Either object ball can be hit first. It's a beautiful way to go.

Shot 2 in Diagram 82 is on the flashy side and not everybody's cup of tea, but it may well be the easiest way to score in the exact position given. You can also go up and down off the right side of the red, hoping to miss the kiss. Another shot is to draw off the white ball for a short angle. The shot diagrammed involves going rail-first off the white and straight across the table with left English. If the red ball is off the rail as drawn, the target is big. The shot is not difficult to judge when the cueball is close to the first ball. With more draw and a fuller hit, you can bring the cueball across the table and into the corner as shown by the dashed line to count on a ball near the end rail.

The shot in Diagram 83 is another beauty from the 1991 U.S. National. There are a couple of up-and-down patterns to consider as well as a "plus two," but the position of the cueball makes them difficult. Lee's solution is elegant in its simplicity. All it takes is knowing where to hit the first rail, which depends on whether you prefer a running ball or a dead ball. Any decent player can bank the cueball once across the table with good accuracy, which makes shots like this feasible. (After the game in which he made the shot, Lee set it up again and demonstrated it to George

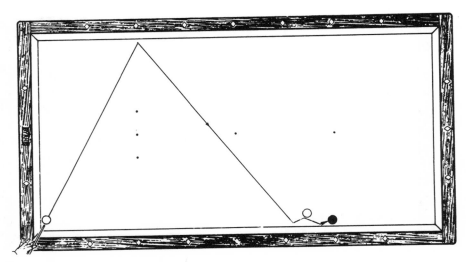

Diagram 83

Ashby, who made it on his first try. Lee held out his hand and said, "Five dollars, please.")

The shot in Diagram 84 may not look like much, but most players would try an up-and-down shot, trying to hit the second rail at A and the third rail at B. Because of the position of the red ball, a better choice is to go around the table as shown. The red ball is huge. Khalil Diab, the highest-rated player in Northern California, convinced me of this.

The shot in Diagram 85, if hit correctly, sends the cueball on such a remarkable path that it can be included in a program of exhibition shots. The action is old hat to every top player, but a surprise to many others.

Diagram 84

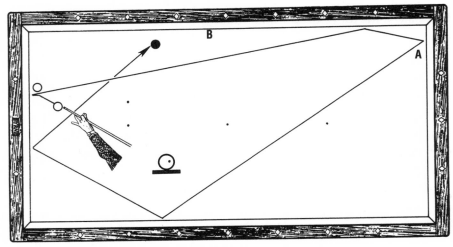

Diagram 85

Use right English and kiss the cueball to the left so that it hugs the rail. If you can get the cueball started in that direction, there are several ways to score. The first object ball must be frozen, or close to frozen, in the corner; if it isn't, look for an up-and-down pattern instead.

As flashy as they seem, none of these shots is especially difficult. The pressure of competition might cause you to overlook them. Don't.

Five dollars, please.

Choice of shot is one of the crucial factors in three-cushion play. All the technique in the world isn't going to help much if you choose the wrong shot to begin with. How many times have you seen a shaky old guy with fuzzy eyesight beat an inexperienced young hotshot? When it happens it's usually because the crafty veteran selects shots with the best percentages for scoring, safety, and position. Unless you've played or watched a lot of top-level three-cushion, you are going to overlook a lot of shots and make a lot of wrong choices.

When you are watching players a lot better than you are, pay special attention to their choice of shots. If you don't know why they picked one over another, ask them after the game. You may be sure they'll have a reason, and it may not be obvious.

World champion Torbjörn Blomdahl had the position in Diagram 86 during the international tournament at S. L. Billiards in New York in May 1992. He felt he couldn't get it long enough to make it off five rails, while trying to shorten it up enough to go six rails created too many chances for a kiss. His solution to the problem was to take the English off the ball and

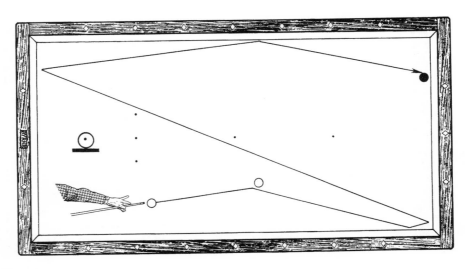

Diagram 86

play it as shown. It impressed me that he jumped on the shot as if it were a big cookie.

The next three shots were made by Sang Lee in July 1993 at California Billiards as he was marching toward his fourth consecutive national title. Consider Diagram 87: ordinary players might try to go thin off the left side of the white with right spin in an attempt to go twice around the table, but even with a great hit, the cueball will probably come into the lower right corner too short off the sixth rail. Another possibility is to go thin off the right side of the white with right spin with the hope of scoring off four or five rails, but a precision hit is difficult when English is used. Lee chose the no-English up-and-down pattern and made it with no problem.

Diagram 87

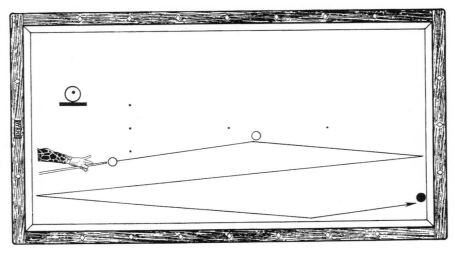

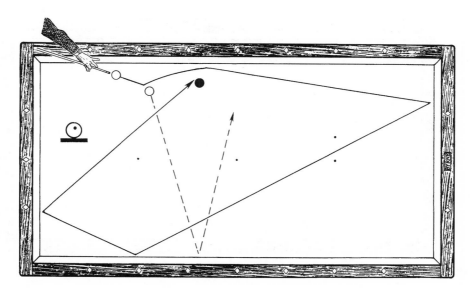

Diagram 88

When faced with the position in Diagram 88, I think most players would go off the red, but there are kiss problems on both the three- and five-rail options. Besides, since the white is not close to a rail, it's a small target. Lee went thin off the white as shown and through the hole, which is only a little wider than a ball. The white crosses the table as shown by the dotted line, presenting no possibility of a kiss, and the cueball takes a long angle toward the red, which is a large target.

The idea in Diagram 89 knocked me out, because it never would have occurred to me. Faced with a shot like this, I think most players would consider only the running English bank shots around the table. Lee

Diagram 89

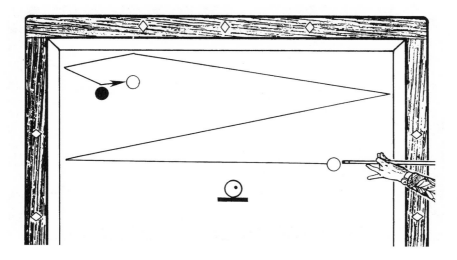

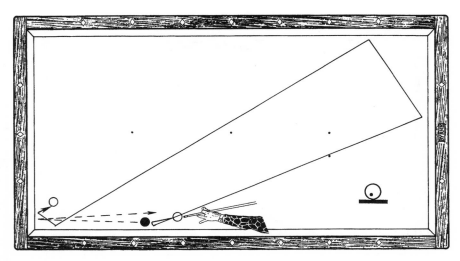

Diagram 90

surprised everybody with a cross-table pattern. As you can see, if you can get through the hole, the white is huge. This is a good example of his wonderful billiard imagination.

In Diagram 90 is an eye-popping draw shot pulled off by the impressive teenager from Spain, Danny Sanchez, at the 1992 S. L. Billiards tournament. He studied it for a long time, finally deciding against going off the right side of the red with hold-up English. Instead, he brought the house down by driving the red in and out of the hole, as shown by the dashed line, and drawing the cueball all the way around the table to score off five rails. What a shot! It was captured on videotape. Call Accu-Stats at 800-

Diagram 91

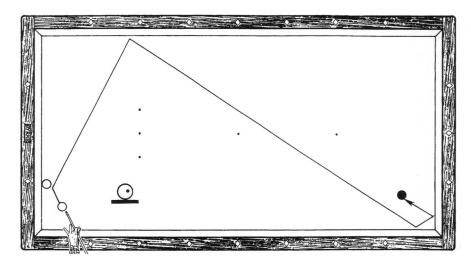

828-0397 and ask for the second three-cushion highlight tape, which was put on sale in 1996.

At the 1993 BCA Trade Expo in Kansas City, one of the 616 booths featured Spanish-made SAM pool and billiard tables. Lee was there, dazzling the onlookers with his magical skill and playing all comers, including such pool luminaries as Steve Mizerak and Mike Massey. During a session I had with him he made the beautiful shot in Diagram 91, a delicate, soft-stroke kiss that backed up to score out of the corner. Would you have thought of it?

The highlight of the convention, in my opinion, came when I quietly challenged Lee to a game of five points. He agreed and because miracles sometimes happen, I won 5–0 in three innings! It's probably the *only* time he's ever been shut out! We continued playing, unfortunately for my reputation, and he scored so many points that I looked around for a disguise.

> "Gaming is a principle inherent in human nature."
>
> —Edmund Burke, 1780
> From a speech in the House of Commons

Fifteen Shots
That Made Me
Gasp

WHENEVER I AM PLAYING POOL OR BILLIARDS and somebody makes an astounding shot, either by luck or skill, I often hear the comment, "There's one for your next book." My stock answer is, "I don't write science fiction." I don't write it, but I've seen a lot of it on the green cloth.

In the diagrams are a dozen surprising shots that I've seen with my own eyes, shots that made mouths, cues, and hopes drop all over the room.

The most fantastic shot I ever saw played in a game is shown in Diagram 92. It was June of 1991 at the Crystal Palace in Las Vegas, an establishment owned by billiard champion Frank Torres. I was playing a pastime three-cushion game with Al Gilbert, while at the next table John Melnichuk was playing with Ira Goldberg. Melnichuk, whose brother Paul is a sharpshooter in both pool and billiards, has a big stroke and a wild imagination, both of which he unleashed in the diagrammed position. He studied the balls for a moment, then said, "Well, I guess I'll jump over the red." And he did! Elevating his cue to about 30 degrees, he skipped off the white to the rail, hopped directly over the red, and spun out of the corner to score. If he hadn't called it, I would have sworn it was a scratch. I was so shaken I had to sit down and fan myself. John got me a glass of water and stayed at my side until I regained control of my bodily functions.

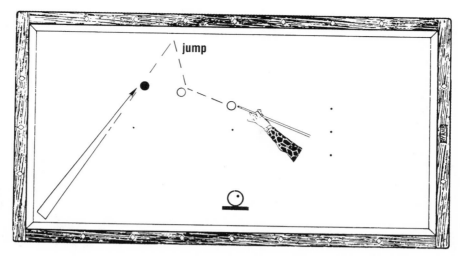

Diagram 92

The shot in Diagram 93 was made against me in a tournament game by former national champion Harry Sims. I thought I had left him safe.

The shot in Diagram 94 was made by former Egyptian champion Nabih Yousri at a tournament fifteen years ago at Yolo Billiards, outside Sacramento, California. What else is there? The path of the cueball will, of course, vary considerably depending on the condition of the cloth and the rubber.

Diagram 93

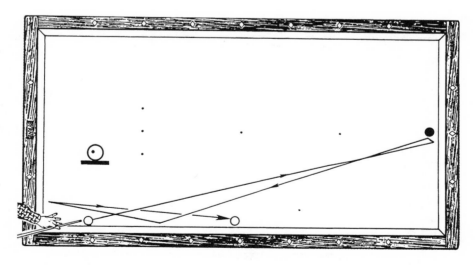

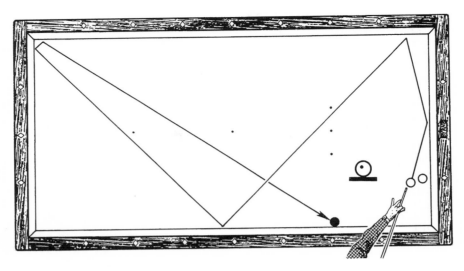

Diagram 94

Scientists have long known that players who practice for hours in the basements of their homes eventually begin to hallucinate. That may explain how Mike Shamos came up with what is known in the billiard underground as "the Shamos massé." Shamos, the beloved historian, collector, and polymath, handles a cue with considerable authority, occasionally running 10 in three-cushion and 50 in straight rail. At the left side of Diagram 95, the cueball and the red are separated by a hair. Hold the cue almost vertical and apply backspin with a touch of right. The cueball touches the red, advances toward the white, then stops and reverses direction, as if sud-

Diagram 95

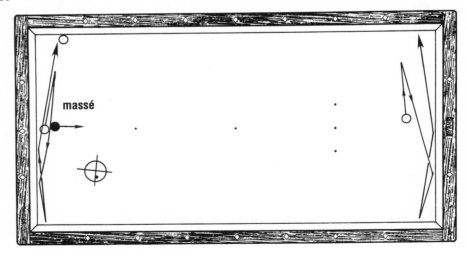

masse

denly remembering the need to hit three rails. The cueball doubles the rail and crosses the table again to complete the count. To make the action clearer, I have drawn the cueball path, somewhat exaggerated, at the right side of the diagram. Shamos says that at the 1991 Billiard Congress of America trade show in Nashville, the Korean trick-shot master Kim Suk Yong made the shot on his first attempt.

The two shots in Diagram 96 are a little more practical. The shot at the top I have seen made in tournament play by both Gilbert and Sang Lee. It would be possible to make the shot by hitting the white ball first and doubling the end rail, but consider the advantage of hitting the side rail first as shown. Then you don't have to get back to the end rail and the red ball becomes big. Use speed on the cueball.

At the bottom of Diagram 96 is a shot I saw diagrammed in a 1990 book by Spaniard Valeriano Parera Sans called *Billar—Mis Jugadas Favoritas* ("*Billiards—My Favorite Shots.*") It's easy when the balls are placed as shown. Elevate your cue slightly and use enough right English to make the cueball touch the long rail twice before hitting the red. *Muy bien!*

The shot in Diagram 97 would give pause to Charlie Peterson, the old-time hall of famer and trick-shot specialist whose slogan was "Show me a shot I can't make." The three balls are not quiet frozen and the cueball is trapped in the corner with seemingly no way out. The solution offered by the Republic of Panama's Guillermo "Mimo" Martinez is to shoot a force-follow with the cue elevated to about 35 degrees. The red will be squeezed

Diagram 96

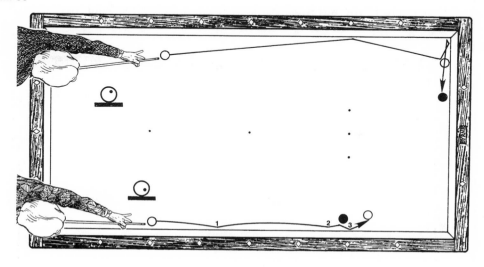

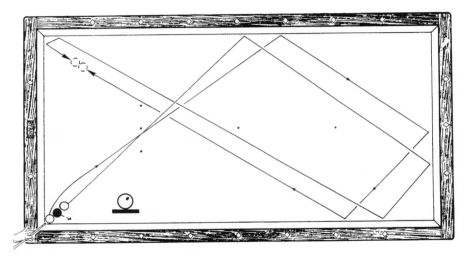

Diagram 97

out of the way to the right while the cueball squirts to the left and then dives forward with maximum follow. The point is scored—if a little luck is added to the required skill—in the upper-left corner. My thanks to Victor Maduro, my Latin American correspondent, for submitting this remarkable time shot.

The time shot at the top of Diagram 98 can be understood by studying the diagram along with the following text. Shoot hard into the face of the white ball with maximum follow. To bring the red and the cueball together in the upper right corner, three things must happen. The white has to get out of the way, as shown by the dotted line, without interfering with the cueball; the cueball must hug the rail as it travels to the upper right corner; and the red must bank to A, then to E, then back to A. A nice

Diagram 98

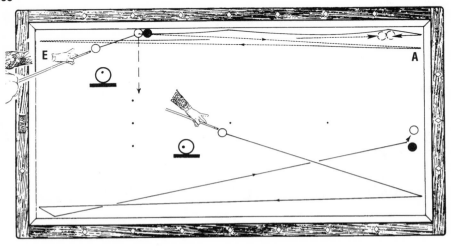

feature is that the red picks up slight left English from the white, which is what keeps it close to the rail as it banks back and forth. My thanks to Mark Viaplana of Barcelona, Spain, who tells me he saw this shot demonstrated by Spain's wunderkind, Danny Sanchez.

The most dominant player in the world today, Torbjörn Blomdahl of Sweden, is also one of the most creative. Al Gilbert swears that when Blomdahl was faced with the position shown at the bottom of Diagram 98 in a European meet, he attacked it in a way that surprised everybody watching the game. Nobody could tell what he was attempting to do until they saw the pattern unfold. Extreme left English sent the cueball along the diagrammed path to score. This one requires new cloth—otherwise there won't be enough spin left to get the needed action out of the corner. Blomdahl isn't handy as I write this, so I can't ask him why he didn't play it some other way.

When I attended the 1991 World Nine-Ball Tournament in Las Vegas, I was happy to run into jovial George Rippe, founder of the Golden Cue billiard room in Lawrence, Massachusetts, whom I hadn't seen in years. Rippe has a Godzilla stroke, is an addict of power shots of all kinds, and is spending his retirement years destroying tables from coast to coast. He has invented dozens of shots that can be made only by an anointed few. The shot in Diagram 99 resembles a pool trick shot I called the Resistance Draw in *Byrne's Treasury of Trick Shots,* page 140, but Rippe's billiard version is far more spectacular. It's another time shot, illegal in a game because the cueball is frozen to the white. Rippe writes: "Level cue, push through about eight inches to really wind up the cueball."

Diagram 99

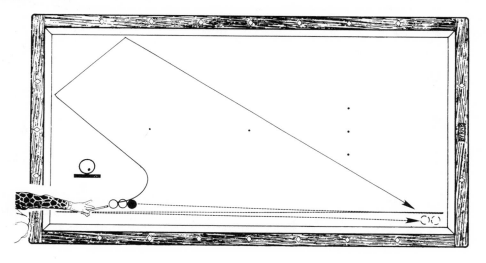

We can thank the Republic of South Korea for the next two shots. Mike "The Amazing" Shamos attended the Billiard Congress of America's 1991 trade show in Nashville, Tennessee, and was impressed with the trick-shot sorcery of the fabulous Kim Suk Yong. Shamos reports that "by far the most unbelievable" shot Suk Yong executed was an eight-rail massé—shown in the lower corner of Diagram 100. I have exaggerated the ball path in an effort to make it easier to follow, but I admit that it is still confusing. Standing at A and with cue almost vertical, Suk Yong delivers a powerful downward stroke to the cueball, which hits the side rail three times and bounces far enough off the end rail *to allow the sequence to be repeated!* There is a similar shot in the standard artistic repertoire with the balls closer to the corner in which a massé stroke forces the cueball into the corner twice. Suk Yong, with the aid of slick cloth, polished balls, and a powerful stroke, has expanded the concept into something truly heroic. In a conversation with Shamos through an interpreter, the Korean admitted that when practicing shots like this he has ripped many cloths and smashed cues to bits. He has even broken balls in two.

The shot at the right side of Diagram 100 is one I saw U.S. National Champion Sang Lee make in a tournament game in 1991 in San Jose, California. How many players would have the confidence, or even the imagination, to try a massé shot in this position? But only by curving the cue ball into the white can a good scoring path be attained. Cue elevation is about 60 degrees. The shot is a good example of the beautiful execution finesse that characterizes Sang Lee's game.

Diagram 100

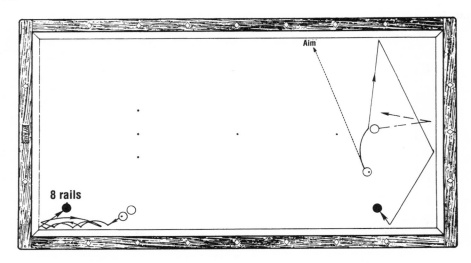

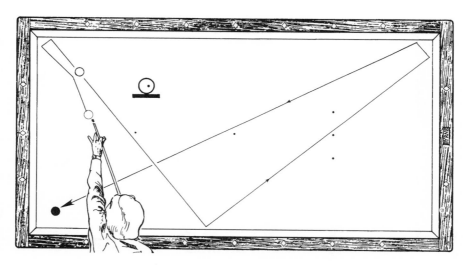

Diagram 101

The shot in Diagram 101 is taken from Heinrich Weingartner's *Billiard, Das Buch Zum Spiel.* It might be possible to make a short angle off the red without getting a kiss and a twice-around off the white might appeal to some, but the shot shown is a good choice on fast cloth. I made it twice the first four times I tried it. You have to hit the fourth and fifth rails close to the corner.

Something similar is the shot in Diagram 102, another length-of-the-diagonal back-up that is best on fast cloth. In this position, it is difficult to hit the white thin enough for a standard four-cushion shot . . . so back up out of the corner instead.

Diagram 102

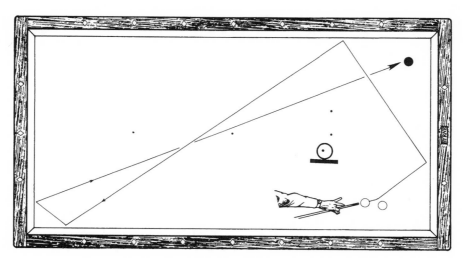

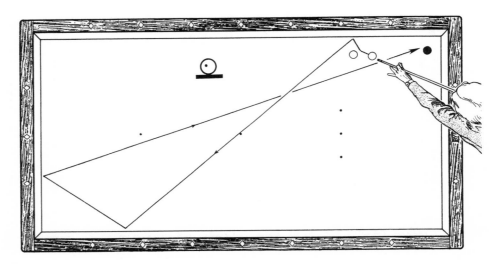

Diagram 103

Finally is a shot that Bud Harris made against me in a tournament at the old Palace Billiards (now closed) in San Francisco over thirty years ago (Diagram 103). Remember this idea when the second ball is big in the corner.

How to Make Your Table Play Longer and Faster

THREE-CUSHION BILLIARDS is much more equipment-sensitive than pool. Worn-out rubber and cloth take the fun out of the game. If the rebound angles are too sharp, experience on good equipment counts for little, and system play requires uncomfortable adjustments. On slow equipment, certain five-, six-, and seven-rail shots can't be made at all.

When the cloth is brand-new, almost any old clunk of a table plays beautifully. When the cloth loses its sheen, rolls get shorter and the players' faces longer.

The test shot outlined in Diagram 104 will help you gauge the behavior of your table. This information can be very important because the correct choice of shot often depends on the equipment, as shown in Diagram 105. On a long table, it's best to go thin off the left side of the white (dashed line). On a short table, that may be impossible with running English. It's best then to take the four-rail route off the right side of the white (solid line). Some players refuse to adapt, preferring to complain about the equipment.

Table mechanics have been trying for decades to make short tables play long. I can remember when the height of the cushion nose seemed to be the key; there was a rush of activity involving sanders and shims. Attention next turned to the angle at which the rubber is glued to the rail. Changing it requires a pass by a routing machine or the addition of a wedge-shaped

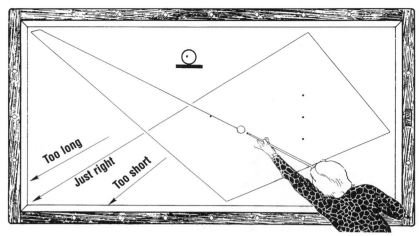

Diagram 104

feathering strip. Lately, a popular cure-all is heat. European tables, the theory goes, play better because they are heated.

Nose height, backing angle, and heat have an effect, of course, as does the amount of sidespin on the cueball. Dr. George Onoda of IBM has studied two other important factors: the liveliness, or elasticity, of the cushion and the amount of friction between the cueball and the cushion. I might add that if the bed cloth is slippery, as it is when it is new, the cueball retains running English longer, which has an effect off the third, fourth, and fifth rails.

Diagram 105

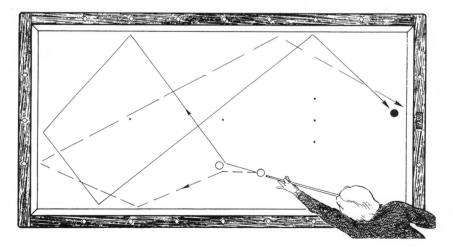

Before listing the ways billiard tables can be made to play better, I want to get technical for a minute. You can skip the next few paragraphs, if you like, without serious damage.

In Onoda's terms, the liveliness of the rubber depends on its coefficient of restitution, or e. If there is no energy lost when a ball hits a cushion, e equals 1.00 and the rebound angle equals the incoming angle (ignoring friction). Since e is always less than 1.00, the rebound angle must be less than the incoming angle. Onoda suggests thinking of the cueball's motion as having two components, one parallel to the rail and one perpendicular to it. Because energy is always lost when a ball hits a rail, the component perpendicular to the rail must be less after impact, reducing the rebound angle.

Interestingly, what this means is that dead cushions play longer than lively ones. The trouble is, too much speed is lost with dead cushions and you can't get the ball around the table.

Onoda has calculated that if the coefficient of friction between the ball and cushion is zero and e is 0.7, then a ball hitting the cushion at an angle of 39 degrees will rebound at 30 degrees.

But friction is never zero. If a cueball hits a rail without English, the friction during the impact—the drag—slows the cueball down somewhat. This increases the rebound angle. The same drag effect also occurs with moderate English in many instances. So reducing friction has the effect of maintaining a longer angle, due to e.

In practical terms, this means that a billiard table will play longer if you decrease the coefficient of friction between the cueball and the rail nose. One way to do it is to use a silicone-based spray on the cueball or the cushions. Onoda discovered a more predictable and longer-lasting method involving medical tape. See below.

Do you sincerely want your table to play longer and faster? Here's what you have to do:

- *Use fast cloth:* Top-grade Simonis (Belgium) or Granito (Spain) is absolutely essential for both the cushions and the bed. Such cloths offer much less resistance to rolling and rebounding balls than cheaper domestic grades.

  Simonis now offers a super-fast cloth, grade 585, just for rails. Bill Glassford of Sun City Center, Florida, reports that installing Simonis 300 on the bed and 585 on the rails changed his table from a diamond short to half-a-diamond long.

- *Use good balls:* Expensive balls have smoother surfaces, which reduces friction.

- *Clean the balls:* Shoot some five-rail banks with dirty balls, then note the marked improvement after you clean and polish them. Ball polish is available at billiard supply stores.

- *Clean the cloth:* Brush the cloth and the rails, vacuum them, and wipe them with a damp cloth. Do it once a day or more often. In particular, remove chalk marks as soon as possible, especially on the cushion, as accumulated chalk dust will increase the friction.

- *Cover the table:* Keeping the table covered when not in use prevents the build-up of dust and dirt.

- *Check the nose height:* The nose of the rails should be as low as possible without causing the balls to jump even slightly. Standard billiard balls are 2 3/8 inches in diameter, with some on the market measuring 2 7/16 inches. The nose height should be 70 percent of the ball diameter, or slightly lower.

  To see the effect of rails that are an eighth of an inch too high, bank a pool ball around a billiard table.

- *Stretch the cloth:* When the cloth is installed, it should be stretched as tightly as possible, and that goes for the rails as well as the bed. If the cloth relaxes after a few weeks or months so that it can be moved or pinched between the fingers, take two rails off and restretch it. Tight cloth offers less resistance to a rolling ball. To stretch rail cloth properly during installation takes three people, two to keep it stretched and one to attach it.

- *Use the right cushions:* Extremely lively rubber is bound to produce short, sharp angles. (To see the effect of dead cushions, stand a book against a cushion and bounce a cueball off it.) Only certain cushions, like K-55, have the right characteristics. European rubber, like St. Michel (France) or Artemis (Germany), is excellent, but it can't be installed on American-made tables without reworking the rails. Old rubber that produces good angles but has lost some of its pep might still be usable if you do what you can to keep the rest of the table fast.

- *Heat the cloth:* Moisture in the cloth slows the balls down and increases the friction at the cushion. Built-in heating elements to keep the cloth dry are standard in top-of-the-line foreign-made tables, but unheard of in American models. Try using a small space heater under the table. On a humid day, go over the cloth with a blow-dryer.

- *Try silicone:* Using a silicone-based spray like Armor All or Gunk on the balls has a dramatic effect. Some players apply it every time they clean and polish the balls; others are against it because the effect wears off fairly quickly. Angles can change noticeably during the course of a single game. To make the effect last longer, spray the nose of the cushion as well as the balls, or apply a light mist all over the bed so the balls keep picking it up as they make their rounds. Do it correctly and often enough and you can keep the cloth playing like new for a long time.

- *Change the rail cloth:* Do you normally change the cloth once a year? Then try changing just the rail cloth at six months. The effect is almost the same as changing the entire cloth.

- *Apply tape:* In 1992, after finding that the ball/cushion friction is a key factor in making a table play long or short, Dr. Onoda experimented with ways to vary it, eventually hitting on covering the cushions with tape. After trying different tapes on a table at Jack and Jill Q Lounge in Brewster, New York, he found that Durapore Cloth Tape by 3M works best. Ordinary adhesive tape and strapping tape don't work well.

   Go to a large drug store or a medical supply store and buy a ten-yard roll of one-inch-wide Durapore tape. Apply it evenly and securely to the cushions so that the nose is snugly covered. Guess what! The balls will act as if the cloth were new, and the tape lasts for weeks and can be easily replaced. Unfortunately, the tape only comes in white.

   If you can't find Durapore, suggests Tom Costello, a California tournament player, go to a paint store and get a roll of two-inch-wide Scotch Branch #2090 Long Mask, which he feels works just as well, and its blue color makes it less obtrusive. When you do finally peel it off, it won't leave a residue on the cushion. Onoda found any masking tape worked well, but did not like the sound of the ball hitting paper tapes.

   Why would you want to peel it off? For one thing, it looks funny. For another, if your practice table plays long, other tables will throw you off.

When Dr. Onoda first found the properties of taping the cushions, he considered designing and marketing a tape that was just the right width, smoothness, and color. He abandoned the idea because the tape companies he contacted weren't interested in making a new product for a small market.

Taping the cushions isn't as good as changing the cloth, but it certainly is cheaper.

- *Shave:* Just before this book went to press, I learned another method of lengthening the angles. Get an electric razor and shave the entire bed of the table and the nose of the cushions. Yes! It works. The green fuzz you'll empty into your wastebasket won't help the razor, but getting it off the cloth will definitely improve the playability of your table.

> "The noble game of billiards is peculiarly in harmony with the mechanical genius of our people; it combines science with gymnastics, teaching the eye to judge distances, the mind to calculate forces, and the arm to execute; it expands the chest while giving grace and elegance to the form, and it affords even to the illiterate a practical basis for the appreciation of mathematical and geometric truth. . . .
>
> "The origin of this delightful game, like the birthplace of Homer, is a contested point, and its antiquity, like that of many elderly spinsters, is involved in considerable doubt. "
>
> —Michael Phelan
> *The Game of Billiards*, 1858

The Evolution of Three-Cushion Billiards

Three early and short–lived versions of the game

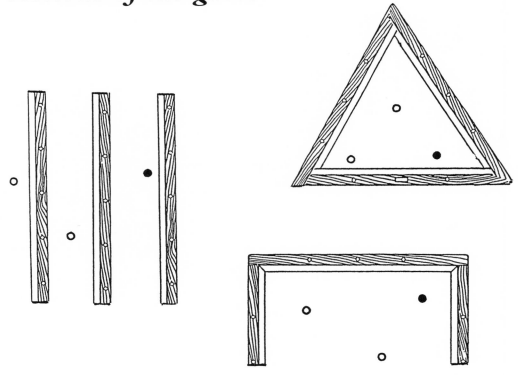

(Graphics by Robert Byrne, idea by Darrell Martineau)

The Games
People Play

Ruth McGinnis, shown here at the age of twenty-one in 1931, was the
unquestioned women's pool champion for three decades and had a high run of 128
in straight pool. At the right is thirty-two-year-old Ralph Greenleaf, the best player
in the world from 1919 to the late 1930s.

(Courtesy of Ray Desell)

Line-up
Straight Pool

WHEN I WAS LEARNING THE GAME a lifetime ago in Dubuque, Iowa, there were three places to play, all on Main Street: The Q, where a man named Cliff Harker awed onlookers with seemingly endless runs in straight pool; Dubuque Recreation, where I and my high-school classmates met almost every day; and the back room of the Union cigar store, which was a little on the scary side because of the gambling.

Our favorite games were straight pool, nine-ball, rotation, and snooker, often with the 6-ball wild. The straight-pool game we usually played was not 14.1 but rather line-up, a version I still prefer, not just because it is slightly easier, but because I like the challenge of trying to pick the balls off the end of the line one after the other, which requires very close control of the cueball.

Line-up rules are the same as the better-known 14.1, with two main differences. Whenever a player misses, the balls pocketed are returned to the table and spotted in a line behind the foot spot—or, if there is no room, in a line from the spot toward the center of the table. The incoming player, therefore, always begins his turn with fifteen balls on the table.

The second difference comes up when you run the table. The last ball does not remain to serve as a break ball as in 14.1, but is pocketed; all the

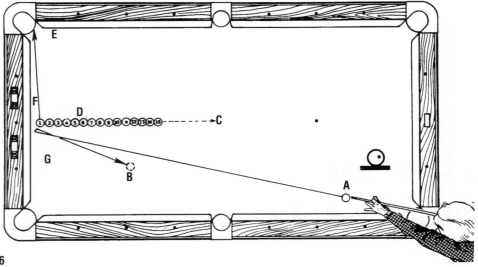

Diagram 106

balls are then placed in a line, as shown in Diagram 106. The player tries to leave the cueball near the foot rail (G would be a good place) so that the run can continue.

Line-up is easier than 14.1 because long runs don't require unpredictable full-rack breaks. After running the table in line-up, you can almost always make at least one more ball and have a chance of continuing the run because the ball at the end of the line near the rail can be made with a rail-first hit. In Diagram 106, the cueball at A is aimed as shown with right English. Making the 1-ball as a kiss off the 2-ball is a cinch. One possible result is that the cueball stops in the vicinity of B and the 15-ball pops out to the center of the table. In addition, the 14-ball might become detached from the 13-ball. You would next try to make the 14 or 15 and bring the cueball to the left end of the table for position on the 2-ball. (It is not necessary to arrange the balls in numerical order as shown.)

After running the table, the cueball might end up in a place like D. From there it is easy to make the 1-ball by banking the cueball to E and F, using enough force to send the cueball through the line to the area near G.

In Diagram 107, the cueball is in perfect position. Running four or five balls off the end of the line before breaking the rest apart requires good control of spin as well as speed and cheating the pocket. If you've never tried line-up before, the following descriptions will help you get the hang of it quickly.

Cutting the 2-ball as much as possible and using straight follow will send the cueball to A for position on the 3-ball. Another possibility is hitting the 2-ball as full as possible with high right, sending the cueball two

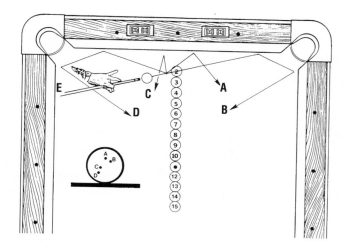

Diagram 107

rails to B. Using left spin and a full, firm hit will send the cueball to C. Draw with left spin will pull the cueball back two rails to D. It might also be possible to use a full hit on the 2 and bring the cueball straight back to E and then out to D. The best path depends on the exact angle of the shot.

In Diagram 108, four balls have been picked off the line and you are faced with the 5-ball. From cueball position B, the correct play is to use follow and enough speed to force the cueball through the line. One possible result is that the 6 and 7 will be pushed forward as shown and the 8 and 9 will be moved off line, leaving you with many options. From position A, the angle is such that the cueball cannot be made to push through the line; it will take a course suggested by the dashed line. Soft to medium speed will leave the cueball near the center of the table, from which it

Diagram 108

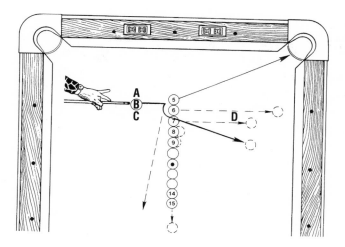

should be possible to make one of the balls dislodged from both ends of the line. Too much speed from position A can send the cueball the length of the table for a scratch in the corner pocket.

From position C in Diagram 108, pocket the 5 straight in and draw back six inches for a force-through shot on the 6. It's dangerous to go beyond the 5 before breaking up the string because the 8-ball, fourth from the spot, is the last one that can be made straight in . . . and only then with perfect position and with the help of sidespin to throw it toward the pocket. By the same token, the ball at the other end of the line (the 15-ball in the diagrams), also fourth from the spot, can be made straight in the side. The balls between the 7 and the 15 must be banked if you have failed to break them loose.

A special situation is given in Diagram 109. You have succeeded in running the table, but you have left the cueball frozen to the rail and uncomfortably close to the 1-ball. If you cut the 1 in the corner, the cueball will drift down the table to an uncertain future. If you angle your cue away from the rail and elevate, you might be able to play the 1 off the 2 and use a nip draw to leave the cueball at A. The danger is that the 2 and 3 may be moved forward, as shown by the dashed circles, just far enough to be makeable from A.

The correct move is to shoot parallel to the rail with follow. The 1-ball will go in off the 2 and the cueball will advance as indicated. Your next shot could well be the 2-ball, which would send the cueball along the dashed line labeled B to a spot near the center of the table. The third shot might be the 15, which will have popped off the end of the line, or maybe the 3-ball, which might now be near C.

Diagram 109

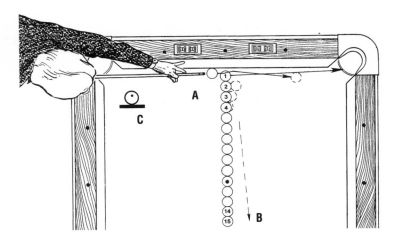

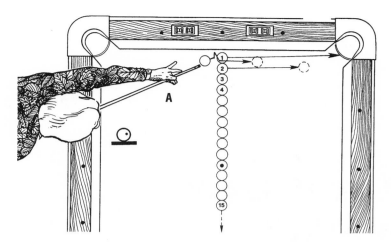

Diagram 110

You have to know the game of line-up pretty well to be aware of the maneuver illustrated in Diagram 110. In some positions of this sort, the best play is to cut the 1-ball and send the cueball all the way to the other end of the table and back for position on the 2. From the position in the diagram, it might be possible to slow-roll the 1-ball into the corner and, with a touch of low left, bring the cueball to A, from where it would be possible to make the 2 and begin the standard pick-off routine. There are certain angles, though, that dictate the idea diagrammed. Use right follow so that the cueball hits the 1, then banks into the 2. Both the 2 and the cueball push through to the other side of the line, the 2 ahead of the cueball. It takes a certain touch.

Line-up straight pool is popular in the Canadian province of Quebec, according to Jean Deshaies, president of the Federation de Billard du Quebec. His personal high run is 200, and he claims to know at least fifty players who have run at least that many. Four who have run more than 350 are Claude Bernatchez, Gaston LeBlanc, Michel Sirois, and Alain Martel. Bernatchez plays nine-ball well, too. In June of 1996, he won a senior tour event at Cue-N-You Billiards in Grayslake, Illinois, topping such veterans as Steve Mizerak, Grady Mathews, Wade Crane, and Bob Vanover.

The Great Game
of Snooker

IF YOU PLAY WORLD-CLASS POOL, why not go to England and go after the really serious snooker money? Tournaments over there with prize funds of $150,000 are common, and the annual world championship at Sheffield pays more than that just to the winner. Top players like Steve Davis, Stephen Hendry, and Jimmy White make over a million dollars a year in tournament winnings, endorsements, exhibitions, and personal appearances.

The reason the pool pros stick with pool is that the snooker pros are unbeatable at their own game. No American pool player has ever been ranked higher than one hundredth in the intensely competitive world of big-money snooker. Even if a pool champion moved to England and played nothing but snooker for six months or a year, the chances are almost nil that he could crack the top fifty.

By the same token, snooker champions have a hard time against our brave warriors when it comes to nine-ball or straight pool. The games are just too different. You would think that players who have such fantastic accuracy in driving balls into narrow pockets (they call it potting) on tables measuring six-by-twelve feet would be unstoppable at nine-ball, but such is not the case.

Most snooker professionals are contemptuous of pool because they feel the pockets are too big and the table is too small. Yet few can play top-class nine-ball. Why?

1. They have lousy breaks. In snooker you seldom have to shoot hard enough to break an egg.

2. They don't fully exploit the freedom wide pockets provide, meaning they aren't good enough at cheating the pocket.

3. They aren't used to using sidespin (except when playing safe) because the accuracy required in snooker doesn't allow it; thus they miss certain positional nuances that flow from throwing the object ball to one side or the other with English.

4. They aren't good at jump shots, because in snooker they are banned.

5. They aren't good judges of the chances of making certain difficult shots on a pool table, so they don't know when to go for a run-out and when to play safe.

6. They aren't used to the size of the table, the speed of the cloth, and the rubber, which affect banking and cueball control.

7. They aren't used to the rules. In snooker, for example, you don't have to drive a ball to a rail when playing safe; you only have to touch it with the cueball.

Pool players are similarly handicapped when trying to play world-class snooker. Their powerful break strokes and skill at jump shots, pocket cheating, and spin are of little value; their cue technique and even their cues aren't suited to a game that places such an enormous premium on accuracy of hit; and they don't know the subtleties of snooker defense.

Defense—that's the key to great snooker. It's the only game that awards points for a good defensive play. Before looking at some sneaky snooker safeties, a recap of the rules for newcomers:

Snooker is played with fifteen red balls, each one worth one point, and six numbered balls ranging in value from two to seven. Players first must make a red ball before they can make a numbered ball. The reds stay down when pocketed, the numbered balls (called the colors) respot. When the reds are gone, the colors then must be pocketed in numerical sequence.

If the incoming player has reds on the table and he fails to hit one, he loses four points . . . or five, six, or seven points if the cueball first hits the 5-, 6-, or 7-ball.

The highest possible run in snooker is 147, which results from making a 7-ball (the black ball) after every red followed by sinking all the numbers. The top pros have done it dozens of times; Willie Thorne once ran

147 while on crutches with both legs in casts after a car accident. Runs of 100 or more, called century breaks, are so common in England that they often go unremarked.

Let's take a look at some defensive plays that separate the adults from the children. Diagram 111 shows how the balls are arranged to begin, with the cueball in the D. (In snooker, the kitchen is the D, not the entire area behind the line crossing the width of the table.) The most often played opening shot is to send the cueball off the pack's corner ball and back to the head rail, called the baulk cushion. With luck, the cueball will stop behind one of the colors, forcing the incoming player to bank for a red.

A common type of defensive shot is given in Diagram 112. Go thin off a red and bring the cueball back to the baulk cushion. If a ball at point A blocks the path, you might be forced to lag the cueball softly to the reds at point C. It isn't a foul if you hit the reds. This doesn't put your opponent in any trouble, but at least you avoid selling out.

In Diagram 113, it is smart to take a chance on cutting the far red in because if you miss, the cueball will be miles from the nearest red; if you make it you will probably have a shot at the 2-, 3-, or 4-ball. Let's say the cueball comes to rest close to the rail as shown, making it risky to try to pocket another ball. The best play here is to roll the cueball softly against and behind the yellow ball, which is not a foul in snooker; your opponent now has to bank for red, with little chance of controlling the outcome.

An amateur player faced with the position in Diagram 114 might hit the red thin and try to leave the cueball near point D. The pro will hit the red full, spreading the cluster, leaving the cueball at E, making a return safety very difficult.

Diagram 111

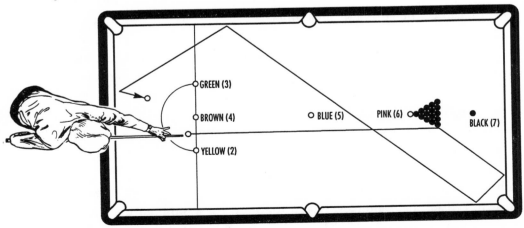

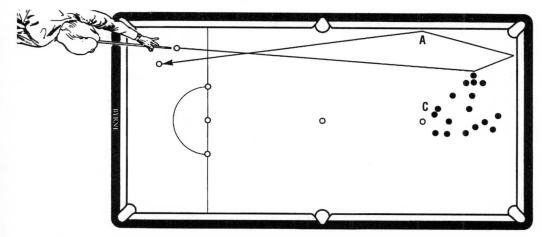

Diagram 112

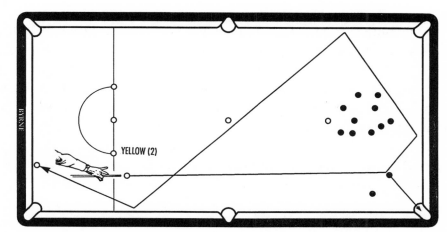

Diagram 113

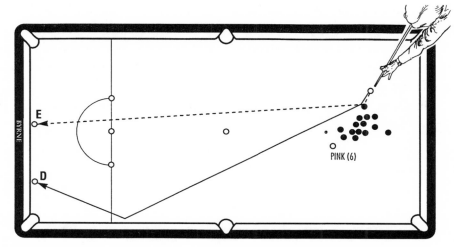

Diagram 114

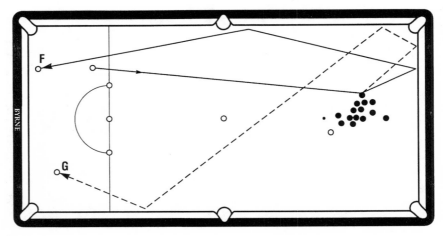

Diagram 115

One more example of devilish safety play is given in Diagram 115. An inexperienced player might simply hit a red thin and bring the cueball to point F . . . which is okay, but gives the next player too much freedom in returning the safety. Better is to hit the red fuller with slight left so that the cueball follows the path shown to point G. A return safety is now difficult because the pink ball blocks the right side of the pack.

In snooker, you are safe if your opponent is far from his work, because the pockets are so narrow and because it is so hard to run a ball down a rail into the corner. In the United States, by the way, snooker tables are usually five by ten and have very tight pockets, sometimes so tight that it is impossible to make a ball on a rail. Such tables are better suited to golf than snooker. In England, the pockets are slightly wider and the balls slightly smaller, but the tremendous size of the table makes long-distance leaves an effective weapon.

Next time you're in England, don't fail to take in a pro snooker tournament. You'll see why snooker is so popular and why there is so much money behind it.

Snooker: another great game that nine-ball has almost killed in the United States.

Watching Snooker
on the Telly

In December of 1995, Norman MacLeod, a snooker and billiard enthusiast in England, sent me a newspaper column from his collection of memorabilia. The piece appeared on April 22, 1987, and refers to some of the then-prominent snooker champions: Ray Reardon, Willie Thorne, Steve Davis, Kirk Stevens, and Joe Johnson. It's a pleasure to be able to reprint it here. My thanks for permission to the author, Oliver Pritchett, and to the **Daily Telegraph.**

IT IS THE GRAVITY OF THE WHOLE BUSINESS that makes it so absorbing. Those serious men in waistcoats, the reverent coughing from the audience, and the whispered moralizing of the commentators all combine to make it addictive.

If ever the revolution comes to Britain, the authorities will not need to play solemn martial music over the radio. They can simply put out seventy-two hours of continuous snooker on BBC television. The whole nation will be calmed by watching Ray disturbing a pack of reds, Willie getting a good angle on the green, Steve screwing back, and Kirk putting a terrific amount of side on the cueball.

The unavoidable Embassy World Professional Snooker Championship is here again, and I have to confess I am hooked, staring for hours at the screen and that headache-green table, listening to the clink of the cueball on red and the occasional thuds of the yellow ball into the corner pocket.

It is not the game which is interesting, but the ceremonial. There is that severe man in white gloves who appears to be trying to strangle the black ball before he puts it back on its spot. There is the pleasure of speculation, too. Have you noticed that the match at the next (unseen) table always seems more exciting? While you are watching Joe playing his nineteenth safety shot, there is suddenly an explosion of applause from the other match. Has Kirk got nicely on to the blue or has Jimmy got a fine cut on the pink? Terry sits deadpan while his opponent clears the table. Is he still brooding about the difficult red he missed?

The commentators are marvelous. One of them affects a John Arlott growl and has a tendency to portentousness. The other suffers from bouts of pessimism.

They are like two men leaning over your garden fence, telling you your guttering is about to fall down, or looking into your car engine and not holding out much hope for your carburetor.

"That leaves Willie needing snookers," they say. "Steve is a bit unfortunate to have landed there," they murmur. "Joe won't be happy with that shot," they lament. "That is not the angle Kirk would have liked," they mourn. Every so often Willie or Kirk or Steve or Joe will stand beside the table, looking remarkably serene considering that they are working out the next seventeen shots of the break, and the commentary-box Jeremiahs will declare that they are "under pressure."

It is an allegory of course. That is the excuse for watching. Don't you find that, in life, you always seem to require 88 points when there are only a possible 59 points left on the table? We all have that feeling when we wake up in the morning that we require snookers if we are to survive the frame of life.

Every day we discover we have left ourselves in an unfortunate position: we are not happy with the angle and the only thing to do is to go for safety. When we are under pressure, the pink always seems to teeter on the brink of the top right-hand corner pocket and refuses to go in. Why does the other chap always seem to get the big breaks while we sit it out and brood? There could be a sermon in all this.

Meanwhile, I spend the evenings slumped on the sofa, watching this lesson in life from the Crucible Theatre in Sheffield, with a bottle of claret to help me survive the pressure. The hours pass and I steadily sink the red. As midnight approaches, I find myself, as they say, tight against the cushion.

Snooker Snafus

Snooker is the number-one television sport in Great Britain and Ireland, and hundreds of hours are aired every year. With so much action to describe, it is inevitable that the weary commentators will make an occasional slip of the tongue or mind. Having done some narration myself, I know how easy it is to blunder into such locutions as "There aren't many last chances left" and "It was an incredible performance and very convincing."

Many British viewers make it a hobby to catch the flubs of the announcers. Favorites are submitted to the magazine *Private Eye,* which presents them in a regular column. A generous sampling was also given in *The Book of Snooker and Billiards Quotations* compiled by Eugene Weber and Clive Everton. (Everton is editor of *Snooker Scene* and well-known for his perceptive snooker narration on television.)

Following are quotes from the last ten years that I found particularly amusing.

- "He won't feel the pressure as much as the more less-experienced players."

- "Steve Davis is acknowledged by his peers to be the peerless master."

- "It's almost impossible to miss, but hitting it is another matter."

- "One of Stephen Hendry's greatest assets is his ability to score when he's playing."

- "If you didn't see Davis against Hendry last night, then you can see them again now."

- "This match has gradually and suddenly come to a climax."

- "There are just enough points left for Tony to pull the cat out of the fire."

- "This said, the inevitable failed to happen."

- "Jimmy White has that wonderful gift of being able to point his cue where he is looking."

- "Well, velour was the better part of discretion there."

- "Sometimes the deciding frame's always the toughest to win."

- "There is, I believe, a time limit for playing a shot. But I think it's true to say that nobody knows what the limit is."

- "The audience is literally electrified and glued to their seats."

- "Griffiths has looked at that blue ball four times now and it still hasn't moved."

- "That's inches away from being millimeter perfect."

- "It's times like these that you have to clench your teeth together and say a prayer."

- "That's the third time he's done that this session: missed his vest pocket with the chalk."

- "The audience is standing to relieve themselves."

- "Here we are in the Holy Land of Israel, a Mecca for tourists."

- "When Higgins has his tail up, he's a hard nut to crack."

- "One mistake here could win or lose the match either way."

- "I am speaking from a deserted and virtually empty Crucible Theatre."

- "Griffiths is snookered on the brown, which, for those of you watching in black-and-white, is the ball directly behind the pink."

- "Ninety-nine times out of a thousand times he would have made that ball."

- "That's a brilliant shot, and the odd thing is his mum's not very keen on snooker."

- "The big prize money is hanging there like a carrot waiting to be picked."

- "The formalities are over and it's down to business. Steve Davis is adjusting his socks."

- "He's forty points behind and there are only fifty-one left on the table."

- "The game could have gone either way, but it didn't."

- "That shot knocked the stuffing out of his sails."

- "After eleven days, he's still sharp as a button."

- "I'm monosyllabic, if that's the word."

- "I'm speechless! That says it all!"

- "As for you, I don't know about me, I'm ready for bed."

The Italian Game
of Five Pins

AREN'T YOU GLAD you misspent your youth? No matter where you go in the civilized world you'll find people bending over tables, poking balls with sticks. You won't always know what they're doing, but they'll be having fun, and chances are that the best players in the country will be making good money in tournaments for the first time in their lives without having to hustle for pennies, or in the case of the Italians, lira, which are worth even less. Skill at cue games is now socially acceptable.

The hot game in Italy and several other countries is five pins. In 1993, Italian television stations devoted some six hundred hours to it, mostly live, and the series of ten qualifying tournaments leading up to the world championship carried a total prize fund of $1.5 *million* . . . that's dollars, not lira. First prize in the final tournament was $106,000, won by Salvatore Manonne of Italy in a thrilling cliff-hanger against a twenty-one-year-old whiz kid from Argentina named Gustavo Zito, who became champion the following year.

Three 61.5 mm balls are used, a red one and a cueball for each player. A small red wooden pin is placed on the center spot, flanked by four white pins. Players make points mainly by knocking pins down with the white object ball (the other player's cueball). The scoring in brief: each white pin counts two points; the red alone, ten points; the red with one or more white pins, four points; a billiard from the white ball to the red is four points; driving the red into the white ball is three points.

A rule that is not present in any other cue game that I can think of is that each player gets only one stroke per inning; even if you score you don't get to shoot again. Although the players sometimes ponder the position for a minute or more, the one-stroke feature gives the game an attractive punch and counter-punch quality.

Like chess—or one-pocket—defense is crucial. Players pick shots and speeds designed not only to knock pins down, but to leave the two cue-balls on opposite sides of the pin cluster in order to force the opponent to kick. Statistics show that top players leave their opponents a direct shot at the object ball only 55 percent of the time.

According to Maurizio Cavalli of Padua, who has been educating me by mail, Italians consider the pin game ideal for television. The rules are simple and the three balls are easy to follow. The blend of offense and defense is intriguing and clever, and the players often resort to multiple rail kicks and banks. Large audiences watch with rapt attention, applauding spectacular shots as well as nuances.

And the audiences are really *large*. In both Italy and Argentina, the countries where the game is most popular, thousands of fans pay to see important matches. Uncounted millions watch each year's tournaments on television, and ratings are very high for the finals, which were staged in 1993 at the posh theater Palais Croisette in Cannes, France.

A decision made ten years ago by the Italian Billiard Federation helped start a boom in five-pin play. Growth of the game was hindered because it was played on tables with small pockets that were rare in other countries. The federation decided to require standard five-by-ten-foot billiard tables and billiard balls. The equipment change worked wonders, and it had an unexpected side effect: three-cushion also became more popular, fueled in part by the international success of Italy's own Marco Zanetti, the world's fourth-ranked three-cushion player.

Another decision helped: the organization in 1987 of biathlon tournaments in which players compete in both five pins and three-cushion. Guess who won the first biathlon tournament? Torbjörn Blomdahl of Sweden! The greatest three-cushion player of all time, who plays excellent nine-ball and snooker, showed that he doesn't care what the rules are: if the game involves a cue and balls and a table, he will play the role of destroyer. (Blomdahl has since returned to three-cushion full time.)

Three-cushion also gets a lot of television time in Italy. In 1993, RAI, the national network, decided to televise the finals of all six World Cup events, one of which was held in Bolzano, Zanetti's hometown.

Pool in Italy has become nearly as popular among the general population as five pins, but is not as highly regarded, just as in England the snooker players and fans tend to look down their noses at the pool crowd. Cavalli feels that pool is hampered as a television attraction because it looks too easy: the players hardly ever miss a shot they try to make. Three-cushion and five pins, by contrast, seem more difficult than they really are, and look good on the tube because of the many multiple-rail banks and the use of sidespin. Snooker comes across better than pool because of the huge, challenging table, but is not played much in Italy.

The road to the world championship in five pins in 1993 was a bit unusual; something similar could be followed in the United States to determine a national nine-ball champion. After ten preliminary tournaments, the participants were ranked according to a point system and the top eight met for round-robin play. The highest four finishers advanced to a single-elimination final.

As it turned out, the four leaders at the end of the ranking tournaments also finished first through fourth in the round-robin. They were Riccardo Belluta, thirty-one, who has twice won the Italian title and is author of a 1989 book on the game called *Il Billardo—Guida Pratica Completa;* followed by the Argentinian champion Zito; and two more Italians, neither of whom had ever won a national title, Vitale Nocerino, thirty-one, and Mannone, thirty-five.

Mannone eliminated an off-form Belluta, and Zito sidelined Nocerino to set up what Signor Cavalli assures me was the greatest world-title battle in the history of five pins, an intense duel that lasted four hours. It was a race to five of fifty-point games. Zito had lost to the more experienced Mannone three out of four times in the earlier competitions, but took a commanding 41–18 lead in the ninth and deciding game. If he could score nine more points, he would be the youngest world champion since Ricardo Fantasia of Italy was crowned at age twenty-six in 1978.

What's this? Zito cracks under the pressure and leaves his opponent an opening! Mannone makes a series of brilliant shots, three times knocking down the red pin alone, always leaving the balls dead safe. Zito fails to score another point and the title goes to Mannone.

For the season, Mannone made $164,000 in tournament prizes; Zito, $126,000; Belluta, $108,000; and Nocerino, $100,000. The eighth player on the money list, Nestor Gomez of Argentina, earned $56,000. By comparison, the leading money winner in the United States for the year 1995 was Efren Reyes, who won $69,000 in the fifteen-event men's pro nine-ball tour. Efren! You're playing the wrong game!

THREE GREAT FIVE-PIN SHOTS

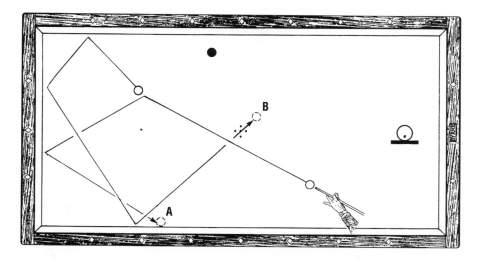

Diagram 116: The object is to score by driving the white object ball through the pins. Here Salvatore Mannone, playing Gustavo Zito for the 1993 world championship, banked the ball three rails, knocking down the center pin alone, good for 10 points. By carefully controlling speed, he left the balls at A and B for a safety. For Zito's response, see the next diagram.

Diagram 117: The pin cluster blocked a direct shot, so Zito went for a two-rail kick, banking the object ball off the side rail and through the pins and returning the safety.

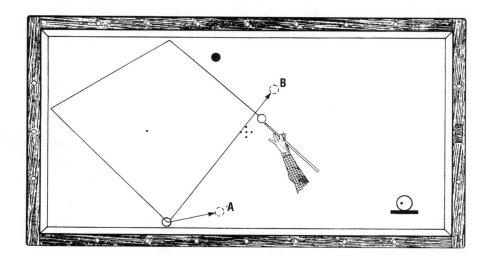

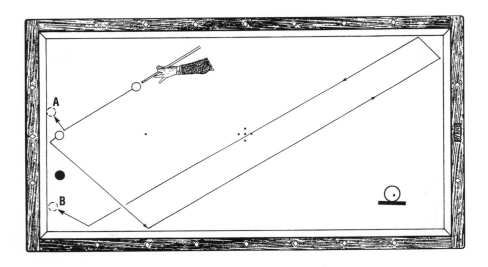

Diagram 118: The red ball can be used for safety play as well, as in this brilliant example from Riccardo Belluta, whose hometown of Milano is the center of five-pin play. Drive the object ball four rails and through the pins, leaving it at B. By killing the cueball, it stops at A, and the opponent is left without a prayer.

"Look, ladies, at the billiard table as a means of domesticating your husbands . . . as a means of making home so agreeable that they will seldom care to leave it except on business or in your society."

—Michael Phelan
The Game of Billiards, 1858

Straight Billiards, the World's Favorite Game

WHAT IS THE MOST POPULAR CUE GAME in the world? It's not pool, friends, and it's not snooker or three-cushion, either. It's straight billiards, the game in which a point is scored when the cueball strikes two object balls. No rail contact is required. It's the game of choice all over Europe, Latin America, and Japan. (In Asian countries, a fourth ball is sometimes added.)

Straight billiards was the most popular cue game in the United States, too, a hundred years ago. What killed it was that a handful of players—notably Jake Schaefer, Sr. ("The Wizard"), Frank Ives, and George Slosson—became so good at it that they almost never missed, which made tournaments impossible at the professional level. It was hard to keep audiences awake when a man was running 500 and out without ever moving the cueball more than two feet. New games were dreamed up to provide a better challenge, games like cushion caroms, in which the cueball must touch at least one cushion before reaching the second object ball; three-cushion, in which the cueball must contact three or more rails before reaching the second ball; and several kinds of balkline, in which restrictions are imposed by lines drawn on the cloth. In England and the nations of its empire, the big game a hundred years ago was a combination of pool and billiards (now called English billiards). Why this group of nations gradually converted to snooker while Americans took up pool and continental Europe and Japan stuck to carom billiards is an interesting question, but beyond the scope of this discussion. Here I will merely introduce the game of straight billiards to those who may not be familiar with it. It's a rich, intriguing game, full of subtleties and nuance. Raymond Ceulemans has said that until Americans master it, they will never be serious threats in world three-cushion play.

The secret of the game is to get the balls close together (by a so-called "gather" shot) and then keep them together. One technique for keeping them together is the rail nurse, called "the American series" in Europe after the nineteenth-century Americans who perfected it. By shooting very softly the balls are kept in a cozy clump close to the rail. Sometimes the cueball moves only an inch or two. A hundred points can be scored while the three balls advance only a few feet along the rail. In Diagram 119, Shots 1, 2, 3 and 4 give the idea. The ideal position is Shot 1, with the object balls side by side forming an angle of 45 degrees with the rail. One possible play here is to aim rather full on the red in order to kiss back off the edge of the white. The kiss "squeezes" the red, holding it onto the rail. Note that the object balls move just a fraction of an inch. It is important to shoot hard enough to get the cueball "outside" the white, that is, closer to the center of the table. The resulting leave will be somewhat similar to Shot 2. Hit the white very thin and land rather full on the red. To make the red move to the right despite the full hit, use left English. The leave will be like Shot 3, which in turn can lead back to Shots 1 and 2. In Shot 2, landing thin on the red might result in a "line-up" like Shot 4, which calls for a massé. To make this masse, elevate the cue to 80 degrees, make sure the tip is well chalked, and use minimum speed; it is not enough to score the point, you want to keep the three balls in a small cluster.

Shot 5 in Diagram 120 is the chuck nurse position, which is very much to be desired. Shoot full on the red, delicately. Done right, the cueball kisses back to the white so softly that neither object ball moves at all. If the white accidentally gets nudged to the right, the red can be moved to the right on the next shot by using a little left English. W. A. Spinks, of Los

Diagram 119

Diagram 120

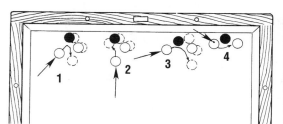

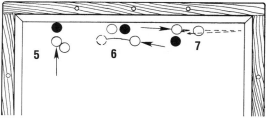

Angeles, ran 1,000 points with this nurse in 1912 and quit with the balls in perfect position.

Shot 6 is the edge nurse. If one ball is frozen to the rail, it is the anchor nurse. In either case, master players can run hundreds of points without losing the position.

Shot 7, one of many strategems, is the block shot. Draw back softly from the white to the red, but in such a way that when the white ball comes back it is stopped in its tracks next to the red by colliding again with the cueball.

Shot 11, Diagram 122, depicts a "short drive" gather shot. The red ball is banked once across the table, while the white is bumped toward the corner. The speed is such that two object balls come to rest close to each other. (A "long drive" is when the first ball is banked the length of the table.) The position in Shot 11 is the goal in the previous three shots. In other words, Shots 8, 9, and 10 (Diagrams 121 and 122) are handled in such a way to set up a gather on the following shot.

Shot 8 is called a "slip through." The important thing is to get beyond the second object ball. In Shot 9 you must land thin on the white ball to get beyond it; if you hit the white ball too full, the cueball will end up between the object balls, which is much inferior.

There are many gather shots that require using the entire table, some of them played with a hard stroke. Shot 13, in Diagram 123, is clever. The cueball hugs the rail to hit the red while the white is driven four rails. The better the player's control of speed, the smaller will be the resulting cluster. In Shot 12, the white ball is driven three rails around the table to rejoin the red while the cueball banks one rail. A subtlety here is that right English is used to kill the cueball's speed.

Straight billiard players in Austria sometimes stage competitions in gather shots using a format devised by Heinrich Weingartner of Vienna.

Diagram 121

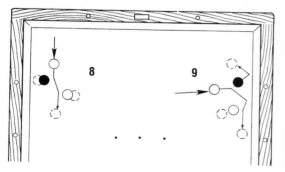

Diagram 122

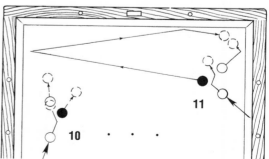

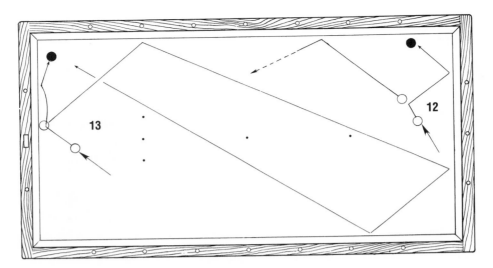

Diagram 123

The players have three chances to make seventy-five different shots, which are graded in difficulty from 4 (easy) to 11 (hard). The object is to make the point and leave the balls within a one-diamond square, as shown in the next series of diagrams.

Shot 1 in Diagram 124 is a slow follow, driving the first ball three rails. Don't hit the cueball too high or the action will be too lively.

Shot 2 is a slow draw. To be successful the cueball must just barely reach the red ball.

In Shot 3 (Diagram 125), the cueball goes four rails before entering the square while the first ball banks once across.

These first three examples are among the easiest in the competition, carrying a difficulty factor of 4. The next two shots are considered medium hard and are worth 7 points each.

In Shot 4, Diagram 126, the white ball is driven three rails the long way while the cueball goes once across. Notice how the speed of the cueball is killed by sending into the first rail at a negative angle. Killing speed with reverse English is a common tactic in the game.

In Shot 5, Diagram 127, the white ball closely follows the cueball around the table. In spotting the balls, put the cueball one ball-width farther from the end rail.

Now for a couple of hard ones. In Diagram 128, Shot 6 gets the highest difficulty rating of 11. All you have to do is make the straight draw from the white to the red, just barely reaching the red, while at the same time sending the white on the zigzag path shown.

Shot 7, Diagram 129, it seems to me, should be worth 11, but the Europeans give it only 10. Here again the speed of the cueball is killed off the first rail by the use of hold–up English.

These comments and diagrams provide a small glimpse at the intricacies of a truly splendid game. Anyone interested in straight rail or in the more difficult game of balkline should acquire a copy of *Daly's Billiard Book,* which contains two hundred diagrams and an explanatory text that is a model of clarity. *Daly's* was first published in 1913 and ran through many hardcover editions before going out of print in the early 1930s. A good quality paperback reprint was published in 1971 by Dover Publications, 180 Varick Street, New York, NY 10014.

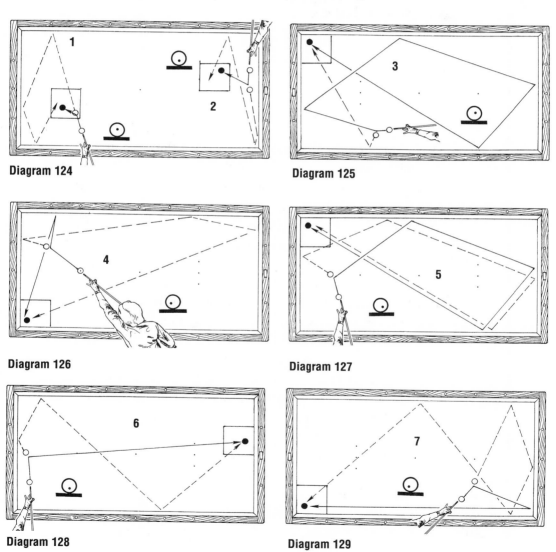

Diagram 124

Diagram 125

Diagram 126

Diagram 127

Diagram 128

Diagram 129

The Artistry of
18.2 Balkline

TO PLAY POOL AT A HIGH LEVEL, you must control the cueball. The best three-cushion billiard players try to control the first object ball as well. In the game of balkline, the movement of all three balls must be predicted down to a gnat's eyelash. Old-time champion Welker Cochran, who once held the three-cushion and balkline titles at the same time, called it the most difficult of all games to master, requiring extraordinary concentration and delicacy of stroke.

To play balkline well, you must estimate carom angles with great accuracy, have a touch for shots that barely move the balls, be able to bank an object ball so that it returns to within a few inches of its starting point, and show total assurance on draw, follow, dead ball, and massé shots of every description. The rail nurses that enable straight billiard experts to build high runs are barred in balkline. Instead, you have to learn how to nurse the balls when they are eighteen or even twenty-eight inches from the rail. Masters can make the balls separate and return to a cluster as if they were on strings.

In 1924, Thomas Gallagher wrote that the game of 18.2 balkline "is the highest standard by which the skill of billiard experts is measured. It is the style of play in vogue for national and international honors. Combining all the beautiful and intricate features of the most fascinating of pastimes, the masterful super-artists who compete at it must employ all their resources and give their best to attain success and eminence."

In 1993, eighty years after *Daly's Billiard Book* appeared, the magic of balkline was captured by Accu-Stats Video Productions (that number again is 800-828-0397). On the tape, balkline is demonstrated by two of the best players in the world, Peter De Backer and Frederic Caudron, both of Belgium. Watching that tape, which features a run of 133 and out, you can't help being amazed at the artistry and skill on display.

Balkline is a carom game played on a pocketless table. It was developed more than a hundred years ago because the top players got too good at the "free" game—now called straight rail in the United States—in which points are scored simply by making the cueball hit the other two balls. You think that's too easy? Put the balls anywhere you want and see if you can run 10.

Without restrictions, the top players could herd the balls into a corner and run thousands of points. In 1874, to prevent crotching the balls in a corner, a "balk" line was drawn on the cloth with chalk to create a triangular zone at each corner within which only two points could be scored consecutively. It wasn't enough of a handicap, especially not after the development of techniques for keeping the three balls in a tight cluster while they are nudged along a rail. In San Francisco in 1890, Jacob "The Wizard" Schaefer, whose son would later become world balkline champion, ran 3,000 points mainly using the rail nurse.

Further restrictions were needed to make competitions feasible among the top players. To hinder the various kinds of nurses, lines were drawn parallel to the rails, first at eight inches, then twelve, then fourteen, then eighteen, thus dividing the table into nine areas. Only one or two points can be scored in any area without driving an object ball across a line. The designation of 18.2 (or 47.2) means that the lines are eighteen inches (or forty-seven centimeters) from the rails and that two points are allowed before an object ball must cross a line; 18.1 means that a ball must be driven across a line on the first point. If the object balls are in different areas to begin with, there is no restriction, and there is no restriction on scoring points in the central area. Essentially the same rules apply today that were imposed in the 1890s.

Players strive for positions in which the object balls are straddling a line so that they are in different areas, yet close together. When it is necessary to drive a ball across a line, the idea is to make it return off a rail and die next to the other ball. It isn't easy.

When Willie Hoppe won his first world championship at age eighteen in 1906 by beating Maurice "The Lion" Vignaux in Paris, the game they played was 18.1 balkline.

The top players soon found ways to get around the restrictions, and the runs mounted once again into the thousands. Players like Hoppe, Cochran, and Jake Schaefer, Jr., would simply get the balls straddling the line at the rail and run points all night by means of the chuck nurse or the anchor nurse, the details of which you will find in Daly's book. It became necessary to add small square areas (today they are seven inches on a side and are called anchor blocks) at the intersections of the lines with the rails. See Diagram 130 for the layout.

Champions then turned their attention to mastering the so-called balk-line nurse, in which the balls are nudged along the line eighteen inches from the rail, as shown in Diagram 131. The key shot is to hit the first ball and land lightly on the second ball while at the same time sending the first ball to the rail and back. The only players left in the world who can do it with any consistency are in Europe.

A still harder version of the game is 28.2 (71.2 in Europe) balkline, in which the lines are drawn twenty-eight inches (seventy-one centimeters) from the rails. Despite the larger areas, both Caudron and De Backer, who appear on the above-mentioned Accu-Stats tape, have runs of 250 and out.

The last world-class tournament in balkline in the United States was held in 1934 at Bensinger's in Chicago, with Cochran the winner, followed in order by Erich Hagenlacher, Willie Hoppe, Kinrey Matsuyama, and Ora C. Morningstar. The winner had a high run of 217 and an average of 32.8. Schaefer beat Cochran in a 4,000-point challenge match in 1938 with an average of 47.19 and a high run of 348.

Diagram 130

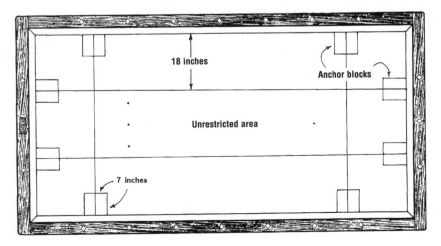

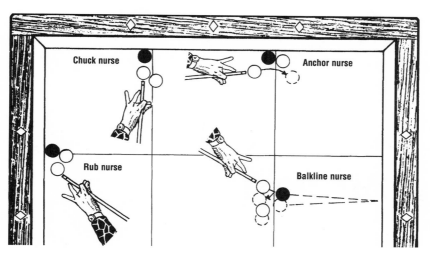

Diagram 131

That was the end of the line for big-time balkline competitions in this country, though balkline still is played in Europe. In the 1960s and 1970s, three lovers of the game on the East Coast tried to keep at least a memory of balkline alive in the United States by playing it a least once a year: The three were Horace Henderson and Clem Trainer of Philadelphia and Ely Castleman of Baltimore. They met at Allinger's in Philadelphia, and when that great old room closed, at the Union League Club. They drew the lines on the cloth with tailor's chalk, played a few hundred points of the great old game, and reminisced about the wonders they had seen and would never see again. (For a touching profile of Trainer and his contributions to billiards, see the obituary by Mike Shamos in *Billiards Digest,* June 1993.)

Only Castleman is left now, and he rarely meets anybody who even knows what the word *balkline* means. There was amazement in his voice when I told him on the phone in October of 1993 about the New York balkline exhibition that had been captured on videotape. I know he ordered a copy the instant we hung up.

Box Billiards

THE CLASSIC GAMES of eight-ball, nine-ball, rotation, straight pool, snooker, three-cushion, and straight billiards are fine, but occasionally something different is needed to keep a player's interest up. Try line-up straight pool instead of rack, snooker with the 6-ball wild, one-pocket, golf on a snooker table, or optional cueball three-cushion (which eliminates safety play). There are challenging and intriguing new games, too, like equal offense straight pool (free break, ten innings only, limit of twenty balls per inning) and "kiss pool" (object balls are pocketed by kissing them off the cueball).

New games or revivals of old games sometimes do more than pep up a player whose interest has flagged; they can keep an entire pool hall from going down the tubes. In the 1930s, the introduction of snooker-table golf kept a lot of rooms afloat until times got better, and it saved a lot of the big six-by-twelves from premature graves. The one-pocket boom served a similar function in the 1950s. Sometimes a variation can become the rage in a particular town or room, keeping everybody's spirits high and the cash register jingling.

If interest is flagging among the three-cushion players in your room, introduce "box billiards." Like snooker-table golf, it is especially good for more than two players. When a game is in full swing, especially when a few vocal personalities are involved, the normally dignified atmosphere around the billiard tables is changed to something more reminiscent of a wrestling match or a street fight. The game seems to bring out the players' natural greed and selfishness. No more Mr. Nice Guy. For a change the noisy bar-pool types at the other end of the room put down their cues and stare in amazement at the suddenly berserk billiard players, who are whooping and hollering in a most uncharacteristic manner.

What does it is money, for box billiards is a gambling game. There is jack in the box. Money changes hands fast, sometimes on every shot, which tends to boost everybody to a fevered pitch. A lot of money is not required; a quarter a point and a quarter a foul seems to do the trick. A quarter isn't much, but if enough of them have to be dished up in a short enough period of time, a man's composure can begin to show signs of unraveling.

The rules of three-cushion billiards apply, with one modification: the box the balls come in is placed in the center of the table as an obstacle. If any ball hits the box in the course of a shot, even if the point scores, the player's inning is over and he must throw a quarter in the box. Two balls hitting the box costs two quarters as does one ball hitting it twice. Not hitting a ball costs a quarter, as does accidentally touching the box with your hand or sleeve.

Whenever a player makes a point, he collects the contents of the box and everybody antes again, including the scorer. After a score, the box is reset in the middle of the table; otherwise it is left wherever it comes to rest after getting struck by a ball.

If a ball comes to rest touching or very close to the box, it is moved a butt-width away.

That's pretty much all there is to it. The high-speed money changing and the surprise fouls get the players keyed up and hysterical. If a player takes a chance for the jackpot by trying a shot that calls for a lot of ball movement, the other players shout "Box! Box!," hoping thereby to influence the course of the balls so that one will hit the obstacle and prevent a payoff.

The educational aspect of the game is considerable, for the shooter must carefully consider the path of all three balls, which is something new for some players. If you are scoring to a ball close to the box, speed becomes critical, another factor some players seldom think about. The game is worth trying just for what it forces you to learn about where the first ball goes.

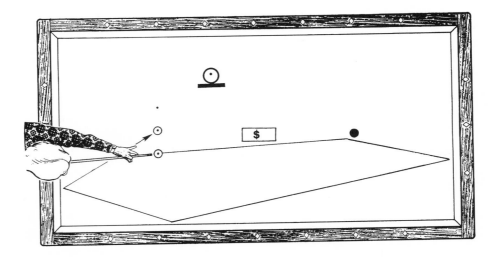

Diagram 132

Diagram 132 is the break shot, which can't be played in the normal way. Soft speed is needed to avoid hitting the box.

A typical problem is shown in Diagram 133. A thin hit (dashed line) hooking the cueball into the corner with draw is risky because too much speed is required for comfort. A five-rail shot is nerve-racking for the same reason. On both shots it would be hard to keep the white ball from banking into the box. Still, a chance is worth taking because a foul only costs a quarter and there might be two or three dollars in the box. A good

Diagram 133

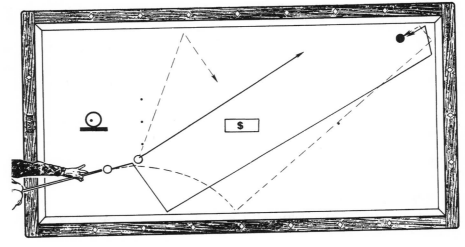

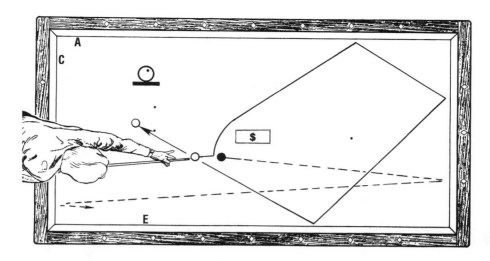

Diagram 134

choice is the spin shot as shown by the solid line, driving the white around the box.

In Diagram 134, the cueball curves around the corner of the box into a scoring path. Make sure you drive the red into the end rail, not the side rail. A short angle off the white, A–C–E, is too dangerous.

> "If there were no gamblers, how drab and dull would mankind be!"
>
> —Tristan Bernard (1866–1947)

A Game of
Safeties and Kicks

MANY OF THE CLASSIC CUE GAMES are in trouble. Eight-ball and nine-ball, advancing like sludge and smelling of sulphur, are destroying everything in their path. Interesting new games are put forward from time to time, but they are faced with a wall of inertia. The suffocating weight of league eight-ball and tournament nine-ball is too great to overcome.

I sketched the rules of nine "alternate games" in *Byrne's Advanced Technique,* including several especially good ones, Equal Offense, Kiss Pool, and Honolulu (pages 73–77). Here I'd like to introduce an intriguing game so new it lacks a name. I'll call it Hooked. You can call it Kick, or One-Ball, or Hide and Seek, or whatever you want. But don't just name it, try it!

Hooked was invented in 1993 by Glen Farr and a few of his pals in Bridgeport, Ohio, and independently by John Delaveau, head referee of the Pro Billiard Tour, in New York. Play it for a while and you'll improve your ability to lay down safeties as well as your ability to escape them. At first glance, passersby will think you are playing nine-ball, for the first nine balls are used and they are racked in the familiar diamond at the start.

The 1-ball must be hit first, as in nine-ball, but the method of scoring and winning is utterly different. You score a point when, and only when, your opponent fouls, and the best way to make that happen is to lay down a good safety. The first player to get nine points wins. Delaveau suggests five, Farr nine. The rules are relatively simple:

1. Use a nine-ball rack. Lag for break.

2. After the break, all pocketed balls are respotted, including the 1-ball. In Ohio, the 1-ball is always spotted in front of other pocketed balls, while it goes behind them in New York. Making the 9-ball on the break has no significance. All nine balls are always on the table when you or your opponent shoot.

3. The object is to hide the 1-ball. If you pocket the 1-ball, it spots and you shoot again. If you hit the 1-ball first and make another ball, the pocketed ball is spotted and you shoot again. But in New York you never shoot twice.

4. If you are hooked and you successfully hit the 1-ball and drive a ball to the rail after the contact, it is your opponent's turn to shoot. He will, of course, try to hook you again.

5. Fouls are failing to hit the 1-ball first, failing to drive a ball to a rail, scratching, knocking the cueball off the table, touching any ball with anything other than the tip of your cue, and failing to drive at least two balls to a rail on the break.

6. After the break, the incoming player has the option of pushing out if he is hooked. That is, he can elect to roll the cueball without penalty to a position from which you can see both sides of the 1-ball. You can either accept the position or make him shoot again.

If you are hooked and have to bank for the 1-ball, it is usually not enough simply to hit it. You should also try to make it hard for your opponent to hook you again.

If you don't see a good way to play safe in Ohio, consider pocketing the 1-ball and shooting at it again when it is spotted. To get a good angle for laying down a tough safety, it might be necessary to make the 1-ball several times or to make a combination using the 1-ball.

On the opening break, it's not a bad idea to spread the balls lightly and leave the cueball behind the pack, forcing your opponent to push out.

In conventional nine-ball, ball-in-hand anywhere on the table is a devastating penalty for a foul. To be a strong nine-ball player under today's rules you must be very good at hiding the cueball and escaping from safeties and snookers, yet how often do you see anybody practicing those aspects of the game? Playing Hooked will help you develop essential skills and have fun doing it.

A note about how the game was invented. Farr says he got the idea after watching videotapes of a match between Efren Reyes and Earl Strickland and a $50,000 "Challenge of Champions" between Buddy Hall and Johnny Archer, both of which had a lot of interesting safety exchanges. Delaveau recalls that his vision came while watching Johnny "The Legend" Ervolino and Mary "Ruby Alabama" Hurt play nine-ball at Amsterdam Billiards in New York City. To make the match even, Ervolino suggested that his only way to win would be to catch her on three fouls. That planted a seed.

In answer to a query from me, Delaveau replied: "I can honestly tell you I've never heard of Glen Farr nor Bridgeport, Ohio, but I greatly admire the man's dynamic intelligence for having dreamed up the same game I did."

Rotation Eight-Ball and Double Position

Is conventional eight-ball too easy for you? Try Glen Farr's rotation eight-ball. Once the groups of balls have been determined, the balls must be contacted in numerical sequence within each group. Combinations and billiards are okay, as in nine-ball, provided the low ball is hit first.

Another of his ideas is "Double Position" nine-ball. (The concept can be applied to almost any pool game, especially straight pool.) The player must call the ball and pocket not only for the shot at hand, but for the next shot as well. If you fail to make the second shot as announced, the previous shot is nullified and the ball spotted. Play this for a while and your cueball control is bound to improve.

The Players
and Their World

**Former Swedish model Ewa Mataya Laurance zeroes in on the tough
Passing Lane shot during an exhibition at Buffalo Billiards
in Cotati, California, in 1993. She was Player of the Year in 1990 and won the 1994
Women's World Nine-Ball Championship in Chicago.**

(Photograph by Jeff Vendsel, courtesy of the *Argus-Courier,* Petaluma, California;
inset photograph by James McNeilly)

A Carnival
of Characters

AT THIS VERY MOMENT, in all likelihood, George "The Ripper" Rippe is trying to set a new billiard high-jump record. Rippe, the gregarious owner of The Cue Club in Lawrence, Massachusetts, is a big man whose stroke has launched a thousand balls. To reach his latest goal, he uses two uprights with nails at half-inch intervals and a crossbar that spans the width of the table. Over and over he sends the cueball off a ball frozen in the corner (see Diagram 135) over the crossbar and around the table three rails to score on the red. Each time he succeeds he moves the crossbar up another notch.

George's partner, Ray Desell, sent me a breathless bulletin: "He cleared 10 inches easily, then 11. He failed when he tried to set a new record of 14 1/2 inches. The record was set in 1963 at the Pemberton Hotel in Pittsburgh by "No Neck" Nolan and tied in 1973 by "The Seldom Seen" Kid. Ripper wants this one bad."

Other bulletins arrive almost daily from Duluth, Georgia, where power-stroker "Fast Larry" Grindinger solidifies his claim of having hit more rails on more different kinds of tables in more different ways than anybody in history. He has rocketed off ten and eleven rails on pool, billiard, and snooker tables, and, even more amazing, he has done it one-handed.

Some stunts are downright dangerous. Hitting ten rails on a pool table using the pattern shown in Diagram 136 is only possible, Grindinger

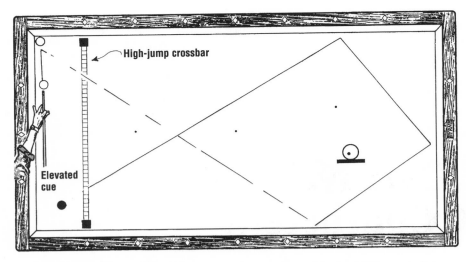

Diagram 135: The set-up for "high-jump billiards." The idea is to shoot into the ball frozen in the corner with an elevated cue and make the cueball jump over the crossbar and go around the table as shown to score on the red. The record height is fourteen inches.

claims, by making the cueball fly through the air off the first several rails. Best to practice it in a room with rubber walls or on a table surrounded by baseball players.

People have killed themselves trying to set fringe records. In 1979 in Australia, Raymond Priestly tried to become the first snooker player

Diagram 136: "Fast Larry" Grindinger (aka The Great Gunninger) has hit ten rails on a pool table using this pattern. The secret is to jump the cueball off the noses of the first several rails, which makes it a dangerous shot to practice.

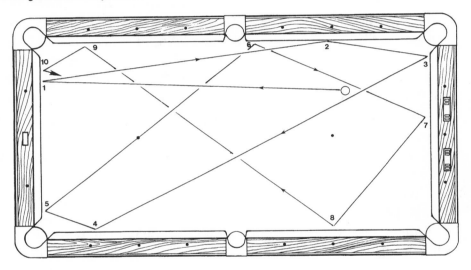

to make a shot while hanging upside down over a table. He slipped and landed on his head. In 1894 the British journal *Billiards* described a man who boasted that he could get a snooker ball into his mouth. He succeeded, but then he couldn't get it out. He was rushed to Middlesex Hospital "amid considerable excitement" and died on the way. Several contemporary American players—George Middleditch and Steve Simpson, to name two—can make pool shots by spitting cueballs from their lips, but they aren't so foolish as to try to put them all the way inside their mouths.

In *The Book of Snooker Disasters and Bizarre Records* (1986), Ray Reardon recalls a scene from his youth when a man trying to win a sixpence put a cueball in his mouth. Doctors had to pull his front teeth to remove it.

Speaking of teeth, the same book tells of a spectator watching a coin-op pool game at the George Hotel in Bridlington, England. He laughed so hard at one player's miss that his dentures jumped out and fell down a pocket. An engineer with the correct keys had to be called from forty miles away to open up the table so the spectator could get on with his life.

But never mind accidents; consider obsessions. It's fascinating, the kinds of things that seize the human imagination. Chicago's Jeff Gates, for example, has invested a tremendous amount of time trying to find out how many balls can be pocketed on a single stroke. At last report he had pushed the total to twenty-four, striving for twenty-six. What an exhilarating day it will be when thirty balls drop! I'd like to be there to share his joy.

Years ago, I heard of a guy whose main focus in life was seeing how many consecutive spot shots he could make on a pool table. All he wanted to do, night after night, was practice spot shots. The game of pool itself had lost its interest.

There are many three-cushion players who sink into a kind of "system swamp," where they become consumed with the idea that the key to the game involves not judgment, not experience, not feel or stroke, but arithmetic. All they want to talk about is how to add and subtract numbers for various shot patterns. Twenty-five years ago an earnest striver from the Midwest published a booklet describing a system that he said God had revealed to him in a dream. I wasn't surprised to learn that God was a system player.

Then there are the finger-flickers. Rives Smith, a prince of a fellow from Texas, is much more interested in propelling the cueball with his hand and fingers than with a cue, maybe because he can do it better than almost anyone else.

Has anyone ever offered to play you one-handed for money? Watch out! John Melnichuk plays very good three-cushion billiards with one arm behind his back; "Machine Gun" Lou Butera once ran 100 in straight pool playing one-handed. Don't forget Ernie Morgan, who is called "The One-Armed Bandit" for a reason.

The late Don Willis is said to have made forty-two consecutive wing shots—rolling object balls down a pool table and cutting them into the corner on the fly. In bank pool, Eddie Taylor claims to have cleared the table—making fifteen banks in a row—six times in his life. Over the course of three games, he made thirty-seven banks before missing. Myron Zownir says he made the 9 on the break six times in a row, but he was practicing alone at the time. In 1989 at the Denver Athletic Club, I made the three-cushion billiards break shot thirty-six times in a row. Or did I lose count?

In 1961, according to Fast Larry, he broke the balls in nine-ball and pocketed every ball but the 9! Eight balls dropped! Naturally, he was left without a decent shot on the 9. Too bad a camera wasn't running at the time.

Did these amazing things really happen? There is no way to authenticate anecdotes. Memory is a treacherous thing. In court of law, hearsay is inadmissible. Eyewitnesses often prove to be spectacularly wrong, even when trying to tell the truth. Always muddying the waters are the braggarts and the self-serving exaggerators. (A certain portly person comes to mind.)

Even if something really happened exactly as remembered and witnesses signed affidavits, is it a world record? There's another quagmire, for no system exists for evaluating and validating extraordinary claims. We don't even have a place to *record* them.

Many mighty deeds depend too much on the equipment to make comparisons meaningful. On a billiard table, for instance, if the cushions are lively, the balls are polished, and a super-fast cloth like Simonis 300 has just been installed, it doesn't take a one-in-a-million stroke to hit eleven rails using the pattern shown in Diagram 137.

Another problem in rating fringe feats is establishing priority. Who did it first? Hard to say when you have only rumors and gossip to go on. In the 1920s and 1930s, Robert Ripley, in his "Believe It or Not" newspaper feature, twice reported that billiard players had hit ten rails but he offered nothing beyond the players' word. (What a brilliant concept Ripley had for a syndicated column! He didn't have to provide proof. You didn't believe him? That was fine with Bob.)

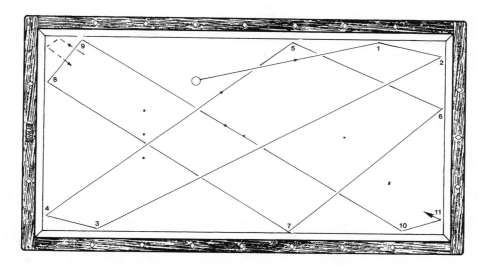

Diagram 137: How to hit eleven rails on a billiard table. It's not so tough when the cloth is brand-new and the rails aren't dead. On slow equipment, the cueball dies after nine rails and comes in short, as shown by the dashed line. The shot is a good test of strength. (Hint: Use a below-center hit on the cueball.)

As far as feats of strength are concerned, Frank Ives was likely the first to hit eleven rails, quite an accomplishment in the nineteenth century, when cloth and rubber were slower than they are today. He claimed he could hit a billiard ball harder than any man in the world. Not even boxing champions could outdo him. Here's a report from *Pearson's Weekly,* October 1896:

> Corbett, Fitzsimmons, Sandow, and other athletes and strong men have competed with him, but he has not been beaten yet. One quick, sharp blow with his cue and the ball flies round the table striking eleven cushions. Fitzsimmons, who strikes a blow that has been compared to a horse's kick, can barely touch nine cushions, while Corbett, whose blows are equally unpleasant, cannot strike more than eight.
>
> There is no trick in Ives's method of hitting the ball; he merely strikes it squarely in the center. Men who are in every way superior to him in strength, if shown exactly where to hit the ball, and if they strike it with all the force they possess, cannot come within a dozen feet of his record. He has consulted eminent physicians on the subject, but they gave him little satisfaction, except to say that his profession had led to the development of muscles which prizefighters and strong men do not use.

As Ives cannot settle the question to his own satisfaction, he has taken steps to enlighten others after his death. In his will, he orders that his right arm be severed from his body and sent to his physician for dissection. The real secret, he thinks, will then be discovered. The rest of his body he desires to be cremated.

During the 1890s, Frank Ives was one of the best billiard players in the world, a master at all forms of the game then popular, including English billiards. According to Willie Hoppe in his 1925 book *Thirty Years of Billiards,* Ives was a champion roller skater, a champion bicycle rider, a horseman of note, and a great baseball catcher before taking up billiards. "Old-time sportsmen," Hoppe wrote, "maintain that he was the greatest all-around professional athlete that ever lived." Who knows what Ives might have accomplished if he hadn't died of tuberculosis at the age of thirty-three; he might have rendered a table completely unfit for further use.

What we need, obviously, are special competitions, perhaps as part of nine-ball tournaments. Let's find out once and for all who can hit the ball the hardest, draw the ball the farthest, control the cueball best. Who has the best break shot, the best jump shot, the best wing shot? Who is the greatest shotmaker? Who can run the table in the fewest number of seconds? Who can dream up the best new challenges?

I would pay to see such an event, and I bet the well-known champions wouldn't sweep the field. Relative unknowns like Rippe and Grindinger would be tough to beat in their several specialties. In basketball, remember, the best free-throwers aren't college or pro-players—they are pudgy middle-aged guys who practice for years and can make hundreds in a row.

We need our own book of records, firsts, and remarkable flukes. The *Guinness Book of World Records* is skimpy on pool, billiards, and snooker, as you can see by looking under those headings. More to the taste of the Guinness editors is how many college sophomores can stuff themselves into a phone booth.

When gathering material for *Byrne's Treasury of Trick Shots* (1982), I contacted Ripley International Limited and bought the rights to reprint ten cartoons that had appeared in the syndicated newspaper feature "Robert Ripley's Believe It or Not." I was surprised to learn that he had published some sixty items relating to cue games. In addition to camera-ready drawings, I was sent copies of the background correspondence. Some people wrote to him over and over again in hopes of making his column, which was tremendously popular worldwide.

He couldn't begin to cope with the volume of his mail, even with a staff of sixty-six researchers and secretaries. Ripley once boasted that he got more mail than anyone in the world and that he had one million unanswered letters.

Robert Ripley was born in 1893 and died in 1949. In the depths of the Depression in the 1930s, he was making $500,000 a year. Before becoming a newspaperman and cartoonist, he had a job polishing tombstones. Believe it or not.

Come with me now and surf through the Ripley files. We'll learn something about the remarkable feats of skill, about curious fixations and coincidences, about trivia and meaninglessness, and about the human trait that dares not speak its name: the need for publicity . . . or, to be kinder, recognition.

(In what follows, my comments are in parentheses. A few of Ripley's non-billiards items are included for flavor.)

- 1701. Duke Maximilian of Bavaria, playing billiards with his chamberlain Barthels, lost $3,600,000 in a single afternoon and was deposed as a result.

- Two Frenchmen named Lenfant and Mellant, after a bitter quarrel over a billiard game in 1843, fought a duel to the death at Maisonfort, France, with billiard balls. Lenfant was killed by a ball that struck him in the forehead.

- Miss Frances Anderson of Newton, Kansas, called herself the Women's World Champion. When she died in 1930, it was discovered that Frances was a man. (The item was sent to Ripley by Anderson's brother, who knew a transvestite when he saw one.)

- 1928. Isidro Ribas can hit ten rails on a billiard table. (The Spaniard Ribas was acknowledged to have one of the most powerful strokes of his day. He could hit the ball so hard that there was talk about having his arm examined by doctors to see how it differed from ordinary arms. Jay Bozeman, ninety years old in 1996 and still playing, told me he once saw Ribas make a five-cushion massé shot *one-handed*.)

- Jake Schaefer ran 400 points from the spot in a match with Hagenlacher, who lost without playing. Chicago, 1925. (It would have helped if Ripley had informed his readers that the game was

18.2 balkline. Schaefer had to share cartoon space with A. H. Perry of Coushatta, Louisiana, a rural mail carrier, who made his daily rounds with a bluejay perched on his head.)

- 1928. Ralph Greenleaf won the world's pocket billiard championship eleven times with the same cue. He has used it for seventeen years.

- 1931. Willie Hoppe ran 898 points in 18.2 balkline.

- 1931. The Greatest Player in the World, The Masked Marvel, a disguised pocket billiard expert, has lost but twelve games out of 1,512 played in three years. (Traveling masked marvels were popular, and several were at work in various parts of the country at the same time. One was Leon "Behind the Back" Yonders, who played the role for fifteen years.)

- 1930. Otto Reiselt makes a six-rail bankshot in three-cushion billiards without touching any of the 120 other balls placed on the table as obstacles. (Ripley carelessly drew the shot on a pool table, which brought letters of protest from all over country.)

- 1930. Common cottage cheese, when moistened with 40 percent formaldehyde, becomes so hard that pool and billiard balls are made from it. (So that's what my mother put in those sandwiches!)

- 1931. Willie Hoppe made a run of 25 at three-cushion billiards in San Francisco in 1918.

- 1934. Four pool balls were balanced on top of each other by Cyril Ball, Eugene, Oregon. (I choose not to believe it, unless the balls were doctored.)

- 1939. Four billiard balls were balanced on top of one another— witnessed by Roy King, Los Angeles, California. (Maybe it could be done with ivory balls, making use of the "eye" and defects in the grain.)

- 1938. Earle Barryhill, Sapulpa, Oklahoma, ran all the balls in succession in a snooker game for a total score of 117. (That was a heck of a run for an American amateur player. The world pro record at the time was 138.)

- The fastest-breaking curve ball ever thrown! Robert McCullough, pitching for a semi-pro team in Mt. Vernon, Ohio, September, 1938, broke his arm in four places on one pitch.

- In 1935 at the Boat and Sport Show in Chicago, Charlie Peterson made 20,000 points in straight billiards in 101 minutes and 8 seconds. (The method involved trapping the balls against a rail and more or less vibrating the cuetip against the cueball; fouls were ignored. In a letter to Ripley, Peterson claimed a distance record: he shot an ivory ball down a concrete runway at Navy Pier and followed it to a stop 334 feet 2 inches away.)

- 1936. Julius Shuster of Jeanette, Pennsylvania, picks up ten pool balls in each hand from a flat surface and turns his hands back and forth without dropping any. (He later toured with a Ripley troupe of off-beat performers.)

- 1938. Sam Sicherman, shooting the cueball from his mouth on every shot, makes a run of 15.

- 1949. Stanley Stonik, after practicing one-handed pool playing for twenty-five years, runs 46 in straight pool. (He taught Lou Butera.)

- 1937. Jack Hill, a specialist in "Chinese" Pool, can hold two cues side by side and scoop sixteen balls off the table.

- 1931. During an exhibition at Wright's billiard room in San Francisco, Spencer Livsey of Los Angeles jumps a ball from one table to another and makes a seven-rail billiard.

- 1948. Leon Yonders makes 163 balls in four innings in straight pool with the cue behind his back at "Peter Mack's place in Shenandoah, Pennsylvania." (He also claims a snooker record, running all twenty-one balls without the cueball touching a rail, always with the cue behind his back. In a letter to Ripley he writes "I was told I am one hundred years ahead of my time. I was named The Wonder Man, The Ninth Wonder of the World. I hope I make myself clear.")

- 1979. (King Features Syndicate, still running old Ripley cartoons, repeats the claim that Neville Chamberlain, "the British Prime Minister who knuckled under to Hitler," was the inventor of snooker. Wrong! Colonel Sir Neville Chamberlain, who invented snooker while stationed at Jubbulpore, India, in the 1870s, was no relation to the man who became Prime Minister more than sixty years later.)

- 1963. George Osbaldeston, English sportsman, for three successive days played billiards continuously from 8:00 P.M. to 11:00 A.M., then went to the race track and remained there until it was time to return to the billiard table—going without sleep for seventy-two hours. At the time, Osbaldeston was sixty-six years of age.

- 1950. A billiard cue was used for seventy-seven years by William Peall, Hove, England.

- 1949. John McHugh, Twin Rocks, Pennsylvania, can throw three billiard balls into the air at one time and catch them on the back of his hand.

- 1949. Joseph Thomas, Quincy, Massachusetts, has operated a billiard parlor for thirty-five years and has never played a game in his life.

- 1947. Oscar Bayer of Appleton, Wisconsin, playing 50 points of three-cushion on his 50th birthday, March 5, won $5.00, made 5 lucky shots, had a high run of 5, lives on 5th Street and has 5 letters in both his first and last names.

- 1945. Billy Bancroft shoots billiards with his nose. Birmingham, Alabama.

- Harry Lewis makes a run of 46 shooting only with his nose. Date unknown. (How big were these noses?)

- 1941. Joe Kline, Stand Billiard Academy, New York, has played billiards after every meal for twenty-two years.

- 1941. Johnny Layton made four high runs of 70 in pocket billiards in four different rooms on the same night in four different Illinois towns.

- 1941. Billiard ball went through window cutting perfect circle—no cracks. Mrs. E. M. D. Ramsay, Carlsbad, California.

- 1940. Tiff Denton, Kansas City, former three-cushion billiard champion, established the world's record (tournament) run of 17 in 1919—and on March 25, 1940, he equaled the record made more than twenty years earlier. (In the same cartoon, Ripley informs us that one T. A. Peake of Philadelphia has used the same set of false teeth for sixty-six years.)

- 1939. Augie Kieckhefer, ten-time three-cushion champion of the world, was blind in one eye. He changed into a left-handed player to overcome his handicap. (Note: Kieckhefer won only four titles in tournament play; the rest were challenge matches.)

- 1939. Human pincushion: John Arbuckle, Louisville, Kentucky, carries forty-eight pins in his mouth at all times, eating, drinking, and sleeping with them for the past fifty years.

- Irving Crane, pocket billiard star, pocketed 309 balls in succession. He cleared the table twenty-two times. Layton, Utah, February 3, 1939.

- A perfectly polished billiard ball is not as smooth comparatively as the surface of the earth. Proven by microscopic tests.

- James Evans, pocket billiard star, ran the entire rack of fifteen balls from an open break without missing or allowing the cueball to touch a cushion on any shot. Kreuter's Billiard Academy, New York, March 7, 1935. (Must have been a slow news day. More interesting was an accompanying item about Mrs. Ada MacCullough of Detroit, Michigan, who had rubber hair—it would stretch 1 1/2 inches without breaking.)

- Ruth McGinnis, Lady Pocket Billiard Expert, ran 53 consecutive balls. Allinger's Billiard Academy, Philadelphia, December 14, 1931.

- Walter Lindrum, Australian Billiard Champion, made a world's record break of 4,137 against Joe Davis, January 1932. (This doesn't mean much unless you know how English billiards is scored. Lindrum was one of the greatest talents who ever picked up a cue.)

- 1964. Baron Paul Natorp of Vienna, Austria, played a billiard match against himself every day for thirty-two years, carefully scoring each shot.

- 1954. Willie Mosconi of Haddon Heights, New Jersey, playing in an exhibition match in Springfield, Ohio, established a new world record with a run of 526 consecutive shots. Submitted by Fred S. Brown, Port Deposit, Maryland.

- Mark Twain often played billiards twelve hours a day.

- The first billiard match for the championship of the United States, held in a jammed hall in Detroit in 1859, lasted from 7:30 P.M. until 5:00 A.M. the following day. (Phelan beat Seereiter.)

- 1930. The Handless Billiardist. George Sutton, Toledo, Ohio, made a run of 3,000 points. (The game was straight billiards. This is one of the most astounding records in any game or sport. Sutton's arms were cut off just below the elbows.)

- 1933. Harriet Albee made fourteen consecutive spot shots. Doyle's Billiard Parlor, New York, 1932.

- Monticello. Thomas Jefferson's home near Charlottesville, Virginia, was designed by Jefferson with a billiard room in its dome—but before the house was finished, Virginia outlawed billiards.

- John Wesley Hyatt (1837–1920) invented celluloid, the forerunner of modern plastics, to win a $10,000 prize for an inexpensive billiard ball.

- 1945. William E. Bell of Boston, Massachusetts, trying to bank a ball in the side, accidentally sends it off the table. It bounces once on the floor and lands on another table, where it banks in the side.

> "I can remember waking up one afternoon with a terrific hangover. I stared at the ceiling for a long time and then I said to myself, 'McGoorty, what you have turned out to be is a no-good, two-bit, drunken pool hustler.' That didn't depress me at all. Listen, I was glad to have a profession."
>
> —Danny McGoorty
> As quoted by Robert Byrne in
> *McGoorty—The Story of a Billiard Bum,* 1972

My Favorite
Pool Stories

POOL HAS MORE THAN ITS SHARE of colorful characters, and I've been hanging around the game long enough now to have known quite a few of them. One I'm sorry I never met was Don Willis, not only a player of legendary gifts but from all accounts a very entertaining storyteller. All I know about him comes from old magazines and newspapers.

Willis (1910–1984), sometimes called The Cincinnati Kid, was the world's best unknown player. His arena was the road, and he saw no advantage in entering tournaments or having his picture taken, and until he quit the hustle in the late 1960s, only insiders knew what he looked like. His skill was phenomenal, and not just in pool. He was also a world-class juggler and card player. At one time he could claim national titles in horseshoes, Ping-Pong, and pool, having beaten the reigning champions in all three games. As a teenager in Canton, Ohio, he even won the city championship in backward running, which was popular in the 1920s. He once won $500 by beating a man who claimed to be the champion backward-runner of New England.

Pool players are unanimous in praising his cuemanship. Straight pool specialists who played exhibition matches against him in Canton almost always lost, including Ralph Greenleaf, Willie Mosconi, Jimmy Caras, and Erwin Rudolph. In nine-ball he was perfection. West Coast tournament promoter Fred Whalen claimed he saw Willis play forty games of nine-ball without ever missing a shot he tried to make. From 1948 to 1961 he was the road partner of Wimpy Lassiter. What chance did anybody have against those two?

One of his exhibition specialties was throwing a ball down the table and cutting it in on the fly, the so-called wing shot. His record was forty-two in a row, many of them, according to those who watched him do it, at almost impossible angles. Danny McGoorty told me Willis used to practice wing shots using billiard balls on a snooker table.

A reporter once asked him how he happened to take up pool. "I was a wick braider in a lantern factory," Willis explained soberly, "when Edison put me out of work with his lightbulb. I had to do something else for a living."

In describing an extremely fast player: "I've seen him run the eight and nine and hang the seven. Now that's *fast* . . ."

One year he attended a tournament in Florida as a spectator. He was sitting with a group of top players when a promoter handed each of them a pen and a sheet of paper and asked them to list tournaments won and titles held. When the players were finished writing and the papers gathered, the promoter asked Willis why he had claimed only to be the best player on Fourth Street in Canton, Ohio. "I don't play in tournaments and I don't hold any titles." The promoter protested: "But everybody says you're one of the best players in the world! There must be *something* you can say about yourself." "Well, okay," Willis said, with a shrug. He snatched a sheet from the man's hand that was filled with the accomplishments of one of the other players. Across the bottom Willis wrote: "I beat him. Don Willis."

Somebody once asked Willis how good the Eufala kid was. "I never saw him play." "What do you mean, you never saw him play? I heard you just beat him out of a lot of money." "I did, but he never got to shoot."

The story is told that Willis once beat a good player using a bar of Ivory soap instead of a cue. Willis says it never happened. "He wasn't a good player, he was a rank amateur. I could have beat him with half a bar."

Sitting around with players in a restaurant late at night, that's when a lot of good pool stories are told and a lot of good diagrams are drawn on tablecloths and napkins. Sometimes the dinnerware is used to illustrate positions on the table. Willis often told the story of how Johnny Irish, another great road player, lost a game of nine-ball. "He cut the coffee cup in the side and got perfect on the spoon. He cut the doughnut in and went up table for the eight-ball, which was the pepper. Guess what happened!

He got straight in and couldn't get back to the other end for the ketchup! How do you like that for bad luck? Straight in on the pepper!"

One of my favorite pool stories doesn't concern Willis. It was told to me by Don Brink, owner of Raytown Recreation in Kansas City. Years ago, when Kling and Allen's was one of the great big-city poolrooms, a group of old men used to play golf on a six-by-twelve-foot snooker table just inside the front door. One afternoon in the middle of a game, a player dropped dead just as a man came through the door. The newcomer saw the body on the floor, dropped to one knee for a closer look, and satisfied that a death had occurred, straightened up and called across the room to the desk man: "Time off!"

I always smile when I think of what Norm "Farmer" Webber, a former road player who now gives exhibitions, says about Detroit Whitey, a hustler from the 1940s and 1950s. "The last time I saw Whitey he had a rope and was lowering his suitcases down the side of the El Cortez hotel in Miami to his wife in the alley. I hollered at him, asking him what the hell he was doing, and he says 'Just checking out.'"

A dozen years ago or so at a national three-cushion tournament in San Jose, California, an exhibition match to 25 points was arranged between two wonderful old-timers, Norman Wolff and Jimmie Lee, both of whom were in their eighties. They were both strong players despite their advanced ages. Lee, in particular, was a gold mine of billiard and pool lore and taught the fine points of the game to a whole generation of West Coast students.

To everyone's dismay, Lee couldn't hit his hat and quickly fell behind. When the score was about 15 to 1 in favor of Wolff, Lee came to the table, aimed, then stood up and took off his glasses. He turned them over in his hand and said, "Wait a minute . . . these aren't my glasses." I turned to the man seated next to me in the bleachers, George Rippe of Lawrence, Massachusetts, and said, "Wouldn't it have been funny if he had said, 'Wait a minute, I don't wear glasses.'" The remark, for some unknown reason, tickled Rippe so much he couldn't stop laughing and he eventually had to leave the arena to get control of himself, which he was never fully able to do. Several times he came back in and sat down only to jump up and run out with his shoulders shaking and his hand over his mouth. Even now, more than a decade later, all I have to do is mention glasses to render him helpless.

Then there was the time former pro player U. J. Puckett was playing a tournament game against an opponent I will call Smith. Puckett made a push shot that Smith called a foul. Puckett shot again quickly to render the protest moot, which infuriated Smith, who leaped from his chair, blocked Puckett from shooting again, and called loudly for the chief referee. Puckett stepped to one side and waited patiently while Smith strenuously described the shot to the referee and explained why it was a foul. After listening for a few minutes, Puckett returned to the table and said, "That was not a foul." He leaned over and with a sweeping motion of his hands and arms scrambled all the balls. "*This,*" he said, "is a foul."

Danny McGoorty was a fine storyteller, and I greatly admire his anecdote about how Alfredo De Oro beat Welker Cochran in the 1934 world three-cushion tournament. I won't repeat it here because I used it in my biography of McGoorty and in *Byrne's Book of Great Pool Stories* (1995).

One of the best three-cushion players in the United States (not Sang Lee) lives in New York City. A couple of years ago his mother was ill and someone asked, "How's your mother?" Shaking his head sadly, the player replied, "Not so good. She only averages point three."

There's the story I first heard from Derek Knell. A woman is hauled into court and charged with beating her husband to death with a billiard cue. Asks the judge: "How many innings?"

I'll close with a riddle. What can kill you if it falls out of a tree, is green, and has four legs? Read no further if you want to try to guess. Give up? The answer is a pool table.

The Man Behind
the Videotapes

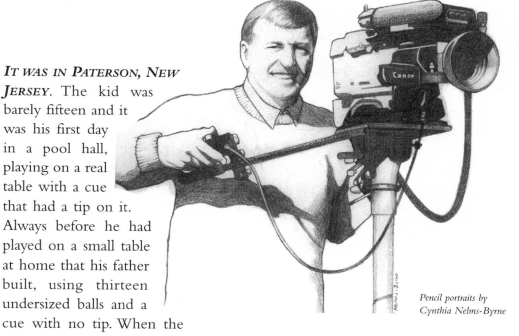

IT WAS IN PATERSON, NEW JERSEY. The kid was barely fifteen and it was his first day in a pool hall, playing on a real table with a cue that had a tip on it. Always before he had played on a small table at home that his father built, using thirteen undersized balls and a cue with no tip. When the

Pencil portraits by
Cynthia Nelms-Byrne

wood at the end of the cue mushroomed too much, he and his older brother Pete simply sawed off an inch. Even on primitive, homemade equipment, the game fascinated him, and anybody who watched him could see that he had a knack for knocking balls into pockets.

On a real table—this was different, this was heaven, and before the day was out he had run 15 in straight pool . . . and he was hooked. He came to the pool hall almost every day after that, brushing tables and vacuuming and doing odd jobs in exchange for table time. Three months later he managed a run of 45. Nine months more of daily practice and he clicked off a run of 93.

Word gets around. When he turned seventeen, a man carrying a cue case showed up. "They tell me you shoot good straight pool. Want a game?"

"I know you," the lad said. "You're Ray Martin. I've seen you play. You're a pro. I'm not going to play for money with a pro. I only play for the time."

Ray Martin, nice guy that he is, agreed to 125 points, and a few minutes later watched in amazement and admiration as his young opponent ran 105 and out. The kid asked if he could keep shooting so he could see how many he could run. "You mean you've never run one hundred before?" "That's right. This is a new record for me." He extended his personal best to 120 before missing.

Running 100 was an almost daily ritual for Martin, one of the best straight-pool artists who ever played the game, but it was a big event for the kid, especially since it came in his first match against a world-class player. It was an accomplishment that Pat Fleming still remembers vividly after the passage of thirty years.

Fleming is an affable, approachable man whose face is that of a Biblical patriarch with a twinkle in his eye. When he laughs, he shows a set of ivory that would make a billiard ball proud. He seems to be without tension, hidden agendas, or limelight lust, and his personality has not been disfigured by ego. His reputation for honesty and integrity is unquestioned among his peers. You can't say all those things about very many people in the pool world (or any world). Despite his low-key approach, he is making a contribution of incalculable value to the game he loves. Life would be a lot less fun and it would be harder to learn to play well without the pool and billiard tapes available from Accu-Stats Video Productions. The tapes are so popular that some customers buy every one. Odd that it all began by accident.

Fleming's prowess with a cue tends to be overlooked by today's younger players and fans, who know him mainly as a tournament director, as president of the Professional Billiards Tour—or as the man videotaping matches at tournaments. To the list of Fleming's attributes must be added diplomacy and tact, for he works closely with Don Mackey, commissioner of the PBT. Pat admits that Mackey is a lightning rod for controversy. "He puts the pro players first and wants them to have as much power as possible. He's a battler, the kind of battler you're glad is on your side and not the other side."

Despite the pressure of running his own business, Pat Fleming still plays national-class pool and could be a force on the nine-ball tour if he turned his full attention to it. After his early inspirational win over Ray Martin, who soon became a good friend, he went on to run 100 uncounted times, most of them unfinished, and once got into the 200s. The need to make a living, however—he married Diane at age eighteen and soon was the father of two children, Patrick and Dara—took precedence. He worked full-time selling tires for Sears Roebuck for eleven years followed by two years at Radio Shack.

He feels his game peaked in his late twenties and early thirties.

"I was probably at my best at the world straight pool tournament in New York in 1981, when I was thirty-one years old. I finished third behind Sigel and Varner and had the highest per-inning scoring average. Sigel ran ninety-seven and out to keep me out of the title match. With the prize money, which I think was three thousand dollars, I was able to do something I had been thinking about for a long time. I bought a computer, quit pool for a year, and wrote a program for rating straight pool and nine-ball players, devoting eighteen hours a day to it. That was the beginning of Accu-Stats. Accurate statistics for pool."

He had been taking computer courses for months, preparing himself for the day when he could put his record-keeping ideas to work. All major sports, he reasoned, especially baseball, depend partly on statistics for their appeal, for setting standards of excellence, for rating one player against another. Why not pool?

A friend invested in the project, enabling Pat to quit his job. His wife, fortunately, kept hers.

The Fleming system was introduced at Barry Behrman's U.S. Open tournament in Norfolk, where it attracted great interest from players and serious fans. The system requires keeping track of the five kinds of errors a player makes in the course of a game—missing, getting out of position, missing a kick, scratching on a break, or failing to lay down a successful safety. A Total Performance Average (TPA) is determined by dividing the number of balls made by the same number plus the number of errors. Pocketing a hundred balls while making, say, ten errors results in a TPA of .909 (100 divided by 100+10). The record keeper must use judgment on occasion (was the player mainly playing safe or mainly trying to pocket the ball?), but judgment is not a significant factor in establishing a player's TPA.

The Accu-Stats newsletter, first published in November of 1984, gave the complete statistical breakdown of major nine-ball tournaments. Twenty-two issues were published over a three-year period. There weren't enough subscribers (500) to offset printing costs, and with such a small circulation, few advertisers were interested. Pat hoped at the beginning that tournament promoters would pay to have Accu-Stats cover their tournaments, but little revenue materialized from that source.

During the publication's run, a lot was discovered about the game of nine-ball. "One of the most interesting things we learned," Pat recalls, "is that the break is not the big advantage everybody thought. The fact that the winner breaks makes it hard to dig out the truth, because since the better player usually wins the rack, he breaks more often. Pat Junior and I went through the score sheets for games involving a favorite and an underdog and found that the favorite won more often when he didn't break than when he did, 64 percent of the time, roughly, instead of 60 percent. Then we studied matches between players of equal skill and found that the breaker won around 48 percent of the time while the non-breaker won 52 percent of the time. Nobody would have guessed it. We studied five major tournaments in detail; breaking was a disadvantage in three of them. In the two tournaments where breaking was an advantage, balls were going in on the break 70 percent and 80 percent of the time, which is much oftener than the average of 60 percent. I guess you can conclude that if the pockets are generous, it's better to break. If they're tight, you're better off if the other guy breaks."

Other facts emerged. The 9-ball goes on the break only 3 percent of the time. Top players scratch on the break 10 percent of the time. As an interesting sidelight, the computer was able to rank players in terms of shotmaking, safety play, breaking, and kicking.

A player's TPA has a powerful predictive value. For instance, when Efren Reyes and Jose Parica came to the United States from the Philippines, most observers ranked them as roughly equal, but Pat Fleming soon was able to tell that Reyes was far superior. His TPA was around .910 while Parica's was around .830. A difference that great means two different classes of player, even though it's hard to separate them by casual observation. In the same way, it was easy to see that Jean Balukas was a fully competitive player because she was racking up TPAs of .900 *playing against men*.

Despite its value, the Accu-Stats newsletter was doomed. It cost too much to gather the figures. For each tournament, as many as twelve scorekeepers had to be recruited, trained, scheduled, and paid. It was the effort to reduce the cost of record keeping that unexpectedly led to Accu-Stats Video Productions. In a last-ditch effort to save the operation, money was spent on a couple of video cameras. Instead of scorekeepers monitoring games, tapes were reviewed quickly after the tournament using the fast-forward button. It worked so well that more cameras were bought until there were a total of six. They were strictly for gathering statistics and the tapes were erased as soon as they had yielded the necessary facts.

Then came a surprise that once again changed the direction of Pat Fleming's life. "In the middle of 1985," he remembers, "at a tournament in Moline, Illinois, Jimmy Hodges wanted to buy the tapes of the semifinal and final matches. He was the first customer. I didn't even know what to charge him. I think I mailed them to him for fifteen dollars apiece. At the next tournament, quite a few people wanted to buy tapes, and eventually we stopped keeping statistics—except for a few selected matches—and were in business just to sell tapes. The quality was terrible. The cameras were fixed in position, one to a table, there was no commentary, and the lighting was poor. But since we were the only game in town, we had customers."

In 1987 it was clear that Accu-Stats had to become Accu-Stats Video Productions. The cameras were upgraded, extra lighting was provided for the featured matches, and a contract was signed with the pro tour covering royalties for the players.

It was Billy Incardona who suggested adding commentary and volunteered for the job. A microphone was purchased at (where else?) Radio Shack and plugged into the VCR. At the Golden Invitational in Phoenix, Arizona, in July of 1989, Bill sat at the railing behind the players' table and provided commentary with Bobby Hunter as his guest. The tapes were a hit.

At the fifteenth U.S. Open in 1990, a second camera was added, one that a cameraman could swivel and zoom. This was a huge improvement and it was reflected in sales. Since then, the equipment had been steadily improved. A Plexiglas booth was devised for the commentators. After the Florida three-cushion tournament in 1992, a big investment was made in Betacam broadcast-quality cameras. Next came the capability for slow motion and instant replays.

To keep expenses to a minimum, the master tape is created on the spot. Pat uses a mixer and watches two monitors while the game is being played, deciding with a flip of a switch which scene will be preserved. Back home, all he has to do is add the titles and credits. "As president of the company," Pat points out, "I am also responsible for stuffing envelopes and taking out the trash. Those chores aren't in anybody else's job description."

The man is a tireless worker, putting in long hours during tournaments. Twice a year he drives with all of his equipment from New Jersey to Nevada to cover the Sands tournament in Reno. I worked with him in

A Short History of the Jump Cue

In 1981 Pat Fleming was experimenting with different kinds of cues for certain shots. A cue of regular length felt awkward on elevated shots, especially massé shots, because the weight at the rear end made the cue feel too light at the bridge hand, so he sawed six inches or so off the butt end of a house cue. While trying a massé shot, he was surprised to see the cueball jump entirely over the ball he was trying to go around. Further practice convinced him that he had discovered a secret weapon, a cue that greatly simplified jump shots. He thought at first that the key was the short length and the forward balance, not the light weight.

At the time, Earl Strickland was exciting audiences with his skill at jump shots using his normal cue. His ability to escape hooks by flying over the interference added a sensational new element to the game. A great jump he made on television during the Caesars tournament in Las Vegas gave him the reputation as the master of the shot.

In a Florida tournament in 1982, Fleming showed up with his secret weapon. To keep it a secret, he taped a fake butt extension on it made of balsa wood. "It looked like a taped base-ball bat at the end. I hauled it out every time I had to jump a ball. Players went nuts wondering how I got such great results. Later that year I came out of the closet and played in a straight-pool tournament without the fake extension, and a couple of times jumped all the way over the rack to pocket balls. I even made a game-winning shot by jumping over the edge of a ball.

"At the next tournament, Ray Martin showed up with a short cue, and a little later, Dave Bollman. I heard that Sammy Jones could jump balls with a shaft, so I asked him about it. He said he'd been doing it for years, and gave me an impressive demonstration. I thought he was using some sort of gimmick shaft until he did it with the shaft of my own cue. He could get over a ball right up close to the cueball, but he didn't have the accuracy I did with my short cue. With a short cue you can even put stop or draw on the cueball.

"Before long every pro player had a short cue and cuemakers were marketing them. But for a while there I had an advantage in nine-ball tournaments, and a lot of players were up in arms. At one U.S. Open, a player argued that since most of the competitors didn't have jump cues, they all should be allowed to use mine!"

October of 1995 on a three-cushion highlight tape, and he thought noth-ing of driving a thousand miles to my home in Iowa to tape some intro-ductory material.

The business is no longer a one-man show. His son Pat, Jr., and his brother Pete are now full-time employees. Pat, Jr., has become a skilled tape editor and computer programmer, and handles the movable camera at three-cushion tournaments. Rick Bouley is the cameraman at pool tournaments. Billy Incardona is the permanent host for pool, with Buddy Hall and Grady Mathews as rotating guest hosts.

Nobody is getting rich, at least not yet. Profits are mostly plowed back in, and professional-quality video equipment is very expensive. On the wish list are a digital editing machine (cost: $50,000) and a Telestrator, which would enable the commentators to write on the screen (cost: $10,000).

With the equipment already on hand and the expertise he and his aides have acquired, Accu-Stats is now a true video production company, able to create specialty tapes, such as Pat's own *Creative Edge,* a selection of inside tips, Anton Riniti's amusing *Magical Menu of Pool Ball Wizardry,* Buddy Hall on nine-ball position play, and Grady Mathews on straight-pool key balls and breaks.

I asked Pat what was next for Accu-Stats.

"We want to add a third camera and another cameraman. That way we can always get a good view no matter what the shot. We want to upgrade our equipment again and move from eight-thousand-dollar cameras to fifteen-thousand-dollar cameras. We want to produce television commercials for people in the billiard industry. With just a few more pieces of equipment we could cover pool events for television networks. Another possibility is to do local live television . . . on any subject. Gathering pool statistics might be revived, too. It's much easier to cover a sport when facts and figures are available to describe what the players are doing."

Pat has a personal goal, too. He wants to play more pool and enter more tournaments. That would be fun for him, but for my own selfish reasons I hope his focus remains on producing more and better pool and billiard videotapes. There are plenty of great players; there is only one Accu-Stats.

At
Thurston's

One of England's most versatile and prolific men of letters was J. B. Priestley (1894–1984), who left an impressive legacy of essays, plays, novels, journalism, and literary criticism. Early in his career, he visited the famous Thurston's Billiards Hall in London to see a title match between Joe Davis and Tom Newman; his description of the competition is wonderfully evocative, full of telling detail about the atmosphere, the players, and the audience. The piece appeared in 1932 in a book of Priestley's called **Self-Selected Essays**

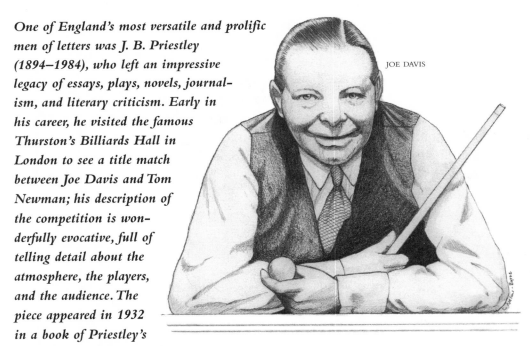

JOE DAVIS

under the title "At Thurston's" and is reproduced here in its entirety.

Newman and Davis squared off for the billiards championship of the world in 1926, 1927, 1928, 1929, and 1930, with Davis winning the last three. Because *the author mentions that both men "have held the title," the match he describes must be the one staged in 1929 or 1930.*

The game is English billiards, the forerunner of snooker, which is still played by a million or so enthusiasts in Great Britain and its former colonies. The table is a six-by-twelve snooker table. Only three balls are used, a cueball, a second white ball, and a red ball. Points are scored by caroming the cueball off both object balls (a cannon); by pocketing (potting) one of the object balls, which is then respotted; or by sending the cueball into a pocket off an object ball, a shot called an "in-off" or a "hazard."

Because two or three ways of scoring can be managed on a single stroke, keeping track of points is often assigned to a third party, called a "marker." The word "top" as used by the English means "follow." And, of course, the English don't call English "English." They call it "side."

With those preliminary comments out of the way, I invite you to lean back and enjoy the reactions of an observant amateur as he watches two great masters of the cue at work.

BEYOND THE VOICES OF LEICESTER SQUARE there is peace. It is in Thurston's Billiard Hall, which I visited for the first time, the other afternoon, to see the final in the Professional Championship. Let me put it on record that for one hour and a half, that afternoon, I was happy. If Mr. Thurston ever wants a testimonial for his Billiards Hall, he can have one from me. The moment I entered the place I felt I was about to enjoy myself. It is small, snug, companionable. Four or five rows of plush chairs look down on the great table, above which is a noble shaded light, the shade itself being russet-colored. Autumn to the cloth's bright Spring. Most of the chairs were filled with comfortable men, smoking pipes. I noticed a couple of women among the spectators, but they looked entirely out of place, just as they would have done among the fat leather chairs of a West End club. I had just time to settle down in my seat, fill and light a pipe myself, before the match began.

It was a match between Davis and Newman, both of whom have held the championship. They suddenly appeared, in their shirt sleeves and holding cues, and we gave them a friendly round of applause, which they acknowledged with something between a bow and a nod. The marker arrived too. He deserves a word to himself. He was an essential part of the afternoon, not merely because he kept the score and called it out, but because he created an atmosphere. He was a young man, whose profile was rather like that of the Mad Hatter; his face was all nose, teeth, and glittering eye; and he had an ecclesiastical dignity and gravity of manner. He handed over the rest of the half-butt like one serving at an altar. To see him place the red on the spot was to realize at once the greatness of the occasion. Best of all was to watch him removing, with his white-gloved hands, specks of dust or films of moisture from a ball. The voice in which he called out the scores was the most impersonal I have ever heard. It was a voice that belonged to solemn ritual, and it did as much as the four walls and the thickly drawn curtained windows to withdraw us from ordinary life and Leicester Square. And withdrawn we certainly were. After a few minutes the world of daylight and buses and three o'clock winners receded, faded, vanished. I felt as if we were all sitting at ease somewhere on the bottom of the Pacific.

Davis had a broad face and wore a brown suit. Newman had a long narrow face and wore a black waistcoat and striped trousers. Davis was the more stolid and cheerful. Newman suggested temperament. Apart from these details, I could discover no difference between them. They were both demi-gods. In the great world outside, I can imagine that one might pass them by as fellows of no particular importance, just pleasant, clean, neat men with north-country accents. But in this tiny world of bright-green cloth and white and crimson spheres, they were both demi-gods. After the first few minutes I began to regard them with an awe that has no place in my attitude toward any living writer. If one of them had spoken to me (and Newman did speak to the man on my left, who was evidently something of a connoisseur and made all manner of knowing noises), I should have blushed and stammered and nearly choked with pride and pleasure. No modern writer could make me feel like that, simply because no modern writer is great enough. It would have to be Shakespeare; and when you are in this remote little world of billiards, players like Messrs. Davis and Newman *are* Shakespeares: they are as good as that. They have the same trick too: they make it look easy. Watching them, you have to use your imagination like blazes to realize you could not do it all yourself.

I do not know whether I have any right to describe myself as a player, but I have played billiards many a time. If I am staying under the same roof with a billiard table, I nearly always play on it, but on the other hand, I never go out looking for billiard tables on which to play. Public billiard rooms are dreary places, even if you find the game itself fascinating, as I do. Moreover, they are too public for my tastes. Once you have a cue in your hand in those places, it appears that everybody who happens to be there has the privilege of advising you. Strangers say, quite angrily: "Oh, you ought to have gone in off the red there!" Then when you try something else: "No, no, no! The white's the game. That's it. Only put plenty of side on. Oh no, too hard!" And they make little clucking noises and laugh softly behind your back, until at last you bungle every shot. This does not seem to happen in any other game but billiards. If you play bridge in a public room, strangers do not stand behind you and point authoritatively to your Queen of Spades or King of Diamonds. Nobody makes remonstrative noises at you when you are playing chess. But billiards is anybody's and everybody's game. The adventures of those shining spheres, as they chase one another over the green cloth, are public property, and the moment you have grasped a cue, you yourself are a public character whose actions can be criticized with freedom. And as I happen to be a very poor performer, I prefer to play in private, almost behind locked doors.

The shortest way of describing the skill of Messrs. Davis and Newman is to say it appeared miraculous when they ever missed anything. Now when my friends and I have played the game, it has always seemed miraculous if anything happened but a miss. The balls always seemed so small, the pockets so narrow, the table so hopelessly long and wide. These professional champions, however, treated every shot as if it were a little sum in simple arithmetic. While they went on calmly potting the red, bringing it back nearer to the white every time, and then collecting cannons by the dozens, we all leaned back and sucked our pipes almost somnolently, secure and happy in the drowsy peace of mechanics and art. It was when they chanced to fail that we were startled into close attention. You could hear a gasp all around you. If the marker had broken into song, we could hardly have been more astonished. The only persons who never showed any signs of surprise were the two players—and, of course, the marker. If Davis, after going halfway round the table with an amazing number of delicious little cannons, all as good as epigrams, finally missed a shot, Newman quite nonchalantly came forward to make the balls do what he thought they ought to do, for half an hour or so. And the things they did were incredible. He could make them curve round, stop dead, or run backward. But if Newman went on doing this for three-quarters of an hour, quietly piling up an immense score, Davis, sitting at ease, nursing his cue, showed no anxiety, no eagerness to return to the table. His turn would come. I tell you, these were demi-gods.

The hall was filled with connoisseurs, men who knew a pretty bit of "side" or "top" when they saw it, smacked their lips over a nice follow-through, and heard sweet music in the soft click-click of the little cannons, and when a stroke of more than usual wizardry was played, they broke into applause. Did this disturb either of the players? It did not. They never looked up, never smiled, never blinked an eyelid. Perhaps they had forgotten we were there, having lost remembrance of us in the following of the epic adventures of the two whites and the red. Of all games, billiards must be the worst to play when you are feeling nervous, for they were beginning a championship match, but they showed no trace of feeling, not a quiver. And when we clapped them at the end of long breaks, they merely gave us a slight nod. "Ah, so you're there, are you?" these nods seemed to say. I felt awed before such greatness. These men could do one thing better than anybody else could do it. They were masters. Their world was a small one, bounded by the shaded electric lights and the stretch of green cloth, but in that world they were supreme conquerors.

To play billiards every afternoon and evening, year in and year out, might seem monotonous, yet I think they must lead satisfying lives. What they can do, they can do, beyond any possible shadow of a doubt. They hit the red and it vanishes into a pocket. They have not to convince themselves that they have hit it and that it has probably gone into the pocket, as we have to do in our affairs. What can I do? What can you do? We think this, we imagine that, and we are never sure. These great cuemen are as sure as human beings can be. I envy them, but my envy is not so sharp that it robs me of all pleasure in their skill. When I am actually in their presence, looking down on the table of their triumphs, my envy is lost in admiration and delight. When the world is wrong, hardly to be endured, I shall return to Thurston's Hall and there smoke a pipe among the connoisseurs of top and side. It is as near to the Isle of Innisfree as we can get within a hundred leagues of Leicester Square.

The Man in Willie Hoppe's Shadow

CONVENTIONAL WISDOM HOLDS that Willie Hoppe was the greatest all-around carom player this country has ever produced. Those almanacs and reference books that deign to mention billiards are apt to cite Hoppe alone and call him the undisputed king. Yet a look at the records shows that for a period of twenty years at least, when Hoppe was supposedly at his prime, Welker Cochran, born and raised in Manson, Iowa, and called early on "The Manson Marvel," was more than Hoppe could handle in both three-cushion and balkline.

Hoppe's overwhelming reputation as an invincible saint was built on talent (he deserved the many world championships he won), his early celebrity (he was considered the best player in the world at age eighteen after beating Maurice "The Lion" Vignaux in Paris in 1906), the extraordinary length of his career (he won his last title in 1952), and on the publicity department of Brunswick-Balke-Collender, which had him on the payroll for decades. Playing billiards was the only profession he ever had, he was a child prodigy, and his personal life was impeccable. It's easy to understand why he came to be considered "Mr. Billiards."

The man who suffered most from the sporting press's adoration of Hoppe was Cochran. He had to get used to "Hoppe Loses" headlines instead of "Cochran Wins." It's not necessary to go back fifty years for examples of the Hoppe mystique. Take the 1993 book *Willie's Game,* by Willie Mosconi and freelance writer Stanley Cohen. On page 143, Mosconi says about Hoppe: "I think he finished fourth in his first world tournament, but he won the title the next year and from that time on nobody could beat him. It takes a lot to stay at the top of your game for three or four decades, but Hoppe's conditioning and his lifestyle helped."

Mosconi's memory is accurate only regarding conditioning and lifestyle.

Until an arthritic condition forced Cochran to retire from competition in 1946, he had won four of the seven world three-cushion tournaments he entered; Hoppe, by contrast, had won only three times in nine tries. In 1945 it was plain to everyone that Cochran and Hoppe were easily the best three-cushion players in the land and a "dream" match was arranged between them—a 5,000-point, thirteen-city, coast-to-coast duel to settle the question once and for all as to who was the top dog. Deliberate safeties were barred to keep the contest from becoming a defensive struggle, a rule that no doubt favored the spectacular Cochran; Hoppe was more of a "manager" than a shotmaker.

The great showdown of 1945 was one of the most exciting and certainly the best-publicized billiard match of all time. The fans saw plenty of fireworks. Hoppe began by making 60 points in twenty-three innings, and after chalking up a run of 20 consecutive points without a miss in Boston, led 1,070–994. In Chicago, Cochran came up with the tour's best game, 60 points in twenty innings, but after forty blocks of the match was trailing 2,304–2,135. In Seattle, Cochran closed the gap to 4,063–4,024, and, playing before his home fans in San Francisco two weeks later, won the match by 50 points with a great finishing rush. The story goes that Hoppe was so angered by the defeat he refused to shake hands with the victor.

Sportswriter Prescott Sullivan, who covered the final matches, said the two players split a purse of $20,000 for their ten weeks of work. When it was over, Sullivan reported in the May 29, 1945, edition of the *San Francisco Examiner,* "Hoppe made a grab for his hat, slammed it on his noggin and scrammed without so much as saying 'See you later, pal.' Cochran, an amused expression on his face, caught a flash of Hoppe's coattail as it swished through the door. 'Same old Willie,' he observed."

The story is similar in balkline. Jake Schaefer dethroned Willie in the memorable 1921 tournament, memorable because of the shock waves it sent through the billiard world, which had come to think of Hoppe as invincible. Cochran, just twenty-three years old, finished third in that event, advanced to second two years later, and took the 18.2 crown for the first time in 1927. Hoppe never again was able to win an 18.2 balkline tournament, as they came to be dominated by Cochran and Schaefer. The final tournament was held in 1934, with Cochran winning again and Hoppe coming in third. Hoppe's best grand average in 18.2 was 45, achieved in 1919. Schaefer holds the American record with 57; Cochran has 54.

Hoppe did not enjoy losing the balkline supremacy he had held since 1906. When Cochran and Schaefer deposed him he reacted by "retiring" from the game! In the middle 1920s his manager released this statement to the press: "Commercialism and the utterly unjust manner in which championship play has been conducted in past years by the concern which controls it have driven Mr. Hoppe into retirement." Newspapers at the time pointed out that the sixteen-year dominance of the game by Hoppe was at the expense of an older generation of players from an earlier era, and that Hoppe had imposed conditions that made it almost impossible for new blood to get a crack at his title.

Commented an Iowa paper: "The only unfairness of the management which Hoppe refers to is the fact that they forced him to meet the younger players which resulted in his defeat. For years Hoppe had all the breaks in the game and dictated his own terms. That is ended now and so he retires to avoid further defeats."

The retirement was, of course, short-lived. For while Hoppe was not tournament champion of anything from 1924 to 1940, he was very active, competing in many tournaments and matches.

Hoppe was a marvelous player—I don't mean to deny it. His exploits as a child prodigy may never be matched. For example, he ran 2,000 points at straight-rail billiards when he was only thirteen years old. His high run of 25 in three-cushion, set in an exhibition in San Francisco in 1918, stood for decades. His best three-cushion tournament grand average of 1.33 was the record until the arrival of Raymond Ceulemans, who had the advantage of faster cloth, in the early 1960s.

Cochran was no slouch as a child prodigy either. He learned the game at age ten in his father's billiard room in Manson. Within two years he showed such aptitude that his father, a good player himself, knew that he had sired a remarkable talent.

Seeking an outside opinion, the elder Cochran took the boy to Chicago, probably the world capital of billiards in those days. There young Welker performed for the famous billiard authority and instructor Lanson Perkins, who was so impressed that he coaxed the elder Cochran to allow Welker to finish his schooling in Chicago, where he could receive his personal coaching. That sounded like a fine idea to Welker and his father, but Mrs. Cochran, back in Iowa, needed a great deal of convincing. Not until Professor Perkins himself, dignified and courtly, traveled to Manson to see the mother was she satisfied that her son would be in good hands.

After only a few months of coaching, Welker was entered in the Chicago 18.2 amateur tournament of 1912. He was a sensation. A newspaper headline in Chicago at the time read: "Youth wins another game . . . Welker Cochran, thirteen-year old cue marvel, takes lead in local tourney." The story began: "Welker Cochran, thirteen-year-old pupil of Prof. Lanson Perkins, took the lead in the Class A 18.2 tournament in Mussey's last night by defeating Thomas 175–174. It was the fifth straight win for the boy, who is making a phenomenal showing in his first tournament. Cochran averaged over 5 points per inning, with a high run of 30." The day before the *Des Moines Register* headlined a story: "Iowa Boy Makes Good at Billiards . . . Welker Cochran of Manson Regarded as Coming Cue Champion." The story stated that Cochran, who had then won his first four games in the tournament, was "the talk of Windy City billiard bugs. The thirteen-year-old billiardist, in his game against Kent, accomplished one of the best performances ever recorded by a player of his age: he averaged 9.7 and had a high run of 37."

W. P. Mussey, host of the tournament, made this statement to the press: "The boy is by far the strongest drawing card in the city. When he is billed to play the place is absolutely packed. I expect to see him average over 15 before the tourney is over." When Cochran won the tournament by beating Conklin, the defending champion, he made headlines in sports pages all over the country.

The *Manson Journal,* December 25, 1912: "The Brunswick people have made a moving picture of Welker in action and it will be shown here in the near future. In a letter to the Cochrans they declare that he will be champion of the world and say that he is the most promising young player in the history of the game." Professor Perkins: "I have seen many promising performers go to pieces when put to the test in a big tournament, but Welker's coolness and skill in the Class A contest convinced me of his real greatness. He will rank above the greats who ever lived."

Cochran continued to improve by leaps and bounds. Shortly after turning fourteen, he averaged 40 in an exhibition match and had a high run of 165. A few nights later he completed a 250-point exhibition in only two innings.

By the time he was sixteen and finished with his education (he attended Lane Technical College in Chicago), he was one of the best players in the country and was asked to join the Champion Billiard Players' League, a group of touring exhibition players that included Jake Schaefer, Jr., Ora Morningstar, Calvin Demarest, and several others. Shortly before turning pro, Cochran had been banned from the national amateur 18.2 tournament when the other entrants objected, not wanting to interfere, so they said, with the lad's education! Said the American amateur champion J. Ferdinand Poggenburg: "There is a feeling among the players that the national association should not encourage boys to play in its premier tournament. It is self-evident to all of us that a boy of fifteen or sixteen should be giving his attention to his studies and thinking of something other than winning billiard titles."

Cochran got his first chance at the world title in the 1919 18.2 tournament, held before huge crowds in the Grand Ballroom of the Hotel Astor in New York. Fans who thought he would upset Hoppe were disappointed. He finished in a tie for second, not bad for a twenty-one-year-old.

The results were the same in 1920.

In 1921 Hoppe was finally dethroned and a new king was crowned, but it wasn't Cochran; Jake Schaefer, Jr., played almost perfect billiards, crushing Hoppe 400–26 to finish first. In his game against Cochran, Schaefer ran 82 on the break and 318 and out on his second shot. Cochran's only shot was a miss, resulting in a final score of 400–0.

According to the system then in force, both the second-place finisher, Hoppe, and the third-place finisher, Cochran, could claim the world title by beating the winner in 1,500-point challenge matches. Schaefer squeaked by Hoppe 1,500–1,468 in March of 1922 at Orchestra Hall in Chicago.

The match against Cochran was scheduled at the same venue two months later. In my collection of billiard memorabilia, I have a handwritten letter that Cochran mailed to his parents on May 10, 1922, from Saint Louis, where he was preparing himself at the Missouri Athletic Club. Here are some excerpts:

Dear Mom and Dad: Both of your letters received OK. Too bad about the car. There doesn't seem to be such a thing as good luck. It's all bad luck. Schaefer refuses to have Hank Lewis referee. He's so dishonest himself he thinks everyone else must be the same. Albert Cutler is going to referee.

I'm still feeling fine. Last night I made 500 pts. In 4 innings: 8–203–63–224. I am playing good every day now. I have decided to leave here Saturday night for Chicago. I will surely send you a night letter every night so you will get it in the morning. Willie Hoppe is coming from N.Y. to see the match . . .

Regarding the match, you know I will be in there doing my best every minute. I may win & I may not, but you can be sure I will have done my best. You must get the breaks to win World's Championships. Believe me, Schaefer had them in the tournament & also in his match with Hoppe. The question is, how long can it last?

I will sure win it some day & this may be the time. I hope so at least. . . . I will not write again as I will be a very busy man May 16–17–18 & after that I will either be the champ or the chump. Ha.

Oodles of love to all, Welker

Schaefer held him off 1,500–1,333.

In the world tournament two years later, Cochran beat both Hoppe and Schaefer, finishing in a tie for first with Hoppe. He lost the play-off game, which must have been intensely frustrating for the Manson Marvel, who was now years behind the schedule his teachers and fans had set for him. He had reached heights of proficiency never before seen, but so had Hoppe and Schaefer.

It was Schaefer again in 1925, setting new records, but in 1927 Cochran won the title outright . . . finally! Schaefer edged Cochran for first place in the next tournament, held in 1929, while Cochran won the final tournament, in 1934, edging Erich Hagenlacher of Germany for first and leaving Hoppe behind in third.

When balkline began to die in the late 1920s and early 1930s, most of the great players switched to three-cushion. Hoppe entered two national tournaments in 1928 without much success, then hung back until 1934, when he tried again and could do no better than fourth. In 1936 he was mired in sixth place.

Cochran, meanwhile, was going great guns, winning the first major tournament he entered, the 1933 world, and following that triumph with victories in the tournaments of 1935 and 1936. In 1938 he traveled to France and tied for first in a three-cushion tournament with Roger Conti, losing the play-off game. He seemed to lose some of his desire after that, perhaps because he was devoting most of his time to making a success of the billiard room (Graney's Billiard Academy) he now jointly owned in San

MISSOURI
ATHLETIC
ASSOCIATION

SAINT LOUIS.

Regarding the match you know I will be in there doing my best every minute. I may win & I may not but you can be sure I will have done my best. You must get the breaks to win world's Championships. Believe me Schaefer had them in the tournament & also in his match with Hoppe. The question is "how long can it last" I will win it _sure_ someday & this may be the time. I hope so at least. I am sorry you are not feeling better, you will be fine & dandy again soon I'm sure.

I will surely remember the Telegram. I will not write again as I will be _very busy_ may 16-17-18 & after that will either be the Champ or Chump. Ha.

oodles of love
Welker

Cochran would have been crowned balkline champion had he beaten Jake Schaefer, Jr., in a 1,500-point challenge match in May 1922. Here is the last page of a letter he penned to his parents in Iowa before leaving for the match site in Chicago.

Francisco. He entered the great tournaments of 1940, 1941, and 1942 without preparing himself properly, and saw Hoppe win his first three-cushion titles in impressive fashion. Cochran finished fourth twice and second once in those meets, trying to play himself into shape during the competitions.

In 1944 Cochran apologized to his fans for playing below his capabilities and promised them he would go to work on his game. He meant what he said, and showed his old form in the cross-country match with Hoppe. In the 1944 world tournament he took first place again, relegating Hoppe to third place behind runner-up Jay Bozeman.

Cochran made only sporadic appearances after that. He came out of retirement briefly to play exhibitions with Masako Katsura when she first came to this country after World War II, and he made a nostalgic, but not serious, effort in the 1954 tournament in Buenos Aires, won by Harold Worst.

Welker Cochran died in 1960, a year after Hoppe.

He left behind some impressive marks, including high runs of 22 in three-cushion; 638 in 18.2 balkline; and perhaps, most impressive, 383 in 18.1 balkline, in which a ball must cross a line on every shot.

Although Hoppe always got most of the limelight, Cochran occasionally caught a few rays. I have a full-page ad from the *Saturday Evening Post* in which Cochran is shown holding a cue in one hand and a cigarette in the other. The caption reads, "Camels give me *real* smoking pleasure. Under the strain of a championship match, Camels never make me feel jittery or unsure of my 'touch.' The saying 'I'd walk a mile for a Camel' expresses just the way *I* feel, too!"

Cochran's public image was cheerful but reserved, proper, maybe a little stiff. To his family and friends, however, he was the same warm, generous, fun-loving person he was as a youth.

If Cochran's demeanor during tournaments and matches was aloof and cool, it may be that he was merely showing how good a student he was. When Welker was only sixteen years old, he had been drilled on the importance of coolness by his old teacher, Lanson Perkins.

"You see, my boy," the professor told him, "it is as necessary for one to have perfect control over his nerves as it is over the three balls. Those two fellows [Hoppe and Schaefer] are like two pieces of ice. Right now you can make shots as well as they, but you'll never win a championship until you become a block of ice."

So lift your cue in salute to Welker Cochran, a shooting star who blazed a brilliant trail during his time in the sky. Next time you find yourself thinking that Willie Hoppe was in a class by himself, think again. There was another student in that class who got better grades.

Meet Jay Bozeman,
the Vallejo Flash

A REGIONAL THREE-CUSHION TOURNA-MENT was under way in 1990 at the Elks Club in Vallejo, California. Among the spectators was a sandy-haired six-footer with a hearing aid, glasses, and a long cigar. Noticing the body English some of the players were using, he shook his head and said, "They look like a bunch of ballet dancers! If we had jumped around like that in the old days, we would've been thrown out of the joint."

When Jay Bozeman talks, billiard players listen, and when he talks about the old days, he really means *old* days. Bay Area newspapers and the national billiard press were talking about him as a child prodigy when he was in his early teens, and by the time he was fifteen he had already clicked off a run of 17 points in three-cushion.

In 1924, when he was eighteen years old, he played a series of private matches with balkline king Jake Schaefer, Jr., who was being urged by his Brunswick sponsors to take up the more popular game. In the basement of the Brunswick showroom in San Francisco, the lanky fast-shooting young-ster drubbed Schaefer unmercifully day and night for a week. "Why should I play three-cushion," Schaefer asked, "when I can't even beat this kid?" Schaefer didn't even try three-cushion again for eight years. "He didn't know enough about safety in those days," Bozeman recalls. "I rarely played deliberates, but I played shot safety and I controlled the speed of the ball. Shot selection and speed are the two most important things in the game."

Another great balkliner, Welker Cochran, trained with Bozeman before making his three-cushion debut in 1933. The two played a 3,000-point match that Cochran won by just a few points. "I don't remember the score exactly," Bozeman said during an interview in his Vallejo home, "I only remember it was more or less a dead heat. He got better and better as we went along, and by the time is was over, he knew most of my tricks. We went back East together and entered the world tournament. Up until that time only Augie Kieckhefer had averaged 1.000 for a tournament. Cochran won the tournament and I finished second and we both averaged over 1.000. We were a sensation."

Finishing second turned out to be the feature of Bozeman's career. In the 1939 Interstate League, Bozeman's record of 48 wins and 24 losses was second only to Joe Chamaco's 55–17. Bozeman was third behind Willie Hoppe and Schaefer in the great 1940 and 1941 tournaments in Chicago, then tied for second with Hoppe in 1944. After taking five years off, Bozeman came back to play in Hoppe's last tournament, the 1952 World in San Francisco. Hoppe won, Bozeman was second.

Always a bridesmaid, never a bride. In the Pacific Coast Regional the next year, it was Ray Kilgore first, Bozeman second. At the big show in Chicago in 1953, the last of the pro three-cushion tournaments in the United States, Kilgore finished first, Bozeman finished second. In the words of Danny McGoorty, Bozeman was the strongest player never to be world champion.

"I had the damnedest luck," Bozeman said, shaking his head. "A couple of times my tip split right at the end of the tournament and I had to switch to one that wasn't properly broken in. Once, I got stomach poisoning halfway through. In 1935, my ball jumped off the table on an out shot. There was one tournament where I lost one game by two points and two games by one point. Another time I made a force-follow double-the-rail for game point against Hoppe and the referee said, 'No billiard.' In 1953, if Zeke Navarra hadn't 'crotched' the corner on an easy natural, he would have beat Kilgore and dropped him into a tie with me for first.

"I remember a game when the referee stopped play and announced, 'Mr. Bozeman has forty-one points in eight innings.' I couldn't hit my hat after that. The most amazing thing of all happened in the 1936 tournament. There were big windows near the tournament tables, and a cold draft sometimes blew across the ivory balls. I had an easy round-the-table shot, I hit it perfect, and when the cueball came off the third rail, it broke in half! This is the truth! The rule was that if either half had gone on to score, the point counted, but no such luck. Neither half hit the second ball and I wound up losing the game. Have another piece of fudge." (In addition to being a remarkable three-cushion player, Bozeman also makes excellent homemade fudge.)

I remarked that there was nothing wrong with his memory, and his wife, Ethel, agreed. "It's the same with bridge," she said. "He remembers bridge hands from thirty years ago." Jay and Ethel have been married since 1941 and have two grown children, Sharon and Michael.

At the age of nine, Jay was given the chore of brushing the tables in his father's Vallejo billiard room and emptying the spittoons. When that was done, he would practice pool. Within six months he was playing fifteen-or-no-count. A year later he switched to three-cushion. Before long the local newspaper was running stories on the prodigy in their midst, and his proud father was taking him to San Francisco, thirty-two miles away, for exhibitions and matches.

McGoorty, reminiscing in 1970, remembered Bozeman as a "tall, skinny redhead. I watched his style, his flair, his accuracy, and it made me sick to my stomach. He never hesitated a second—before the balls stopped he was ready for the next shot. Sometimes he had a hard time waiting for the cueball to stop spinning. You never saw a guy run so many fives, sixes, eights . . . and when he missed, a look of *amazement* came over his face."

Bozeman's first major tournament victory came in 1928, when at the age of twenty-two he won the National Amateur Championship held at the Buffalo Athletic Club. Four years later he qualified for his first world tournament, finishing eighth in a field of twelve . . . ahead of Schaefer and Tiff Denton. In the 1933 meet, won by Cochran, Bozeman tied for second with the great Johnny Layton, requiring a play-off, which Bozeman won 50–33 in fifty-one innings.

From then on, Bozeman always finished among the leaders in every tournament he entered no matter what the strength of the field. He made 50 points in twenty-three innings in both the 1940 and the 1952 tournaments and had world-tournament high runs of 13 in 1933 and 14 in 1940. He remembers having several good chances of going out in eighteen innings, only to falter at the end.

Once at the start of an exhibition match against Layton, somebody handed him a Rambow cue. Three innings into the game, Bozeman got a run of 20. "I thought I had found a magic wand."

Bozeman is one of the last remaining links to the Golden Age of the game, and his conversation is laced with anecdotes from those legendary years.

Had he seen "Armless" George Sutton? "A fantastic character. His arms were cut off just below the elbows, and yet he could run hundreds and hundreds of points in straight billiards, sometimes in only a couple of minutes. I went to dinner with him during the World's Fair in Chicago in 1933. He looked over the menu and ordered a bowl of soup! I thought he was kidding, or that I was going to have to feed it to him. When it came, he picked up the bowl and sipped from it and never spilled a drop. The waiters were amazed. Somebody came over to the table and asked me for an autograph, ignoring Sutton. He said, 'Don't you want my autograph, too?' The fan was embarrassed and didn't know what to say. Sutton picked up the pen between his elbows and signed his name with the most beautiful penmanship you ever saw.'

What about Robert Cannefax, the early world champion who once sliced the cloth with a penknife to force a room owner to change it? "I never knew him. He died in 1927, just before I went East. He had only one leg. I heard that sometimes he got so broke he would hock it. Yes! Go to a pawn shop and hock his leg. As soon as he got a few bucks, he'd hobble back and get it out of hock."

Bozeman was always a great favorite because of his aggressive approach to the game, the daring way he went for fancy shots, his flashy style, and his fast tempo. Many times he made his 50 points in only thirty minutes. He had a big stroke, and could double the rail from the opposite end of the table even if the first object ball was half a diamond away from the cushion.

But there was no way to make a good living as a player in the Depression years, so in 1937 Bozeman opened his own room in

Vallejo, operating it until 1955. Many of the game's top stars made appearances there. In the mid-1940s, for example, Hoppe came to town for two exhibition games. Bozeman beat him 50–48 in the afternoon and 50–41 in the evening, and in his scrapbook there is a yellowed clipping that proves it.

After the 1953 Chicago tournament, Bozeman hung up his cue and turned to other things, like raising dogs and playing golf. At the age of fifty-five he shot a 76 on the Olympic Club's Lakeside course in San Francisco to become the top qualifier for the National Senior Amateur. In the National, he shot a 77. For years he held the course record at Vallejo's Green Valley Country Club, a sizzling 64 in 1960.

In 1983, at the urging of Bud Wheeler and other members of the Vallejo Elks Lodge, Bozeman started playing billiards again after not touching his cue for thirty years. "You know," he said, remembering the day, "I couldn't even remember how I used to stand at the table. I had to study old photographs of myself." Slowly the old magic came back. You can see it today, watching him play. The upright stance, the flowing stroke, the way he tends to cue the ball low during the warm-up strokes, the aura of stylishness and mastery . . . it's still there. He doesn't have the explosive power that once made him so dangerous, and a failing left eye has cost him accuracy on long shots, but there is much to be learned from studying his shot selection, stroke, spin, and speed.

He plays now for fun. He enjoys passing along the seemingly endless fund of knowledge he acquired from decades of competing against the storied champions of the Golden Age. Top California stars like Allen Gilbert and Khalil Diab are quick to acknowledge how much they have learned from him.

He is very impressed with the skill shown by such modern champions as Raymond Ceulemans and Sang Lee. I sat next to Bozeman for several games at the 1991 U.S. National in San Jose. Whenever Sang Lee made a point, the old curmudgeon would turn to me and smile and nod and raise his eyebrows. "That's how to play," Bozeman would whisper. "I'd like to meet his teacher."

He also wishes he could have played on the equipment used in today's top tournaments. In his day, the cloth and the cushions were much slower and the ivory balls were impossible to keep round. "I watch videotapes of games being played in Europe and I can't help hoping that someday I can play on fast accurate equipment like that."

In 1994, at the age of eighty-eight and with his eyesight and hearing not what they once were, he traveled alone from California to New York

City and found his way to S. L. Billiards in Queens. Many of the top players in the world were there to compete in a tournament and Jay wanted to see some good billiards one more time. He was introduced a couple of times to the spectators, but there were very few who remembered him. Those who did were amazed to see him, not having heard his name in forty years.

He sat ringside day after day watching the tables intently. When one of the players pulled off a shot worthy of Hoppe or Cochran—or Bozeman—in their prime, you could see his smile a mile away.

Back in the late 1940s, sports columnist Bill Leiser asked Hoppe, "If you had to play somebody fifty points every day for a month, who would give you the most trouble?"

Hoppe didn't hesitate in answering: "Jay Bozeman of Vallejo, California." When I recalled that to Bozeman, he laughed and said, "Well, I was pretty good."

No kidding!

JAY BOZEMAN'S WORLD TOURNAMENT RECORD
(Deliberate safeties allowed)

Year	Place	Winner	Bozeman's Grand Average
1933	2nd	Cochran	1.024
1934	5th	Layton	.894
1935	5th	Cochran	1.023
1936	5th	Cochran	.973
1939	2nd	Chamaco	——
1940	3rd	Hoppe	1.009
1941	3rd	Hoppe	1.060
1944	2nd	Cochran	1.160
1947	3rd	Hoppe	.950
1952	2nd	Hoppe	1.000
1953	2nd	Kilgore	.952

Big-Time Billiards
in New York

IN 1992, 1993, AND 1994, American billiard fans had the chance to see extraordinary displays of three-cushion brilliance by the international stars of the game. Sang Chun Lee, U.S. champion every year since 1990, hosted three tournaments at his S. L. Billiards, which is located at 86th and Roosevelt in the borough of Queens.

Torbjörn Blomdahl, five times world champion, and Sang Lee, world champion in 1993, weren't the only stars worth watching. A glittering cast of champions from around the world combined to produce some of the best billiards ever played in the United States.

I had a choice seat for the three tournaments as narrator for the two-camera videotapes produced by Accu-Stats. The tapes of many of the matches are mesmerizing even after several viewings and the passage of several years. In 1995 and 1996, I helped Accu-Stats assemble two highlight tapes featuring the best shots from the three events. Taken together, the tapes are an unprecedented bonanza for students of the game. There is simply nothing like three-cushion billiards when it is played at the top professional level.

Following are my reports of the action.

THE FIRST S. L. BILLIARDS TOURNAMENT

Billiards fans lucky enough to be at S.L. Billiards in mid–May of 1992 will never forget what they saw. World champion Torbjörn Blomdahl led a strong foreign contingent of three-cushion stars to American champion Sang Lee's billiard room in Elmhurst, New York, to tackle the best carom players in the United States; the result was one of the most impressive displays of shot making, precision, and all-around cue artistry in the history of American billiards.

The hundreds of spectators who circled the five Verhoeven tables saw, among other things—

- A run of 22 by Blomdahl.

- Fifty points scored in 16 innings by Sang Lee. That's an average of 3.125 for the game.

- Six players averaging over 1.000.

- The smashing American debut of Daniel Sanchez, an eighteen-year-old Spaniard.

Sang Lee organized and hosted the unusual event, and a generous host he was. Not only did he add $4,000 to the prize fund and give a $500 Schuler cue to the player who traveled the greatest distance (Ji Soo An of Korea), he also paid the expenses of the three seeded world-class players (Blomdahl, Sanchez, and Junichi Komori of Japan), provided trophies and engraved plates to the top finishers, hired a magician from Guatemala to entertain the crowd, and brought in Korean trick-shot wizard Cho Chung Sup for two shows. To top it all off, Lee laid out a tournament-closing champagne and sushi buffet for everyone in the house.

A fever of anticipation began to rise on Sunday, May 10, two days before the tournament started when Blomdahl played a 50-point practice game with Sang Lee. The world champion stepped out to a big lead with a run of 14, and a few innings later ran 18 and out! Urged to continue, he ran 4 more before missing the 23rd by a hair. That run—and what was still to come—was almost enough to make the fans forget their disappointment at the inability of Raymond Ceulemans to attend.

The tournament had three parts. First was an open division of thirty-two players; second was an exhibition round-robin among five seeded players (Blomdahl, Sang Lee, Komori, Sanchez, and Jose Paniagua, the Pan-

American champion from Mexico); and third was a thirteen-man handi-capped round-robin among the five seeds and eight qualifiers from the open division; the qualifiers got a 10-point handicap in 50-point matches with the professionals.

The exhibition round-robin was staged on Wednesday and Thursday nights. Sanchez, who speaks no English but who certainly knows how to apply it to a cueball, stepped off a plane from Madrid to find that his first two games were against Sang Lee, playing in his own room, and Blomdahl, the world champion. The Spaniard is a slightly built, mild-mannered and composed lad with a classic style free of mannerisms. Someone mentioned that Ceulemans said Sanchez already is a 1.3 player, but I for one had to see it to believe it. Sanchez fell behind Sang Lee, then caught fire with two runs of 6 and one of 5 to take the game, much to the surprise and excite-ment of the onlookers, who seldom see Sang Lee lose. He captured the crowd completely by blitzing Blomdahl 50–36 in only twenty-two innings, helped by a run of 14, and cruised past an overmatched Paniagua. He lost a squeaker to Komori 50–46 in thirty-one to finish with a won-lost record of 3–1 and a sparkling grand average of 1.484.

Komori, somehow unaffected by jet lag, was red hot, running 12 and 11, and losing only to Blomdahl. His average was an awesome 1.716 for the four games. Blomdahl's win over Komori 50–44 in thirty-one gave them both records of 3–1. Sanchez, who recently won the world junior championship (for players twenty-one and under), took first place on total points. It was amazing to see a player so young play with such maturity and heart, and it seems a virtual certainty that he will one day be world cham-pion. He is also an expert at balkline, cushion caroms, and straight rail.

Sang Lee, burdened with organizing and managing the tourna-ment, nevertheless managed to average 1.355 in compiling a 1–3 record. Paniagua was 0–4.

The open division was divided into four flights of eight, the top two from each advancing to the finals. Play started Tuesday morning and ended late Thursday afternoon. In flight one, C. Barraza of Mexico and B. Soo Kim of New York were 6–1, sending Frank Torres and Carlos Hallon to the sidelines. In flight two, Al Gilbert of North Hollywood and Ji Soo An of Korea finished on top, sidelining such players as George Ashby and Abel Calderon. New Yorker Mike Kang was impressive in flight three, not los-ing a game and finishing one step ahead of J. Martin of Spain. In flight four, the top two were Adrian Viguera of Chicago and Chris Bartzos of New York.

In the finals, giving up 10 points was a little too much for Sanchez, who lost to Gilbert and Soo Kim by one point, 50–49. The handicap cost Blomdahl two games as well; he lost 41–40 to Soo Kim and 47–40 to Bartzos. Kang beat Komori 44–40. The pros lost a few games straight up to the qualifiers as well: Sanchez, for instance, lost 40–37 to Vigurea and 40–39 to Bartzos; Soo Kim beat Sang Lee 40–36; Gilbert ran 14 and crushed Komori 50–24 in only twenty-five innings. While the handicap took something away from the significance of the games, it did result in many cliff-hangers and an exciting tournament to watch.

In the last round, all Blomdahl had to do was score 26 points against Sang Lee to finish first. He didn't do it. Sang Lee went out in sixteen innings to tie an American record for best game, set in 1926 by Otto Reiselt of Philadelphia. Blomdahl's failure left the door open for Komori, who had only to beat an eighteen-year-old kid to win the first prize of $3,500. But the Japanese champion, rated seventh in the world, watched helplessly as Sanchez, aided by two scratches, rained points and took the game 50–26 in twenty-seven innings. The Komori loss dropped him to fourth place and left Blomdahl alone in first with a record of 9–3. The Swedish champion is a thin, square-shouldered man who stalks the table more like a bird of prey than an assassin. When he gets a bad hit or a bad break, he walks with quick steps to the player's chair and drops into it with disgust. An intelligent and even eloquent man who speaks fluent English, he showed in this tournament why he has the best record in the game since 1986. His grand average was 1.629. Without giving up 10 points to the qualifiers, he would have finished 11–1. "It's hard for anyone to help me with my game," he told Mike Shamos almost wistfully during an interview, for he knows there is room for further improvement. "Playing a good game of billiards is like painting a picture, and one artist can't tell another what colors to use."

One surprise was many-time U.S. Champion Al Gilbert, whose play suggested that he left the pro ranks a bit too soon. After compiling a 1–4 mark, he won seven in a row to finish at 8–4, good for third-place money. He averaged 1.174 and took high-run honors with 14.

THE SECOND S. L. BILLIARDS TOURNAMENT

Sang Lee's second world open tournament was another awesome exhibition of cuemanship. The international carom stars performed at their customary stratospheric level.

Three of the highest-rated three-cushion players in the world were on hand: Sang Lee, ranked second; Dick Jaspers of the Netherlands, ranked fourth; and Frederic Caudron of Belgium, ranked seventh. They all lived up to their reputations by taking the top three prizes, though they didn't have an easy time of it. Caudron excelled beyond his ranking and finished in first, ahead of the higher-ranked Sang Lee and Jaspers.

Also particularly impressive were the South Koreans. The field featured a dozen players who were either from that small nation or who were of Korean ancestry; seven of them made the ten-man finals, including New Yorkers Byung Soo Kim and Michael Kang.

In the field were the current champions of Peru, Uruguay, and South Korea. George Ashby, former American Champion, played well, but narrowly missed making the finals.

The entrants were divided into four preliminary flights of eight for round-robin play, with the top two from each flight advancing to join seeded players Sang Lee and Jaspers in a ten-man round-robin final.

It was impossible to predict who would make the finals, as the flights were well-balanced in strength and the games were short—35 points. The winner of Flight A was an impressive young Korean named Yong Hee Lee, who was undefeated and averages 1.107. Taking second was Belgium's Peter De Backer, the current European 71.2 balkline champion.

Caudron, who is world champion 71.2 balkline, was heavily favored in Flight B, but he was upset in his first game by Chicago's Adrian Viguera, 35–34, in thirty innings, and in his third game by Korea's Ji Soo An, which put him close to elimination. Ji Soo An went on to win the flight, losing one game and averaging .810. Caudron and Viguera tied for second with two losses each, with the nod going to Caudron on the basis of his average, 1.117.

Kang was impressive in Flight C, finishing with a record of 6–1 and an average of .969. At one point he ran a 10 and an 11 back-to-back. He pushed Ashby into third place by beating the former U.S. champion 35–20 in twenty-six innings. Also advancing was two-time Korean champion Hyo Sub Kim, who averaged 1.250.

Flight D was a four-way battle among Korea's Soon Min Hong; a tall twenty-two-year-old from Uruguay named E. Piedrabuena; Belgian D. Van Brabant; and New York's Byung Soo Kim. Soo Kim and Hong prevailed.

When the finals began, the spectators were looking forward to some great billiards as the qualifiers tangled with the two top seeds, and they weren't disappointed. To give every finalist a chance at winning, Lee and Jaspers spotted everybody 10 points on 50. Jaspers, a slender, personable twenty-seven-year-old who speaks perfect English, started with a thirty-three-inning win over Yong Hee Lee, 50–25, while Sang Lee smashed Kang 50–11 in twenty innings. Jaspers topped that a few rounds later by beating Kang 50–19 in only nineteen innings.

The high runs piled up, too. Jaspers had an 11; Sang Lee had two 12s; and Soon Min Hong, a sparkling 14.

In a crucial eighth-round match, Sang Lee handed Caudron his first loss, 50–33 in twenty-nine.

Going into the ninth and final round, Caudron and Sang Lee were both 7–1 while Jaspers was 6–2. Sang Lee could win the tournament by beating Jaspers in the long-awaited face-off between the two top seeds, because even if Caudron beat Kang, Sang Lee's average, which was a lofty 1.772, would be higher than Caudron's which stood at 1.283. If Sang Lee lost to Jaspers, however, then a victory over Kang would give Caudron the title. The only way Jaspers could win the tournament was with a Caudron loss coupled with a lopsided win over Sang Lee that would lift his 1.628 average above Sang Lee's.

The Sang Lee–Jaspers match was sensational. About 150 spectators crowded around the table, with another 50 watching in the bar area on a closed-circuit television hookup from the Accu-Stats video cameras. Jaspers built up an early lead and then thrilled the onlookers with a brilliant run of 15, missing the 16th on a last-instant kiss-out. He won the game 50–30 in twenty innings. Only a late run of 6 by Sang Lee kept his overall grand average, 1.749, above the 1.701 scored by Jaspers.

The game was anticlimactic as far as determining the tournament winner was concerned; thirty minutes before it ended, Caudron took first place by winning his game with Kang. The well-trained, disciplined young Belgian won the title with a grand average of 1.303. Sang Lee and Jaspers were next in line, with records of 7–2.

(Caudron has continued to improve as a three-cushion player since his victory in New York in 1993. In 1995 he won a tournament in Belgium, finishing ahead of Raymond Ceulemans; had a high run of 23; and was elected Belgium's player of the year.)

THE THIRD S. L. BILLIARDS TOURNAMENT

You had to be there to believe it, and even if you were, you might wonder if you were hallucinating. World records were broken and a rising star from Turkey (Turkey?) put on a trick-shot show that had hard-boiled New Yorkers rolling their eyes and shaking their heads in disbelief. It was like being at the circus and wondering which of the three rings to watch—here it was which of the five Verhoeven tables.

The game was three-cushion billiards, and the event was the third annual world open sponsored by S. L. Billiards, world champion Sang Lee's room in Elmhurst, New York, in the Borough of Queens. Thirty-three sharpshooters from across the country and around the world plunked down $500 for a chance to play four seeded players: Lee; four-time world champion Torbjörn Blomdahl of Sweden; Italy's Marco Zanetti, ranked third in the world; and Dick Jaspers of the Netherlands, ranked fifth.

Other players with world rankings were Louis Havermans (twenty-fifth) and Henk Habraken (eighteenth), both of the Netherlands; Tony Carlsen (eighth) of Denmark; and a remarkable billiard prodigy from Turkey named Semih Sayginer, who in two short years has risen from obscurity to become the seventh-ranked player in the world.

Among the major highlights: Sang Lee ran 15 *and* 14 in the same game against Havermans; Sayginer made 50 points in only fourteen innings against Sang Lee, the fastest game ever played in the United States (the old record was sixteen innings, set in 1926 by Otto Reiselt, and tied in 1992 by Sang Lee); Blomdahl set a new world record by beating Sang Lee 60–26 in a blistering eighteen innings; the eight players in the finals averaged a combined 1.370.

The billiard gods were really smiling. Acccu-Stats Video had special lights and cameras set up over one table, and in a wonderful stroke of good fortune, most of the good stuff took place on that table, including the record-breaking games by Sayginer and Blomdahl, the long runs by Sang Lee, and a stunning Sayginer trick-shot show. (For tapes, call 800-828-0397.)

Sayginer, the thirty-year-old Turk, is a dynamic player with prodigious talent and a flair for the dramatic. If he has a weakness, it is occasional impatience and perhaps too great a fondness for shots he knows will electrify the grandstand. He's an exotic figure, with jet black hair pulled into a short ponytail, a narrow band of beard that rings his face, and hypnotic brown eyes. It's easy to imagine him in flowing robes waving a scimitar instead of a cue. He'll win the world title one of these years. Mark my words.

The format called for the four seeded players to play to 60 points against the four players who emerged from the four eight-man preliminary flights: Sayginer, Havermans, Carlsen, and New York's Chris Bartzos—each of whom received a 10-point spot against the seeded stars.

The spot cost Blomdahl a game in the first round of the finals when he lost to Havermans, 50–52. He came back, however, to edge Sayginer, 60–49; both players were in the one-hole for several innings. After crushing Sang Lee, 50–32, in the fourth round, Sayginer was upset in the fifth by Zanetti, 60–43. Zanetti followed with an upset of Sang Lee, but missed his chance to finish third by losing to Chris Bartzos at the end.

If Sang Lee, with two losses, could beat Blomdahl in the last game, both players would finish at 5–2. Sayginer, with a final-round win over Carlsen, would also be at 5–2 and probably would win the tournament on the tiebreaker, which was grand average.

As it turned out, Blomdahl uncorked his eighteen-inning game against Sang Lee to finish at 6–1. Sayginer also won, finishing alone at 5–2. Sang Lee dropped to 4–3. If the young Turk had scored just one more point in his second-round loss to the Swede, he would have won the tournament. His grand average of 1.668 was second only to the winner's 1.682, and better than Sang Lee's 1.610. Among the eight finalists, only Bartzos, a .920, failed to average better than 1.000.

How would you like to be Dick Jaspers? He averaged 1.296 and finished last! Or how about Sang Lee? He averaged 1.373 in his three losses, while his opponents averaged 2.626. Here's another interesting statistic: Sang Lee and Sayginer combined for 82 points in their fourteen-inning game, which means they scored 5.857 points per inning! In the Blomdahl–Sang Lee game, 4.778 points were scored each inning. Both are world records.

A "consolation" round-robin was played along with the main event among the second- and third-place finishers from the preliminary flights. Popular Mike Kang of New York, with a record of 5–2 and an average of 1.013, finished first. Kurt Ceulemans, son of Raymond, finished second.

POSTSCRIPT: A fourth S. L. Open was held in late June of 1996, too late for coverage in this book. The highlights: Dick Jaspers nipped Sang Lee in a thrilling finale to take the title, dropping Sang Lee to third behind Blomdahl. Semih Sayginer was fourth; Raymond Ceulemans, fifth. Ceulemans, who averaged 1.670, lost three games by a total of 5 points. Two world records were set by Blomdahl, both of which were captured on videotape: 60 points in seventeen innings and 60 points in fifteen innings. Both Blomdahl and Ceulemans had runs of 17.

Sang Lee's Amazing World Cup Triumph

IN 1994, SANG CHUN LEE, the genial owner of S. L. Billiards in New York City, scaled an almost impossibly steep mountain. He won the world championship of three-cushion billiards, bringing the crown to the United States for the first time in forty-one years.

The Korean-born Lee dominates three-cushion in his adopted country as no one has since the days of Willie Hoppe and Welker Cochran. The creativity, accuracy, and control that characterize Lee's game made it almost inevitable that he would one day capture the title, but nobody, not even Lee himself, thought it would be so soon.

Lee's prospects were dim at the start of the sixth and final World Cup tournament, which was staged in Ghent, Belgium. Both former world champion Raymond Ceulemans of Belgium and reigning champion Torbjörn Blomdahl of Sweden were ahead of him in ranking points. To win the title, Lee not only had to win the tournament, Blomdahl had to be eliminated in his first match.

Can you believe it? That's exactly what happened.

When play began in Ghent on January 6, 1994, Blomdahl had accumulated 210 ranking points by winning three of the first five tournaments and finishing third once. (Sixty points are awarded for first, 45 for second, 30 for third, and so on down to 12 points for eighth place.) In second place with 150 points was Ceulemans, who had finished first once and second twice. Sang Lee had 130 points based on a win, a third, a fourth, and a sixth. No other player was close enough to have a shot at the crown.

What gave Sang Lee an outside chance at overtaking the leader was that the ranking points were increased by 50 percent for the final event; the winner would get 90 points instead of 60. If Blomdahl reached the round of eight by winning his first game, he would be beyond Sang Lee's reach.

The luck of the draw worked against Blomdahl; he was paired against his Dutch League teammate, the dangerous Raimond Burgman, ranked twelfth in the world. Burgman broke the tournament open by scoring his first career win over the top-ranked Swede. Matches consisted of 15-point sets, race-to-three. Blomdahl trailed 9–1 in the first set after four innings, then ran 14 and out. Burgman won the second 15–14 by running 5 and out. The third set was 15–7 Burgman; the fourth, 15–10 Blomdahl. The decider went to Burgman, 15–10. For the five sets, Burgman averaged 1.422, and Blomdahl, 1.386. If Blomdahl had scored just one more point in the second set, he would remain world champion; that's a measure of just how miraculous Sang Lee's eventual victory was.

With Blomdahl gone, attention turned to Ceulemans and Sang Lee. In his first match, Ceulemans dispatched nineteen-year-old Daniel Sanchez of Spain, 3–1, averaging 1.551 to the teenager's 1.296, while Sang Lee scored a 3–1 win over tough Dutchman Arie Weijenburg, who is ranked thirteenth in the world.

Sang Lee's hopes for the crown, flickering when the tournament began, burned more brightly when Ceulemans was eliminated in the quarterfinals by countryman Frederic Caudron, 3–1, who averaged 1.461 to the Belgian's 1.026.

Sang Lee took care of his quarterfinal opponent, Holland's Henk Habraken, 3–1. His heart must have been beating fast then, for he was two victories away from realizing a lifelong dream.

In one semifinal bracket, Caudron eliminated Italy's Marco Zanetti, 3–2, averaging a lofty 1.550 to Zanetti's 1.461. Sang Lee was up against the superb Japanese master Junichi Komori and won by scores of 15–11, 15–12, 10–15, and 15–11.

So the stage was set: Caudron of Belgium versus Sang Lee of the United States. A win by Caudron would leave Sang Lee with 197 ranking points and Blomdahl would win his fourth World Cup.

While the thirty-nine-year-old Sang Lee would normally be favored over the twenty-seven-year-old Caudron on the basis of his higher world ranking and higher scoring average for the season, the outcome was hard to predict. Sang Lee has reached the finals by averaging only 1.100, 25 percent below his usual standard, while Caudron, ranked seventh in the world, was hot, coming into the final match with a tournament average of 1.400.

With Blomdahl, a packed house, and a cluster of European sports journalists watching every shot, Sang Lee took the first set, 15–4. Caudron came back to win the second, 15–6. It was Sang Lee in the third, 15–6. Fifteen more points for Lee and there would be a new world champion. It was the American all the way, 15–8. In that final match, Sang Lee needed only thirty-five innings to make his 51 points, an average of 1.457. By his victory he became the toast of the billiard community around the world. Photographs of Sang Lee crying during the awards ceremony appeared in scores of European newspapers.

When he arrived back in the United States on January 17, he went to his S. L. Billiards in Queens and found himself the center of a celebration that went on for hours.

Even the *New York Times* was impressed, running a forty-column-inch feature on January 19. "When the gentle Korean-American walked triumphantly through the door," wrote David Firestone, "the parlor's regulars broke into applause, cheers, and even a few tears. . . . He bore with him an engraved silver trophy, $40,000 in prize money, and a thick pile of adulatory clippings from most of the major European newspapers, which had covered every moment of the championship and wrote of him as if he were slightly superhuman. But his trophy and his singular talent seemed lost amid the indifference of his adopted country, for few Americans have even heard of his sport, let alone picked up a cue and challenged its fearsome geometry."

It's the indifference that can now be challenged. You can hardly blame the media in the U.S. for losing interest, over the years, in a game in which the American champion was regularly drubbed by foreigners. It was different forty years ago and more, when it was the Americans, particularly Hoppe and Cochran, who were doing the drubbing. Then the game was news.

Hoppe won the last of his many world titles in 1952. The next year, Ray "St. Paul" Kilgore was the upset winner, edging out the favorite, Jay Bozeman. The last American to hold the world three-cushion title was Harold Worst, who went to Argentina in 1954 and prevailed over a field that included Juan and Ezequiel Navarra, Cochran, and Masako Katsura.

In Sang Lee, the U.S. has a superb champion. At the table he is an elegant figure: always well-dressed and dignified, a perfect gentleman, and a picture of concentration and dedication. His stance is more upright than most billiard players', and his wrist is noticeably loose and free. He relies entirely on instinct and judgment rather than numerical systems; in fact, he argues against the use of systems because they interfere with the development of judgment and feel. Sometimes he takes only a few warm-up strokes before pulling the trigger, sometimes as many as twenty or thirty, but despite his generally deliberate style, his games don't last long because he doesn't need many innings to get out. In winning the last seven U.S. championships, his averages ranged from 1.464 to 1.834. Results like that aren't solely the result of natural talent, though he has that in abundance. Sang Lee works extremely hard at improving his game, often playing eight to ten hours a day.

He's a gem away from the table, too, friendly, unassuming, always willing to discuss shots with other players regardless of their ability, even though he is still not completely fluent in English. His love of the game and his generous nature show clearly in the way he runs his room. Balls are cleaned and the table vacuumed after each game, and most of the tables are the best money can buy—Verhoevens from Belgium.

It's amazing how much he has achieved as a player, as a room owner, and as a positive force since arriving in the United States from South Korea in 1987, when he knew few people and was unable to speak the language. What he will be able to achieve now that he has a world championship under his belt is impossible to say, but it's bound to be good.

Congratulations, Sang Lee! Good luck, good health, and long life! And thanks for settling in the United States instead of Europe; they already have enough good players.

The Man Who Would Be Fats

"MINNESOTA FATS" didn't die on January 18, 1996, as was widely reported. Rudolph Wanderone died, a second-rate pool player and a first-rate media manipulator. Wanderone achieved something unprecedented in the history of literature: he made a career out of impersonating a fictional character. The real Minnesota Fats, the one who never existed, lives on in two novels by Walter Tevis and the movies based on them.

First came the 1959 novel *The Hustler,* then two years later the gritty gem of a movie starring Paul Newman and Jackie Gleason. When the movie was released, Wanderone was an obscure pool hustler known as New York Fats, or Brooklyn Fats, or just plain Fats. He very likely had never been in Minnesota, a state with little to offer a street-smart gambling man trying to scratch out a living at pool and cards. His claim that the book and movie were based on his life was a masterstroke of self-promotion; it catapulted him into the bright lights and out of the sleazy shadowland where he had spent his adult life. That his claims of being the greatest player in the universe were insupportable and easily disproved didn't matter. The public got a kick out of his outlandishness and his sense of humor, and that's what counted. Was he kidding? Was he serious?

His audacity and wild boasts amazed and amused his pool-hall cronies, for they knew he was never a top player. They had to give him credit, though, for seizing an opportunity and giving the public what it wanted. He was a great interview and always provided reporters with laugh lines.

One person who was not amused was Walter Tevis, who protesed until his death in 1984 that Minnesota Fats was imaginary. The spectacle of the bizarre Wanderone taking over his invention was a constant irritation to him, and he killed off the character quickly in his follow-up novel *The Color of Money*. Minnesota Fats didn't appear at all in the movie version of that book. In an introduction to the paperback edition of *The Hustler,* Tevis dismissed the portly pretender's claims. He wrote: "I once saw a fat pool player with a facial tic. I once saw another pool player who was physically graceful. Both were minor hustlers, as far as I could tell. Both seemed loud and vain, unlike my fat pool player. After *The Hustler* was published, one of them claimed to 'be' Minnesota Fats. That is ridiculous. I *made up* Minnesota Fats—name and all—as surely as Disney made up Donald Duck."

The media paid no attention.

Also among the unamused was Willie Mosconi, one of the greatest players of all time and holder of fifteen world titles. When Wanderone claimed that he had cleaned Mosconi's clock many times, Mosconi hit the ceiling. So mad was he that he demanded an opportunity to put the poseur in his place. (Not his exact words.) The champion and the challenger traded insults for months before matching up in 1978 on ABC's *Wide World of Sports* for a showdown hosted by Howard Cosell. It was no contest. Mosconi mopped the floor with Wanderone in nine-ball, eight-ball, and rotation. The next day it was the wisecracking Fats that the public remembered, not the unsmiling Mosconi.

The breathtaking scope of Wanderone's greatest hustle—convincing most of America that he "was" Minnesota Fats—can be appreciated by noting the profound gulf between the man and the figment. Tevis's character was soft-spoken, elegant, sophisticated, a meticulous dresser, neatly groomed, and gracious in defeat; he was a man who retired (in *The Color of Money*) to the Florida Keys to sip Perrier and photograph roseate spoonbills. Does anything in that sentence make you think of Rudolph Wanderone? "In no other sport," pro player Dan DiLiberto is quoted as saying in *Billiards Digest* in 1991, "could a man fool the public like that. But pool has a public that knows nothing, plus a media that knows nothing. He couldn't play; he *wouldn't* play anybody good. [We] used to stand around helpless with laughter when he told his stories about winning millions in India or in the Depression or wherever or whenever."

Fats was remembered by Bill Lyon of the *Philadelphia Inquirer* in a January 21, 1996 column that was widely reprinted. "He had Joe Montana's touch," Lyon wrote, embroidering the myth when Fats was no longer around to do it for himself. "He could make a pool stick sing like a Stradivarius. . . . He could make the ball dance like Magic Johnson. . . ." Who needs a press agent when there are so many volunteers?

For sparking two booms in the game with his books, Walter Tevis was inducted into the Hall of Fame in 1991 by the Billiard Congress of America. Eleanora Tevis, his widow, accepted the award for him. In her acceptance speech at the BCA's annual convention, she repeated Walter's denial that Minnesota Fats was based on an actual person. If anyone, she said, the character represented the author's father, who had never acknowledged his son's success as a writer. He made the character fat "to give substantiality to a very insubstantial man." In the novel, "when Fats turns to Eddie after their final game and says, 'I'm quitting, Fast Eddie. I can't beat you,' that was Walter's way of forcing his father to acknowledge not only that he existed, but that he was a better man than him." Why "Minnesota" Fats? "Walter liked to write against the grain, and as he said, the land of sky blue waters is not where you'd expect to find a great pool player."

Mrs. Tevis reminded her listeners that her husband had written twenty-nine short stories and six novels, and whenever the story is about a young contender and an older established pro, "that pro is almost invariably a fat man."

Again, the media paid no attention.

The money and fame that came to Wanderone brought a host of pool players forward claiming to be models for Fast Eddie Felson, the character portrayed by Paul Newman in both *The Hustler* and *The Color of Money*. In my thirty years of writing about the game, I've heard of at least half a dozen, some of them with wildly inappropriate histories and ages. When I lived in the San Francisco Bay Area, I remember seeing a newspaper obituary datelined San Jose, California: "Edward 'Fast Eddie' Pelky, the famed pool shark portrayed by Paul Newman in *The Hustler,* is dead." The writer deplored the fact that Pelky had never received a single cent in royalties. Quoting Eleanora Tevis again: "Fast Eddie probably had something of all the ambitious young pool players that Walter had ever seen, but if Fast Eddie was based on any one person, it was Walter himself. Not as a pool player—Walter was good but not great—but as a young writer who could write like a streak, who wrote the first half of his novel, *The Hustler,* in a long weekend; a young writer [pitting himself] against older, established writers and testing himself against the novel form itself."

Wanderone in his playing prime, before the book and movie, was a fairly effective hustler, especially in games like bank pool and one-pocket and even three-cushion billiards, which depend as much on strategy and clever defensive plays as on shot-making skill. He hated Mosconi's best game, straight pool, which calls for precision, delicacy, and concentration. "Straight pool," Wanderone said in his usual style, "is a *cancer.*"

His hustling technique was to never stop talking, driving his opponents crazy with an endless string of baloney, making them so mad they couldn't shoot straight. He liked to challenge better players when they were exhausted from all-night marathons. He infuriated them, goaded them until they gave him unfair handicaps. He knew how to make a match and he knew when to quit. Against top players in a level game with no talking allowed, he had little chance, and he was smart enough to avoid such contests.

The late Danny McGoorty, a close observer of the pool-hall subculture, said that "there were always at least twenty people in the country who would have been glad to swim a river of shit to play Fats for money. Fats won a lot of games in his life, but it was mainly because of the heavy hustle he used. He was afraid to rely on his game alone; he had to constantly irritate the other guy."

Despite the obvious superiority of Mosconi as a player, it was Fats who was given his own television show—*Celebrity Billiards with Minnesota Fats*—matching his mouth and his cue against the likes of Zsa Zsa Gabor, Milton Berle, and Nanette Fabray. By then he was a kind of urban myth, immune to analysis or criticism. Once you achieve celebrity status in America, criticism only adds to your fame. "Even playing Zsa Zsa," McGoorty said, "he wouldn't let her shoot in peace, kept bothering her and distracting her. If a man is afraid to play fair with Zsa Zsa, how do you think he would have done against real players like Wimpy Lassiter, Washington Rags, or Big-Nose Roberts?"

I included McGoorty's remarks in my 1972 book *McGoorty: The Story of a Billiard Bum*. It was the first time anyone had called Fats's bluff in print. A couple of years later I was in the bleachers at a pool tournament in Sacramento, California. Fats had been hired to entertain the crowd with his patented mixture of easy trick shots, tall tales, and challenge matches with spectators. He was very funny that night. He deliberately threw games of eight-ball to youngsters from the crowd, then handed them pins that said: I BEAT MINNESOTA FATS. Somebody shouted a question: "How good was Danny McGoorty?" Fats answered: "He couldn't beat Mickey Mouse, yet some idiot wrote a book about him."

Wanderone's mouth was indeed a formidable weapon, his cue no more frightening than a sprig of mistletoe. He ridiculed pool champions who played in tournaments for trophies. "If I wanted a tin cup," he often said in his W. C. Fields drawl, "I'd go to a store and buy one." Try for a first prize of, say, five thousand dollars? "The way I eat, five grand wouldn't even keep me in radishes." Think of a great champion in any form of the game, from any country or era, and ask Fats if he knew him. His Lardship (one of the many sobriquets the press dreamed up for him) would likely answer: "Know him? I beat him out of every nickel he ever had." He claimed he once parachuted into Arabia to fleece a sheikh.

One of his funniest bits was describing competitive eating contests. His Heaviness said he could out-eat anybody and often won big bucks proving it. One spiel involved a challenger named (what else?) Tiny, a giant of a man who had to be brought to the restaurant on a flatbed truck. While waiting for the contest to begin, Wanderone warmed up by eating a leg of lamb. Tiny was so big his backers "couldn't get him into the joint until they smeared chicken fat on the door." Details like that kept his fans in hysterics.

Eating big was something he started as a infant. In 1996, he told writer Tom Fox that when he was two years old his mother and three sisters "used to plop me on a bed with a jillion satin pillows and spray me with exotic perfumes and lilac water and then they would shoot me the grapes."

Give Rudolph Wanderone high marks as a comedian, as a talker ("I won two world speaking titles in Canada alone . . ."), as a sideshow, as a generator of publicity. When he wasn't in his bragging mode, he was often charming, even sweet. I found his policy of losing to children at his exhibitions especially endearing. Even his nemesis Mosconi learned to think of

Howlers from the Fat Man

- "I outdrew the Pope in Rome and that ain't even good pool country."
- (On the Carter-Ford debates) "I could beat the two of them with a rope tied around my tongue."
- "When I was eight years old, I was a grown man, playin' cards or shootin' pool or chasin' broads."
- "I fought in two revolutions, the British West Indies and Cuba. Just happened to be there. I shot outa the windows of the hotels."
- "I won the Man of the Year in Industry award even though I ain't worked a day in my life."
- "I've never lost and I've been hustling around saloons since I was two or three years old."
- "There's nobody left on earth who can beat me. *Apollo 14* tried to find somebody on the moon, but they couldn't."
- "Putting pool players in tuxedos is like putting whipped cream on a hot dog."
- "My zip code? It's unlisted."
- "My philosophy of life is that every day is Christmas."
- "I'm not human. Never was."

—With thanks to Ray Desell

him in an almost friendly way by realizing that he was primarily an entertainer, not a real player to be taken seriously. How can you continue disliking a man who revives your career and makes you a lot of money on television?

Toward the end, Fats seemed irretrievably lost in the fanciful world he had created for himself, a victim of his own hyperbole. He was like a sketch comic who had lost the ability to step out of character when the sketch was over.

He was a hustler and never held a conventional job. He loved animals and collected strays. He was a soft touch for children and moochers. Writer George Fels quotes Wanderone as saying that he knew from an early age what he wanted to do in life: nothing. "And that's all I've ever done. Done it better than any man living."

It's probably a blessing that Walter Tevis preceded him in death. The Associated Press and CNN obituaries of Wanderone said that he achieved world fame when he was portrayed by Jackie Gleason in *The Hustler*. If Tevis had lived to see that, it would have killed him.

The Books of the Game

Photo for poster announcing publication of the game's biggest and most beautiful book, *The Billiard Encyclopedia* by Victor Stein and Paul Rubino.

(Photograph by Francis M. Esposito, reprinted courtesy of
Victor Stein and *The Billiard Encyclopedia*)

The Billiard Encyclopedia
An Illustrated History of the Sport

by Victor Stein and Paul Rubino

Second edition, 1996, 558 pages, $139.95 plus $7.50 mailing. Published by Blue Book Publications, Inc., Minneapolis, MN.

WHAT A STUNNING, SUMPTUOUS, and unbelievable book this is! Stunning because of its size—the enlarged second edition has 558 large-format pages (9 1/2 x 13 inches), weighs in at nine pounds, and contains a staggering total of 800 illustrations. Sumptuous because of the quality of the paper, binding, and layout, the high-resolution photos, the hang–the–expense use of color. Unbelievable because it was produced by just two men without grants from the government, trade associations, or manufacturers; two men who had never written anything for publication before and who had no training in publishing or historical research.

When they started gathering information in 1988, I was skeptical that two people working alone could produce the monumental book on the history and equipment of the game that they had in mind. What I failed to consider was the power of obsession. "The book" took over the lives of New Yorkers Paul Rubino and Victor Stein for six long years. The deeper they got into the subject, the deeper they were drawn, and before they knew it, they were working sixteen hours a day pursuing a goal that seemed to recede as they approached it.

Their early interest was centered on cues and cuemakers (Rubino has been making cues for fourteen years), but so much interesting artwork and history came to light that they gradually expanded the scope of their research. Some two hundred pages, nevertheless, are devoted to cues and

cuemakers. A major effort was made to trace billiards to its ultimate begin-
nings, which led them to chase stick–and–ball games all the way back to
ancient Greece and even to ancient Egypt. Their questioning, in fact, led a
leading Egyptologist, Dr. Robert Steven Bianchi, to take a new look at the
significance of ball games and ball ceremonies in those distant times,
and Bianchi contributes a fascinating essay on the subject to *The Billiard
Encyclopedia.*

The various ground games played with sticks and balls resemble modern billiards in some ways, but it was not until the late 1400s that tables
were used. Ground billiards can be said to be the precursor not only to the
game as we know it, but also to field hockey, ice hockey, croquet, golf, tennis, and baseball. The sixty pages the authors devote to early history—with
dozens of photos of rock carvings, tapestries, paintings, and artifacts—is
historical spadework of a high order. Professional historians should be asking themselves why it took two amateurs to do it. Of course, the authors
aren't ordinary amateurs. They are lovers of the game who threw their
hearts and souls—and money—into creating a book that would reflect the
glory of the game itself. At the end of five years they had accumulated thirty thousand photographs, including eight thousand color slides. Most they
took themselves, some were borrowed from collectors and museums, some
were taken at their direction by professional photographers at rates of up
to $1,500 a day.

Speaking of expenses, the cost of initially producing 2,500 copies of
the book, not counting five years of lost wages, was in the neighborhood
of half a million dollars. Making plates and separations for a color photograph, for example, costs around $190 . . . *and there are 520 of them.* Printing
a top-quality art book such as this is extremely costly, even if you try to
cut corners by having the printing done in Asia. No corners were cut in
this case; the authors turned to the best art-book printer in the country,
the Steinhour Press in Lunenburg, Vermont.

Leafing through this magnificent tome is like participating in a ten-
course banquet, each one a pleasure to the eye and mind. The ten courses
are The Evolution of Ancient Bat-and-Ball Games; Development of the
Pastime and Sport; The European Story; The Norman Clare Museum at
Thurston's; Billiards in America; Tables, Cloth, and Balls; Cue Construc-
tion; Legendary Cuemakers; Current Cuemakers; and Collecting.

I was particularly struck by the hundreds of superb photos of cues and
tables; the artistry and craftsmanship are inspiring. If you aren't particularly interested in cues and tables, you will be when you see what can be
accomplished by the great masters.

This is not a book about the champions of snooker, billiards, and pool, though many old-timers are pictured, nor is there much on the state of the game today. Neither is it a book of instruction. The second edition (1996) includes an index, a painful omission in the first edition (1994).

What it is, is a celebration in grand style of one of the world's oldest and most popular games, its art, its implements, and its colorful history. Stein and Rubino have given us a gift that will never be matched. Beside it, every other book on the game seems puny, including my own.

Yes, $139.95 is a lot to pay for a book. In this case, it's a bargain.

For more information, contact Blue Book Publications, Inc., 8009 34th Ave. S., #1391, Minneapolis, MN 55425, or phone 800-877-4867.

"We are happy to see that the development of the game of games— Noble Billiards!—in this country is such as to rejoice the heart of everyone who knows the value of the tasteful, thought-requiring amusements in forming the character of a people."

—Michael Phelan and Claudius Berger
The Illustrated Hand-Book of Billiards, 1874

The Science of
Pocket Billiards

by Jack H. Koehler

262 pages, $26.95 (hardcover), $22.95 (paperback), 8 1/2 x 11 inches, 1989. Sportology Publications, 25832 Evergreen Road, Laguna Hills, CA 92653.

JACK KOEHLER, A RETIRED GOVERNMENT HYDROLOGIST and an amateur pool player from Laguna Hills, California, spent five years of research on his home table before writing this treatise on the science of pool, and the results are impressive.

The book has 262 pages, 33 photographs, and 227 drawings and covers all the major phases of the game, including especially bank shots, rail shots, combinations, oversized bar-table cueballs, and systems. Much interesting material is presented on friction, throw, cueball deflection resulting from sidespin and ball collisions, margin of error for various types of shots, practice methods, and more.

Koehler is not a top player and is not well-known even to players in Southern California, much less to other scientists and engineers who write about the game, but he has a scientific background and knows the physics of pool. To check his intuition about what happens on certain kinds of shots, he constructed various types of ramps and jigs that enabled him to run thousands of controlled trials. With the data generated, a home computer was used whenever possible to check and to predict results. He spent six months, for example, running balls down ramps before writing his chapter on rail shots.

Not only did Koehler do all the research and writing, he also took the photographs and made the diagrams. No awards for graphics, layout, or design are deserved, but the drawings are clear and the substance is there along with plenty of supporting data. The text is not typeset, but rather consists of photocopied double-spaced typing.

Purchasers get a large tome full of information that has never been written about at such length.

While there are tips for beginners, the book would be too much, in my opinion, for players who aren't already serious students. You have to be willing to pay close attention to a fairly dry text and be willing to study charts, graphs, and tables full of lines, arrows, and measured angles. The author (and typist and artist and researcher) offers some ingenious practice methods, especially for the break shot, that would be of great help to players at any level.

My quibbles on technical matters are minor. I don't agree that a flexible shaft reduces cueball deflection and I think Koehler's analysis there is faulty. And while moving the body forward on the break shot can increase cueball speed slightly if the timing is right, the loss of accuracy makes such advice arguable.

The Science of Pocket Billiards is a fine and useful piece of work, especially considering that it was written by a man working without interaction with top players or other researchers. Nothing like it is available in any language. While it could have been improved by peer review, it is a welcome addition to the literature of the game and belongs on your shelf.

Other
Recent Books
Worth Noting

TWENTY YEARS AGO, students had a hard time finding good books on pool or three-cushion. There were aging classics like *Willie Mosconi on Pocket Billiards* (1948, 142 pages) and *Billiards As It Should Be Played* (1941, 78 pages), excellent works in their way, but devoted mainly to styles of play that had fallen out of favor. I wasn't crazy about *The Game of Billiards* (1964, 166 pages) by Clive Cottingham or *How to Win at Pocket Billiards* (1970, 256 pages), both written by amateur players, but they weren't bad and I was grateful for them. It was what I perceived as weaknesses in those four books—in style, scope, depth, layout, and illustrations—that led me to devote a year of my life to writing *Byrne's Standard Book of Pool and Billiards* (1978, 332 pages). In that book I gave capsule reviews of a dozen books (pages 329–333) that could be found by diligent searching in bookstores, secondhand stores, and billiard supply stores.

The literary picture is far different now. Publishers have discovered the billiard market, and books of instruction, reference, and biography are popping up like spring flowers. The last half-a-dozen years or so have been especially fruitful, as the following pages attest.

STEVE MIZERAK'S COMPLETE BOOK OF POOL
by Mike Panozzo and Steve Mizerak

(softcover, 196 pages, $11.95), Contemporary Books, Chicago, 1990. Introductory instruction with a look at history, game rules, cue care;

256

lots of unusual photographs from the archives of *Billiard Digest* magazine, of which Panozzo is the editor.

POOL
by Mike Shamos

(softcover, 130 pages, $12.95), Friedman/Fairfax Co., New York, 1991. A breezy overview in large format and on glossy paper by the game's foremost historian and collector. There are 120 photos, most in full color, selected from the fifteen thousand images in the Billiard Archive, Pittsburgh, Pennsylvania, Mike Shamos, Curator.

THE ILLUSTRATED ENCYCLOPEDIA OF BILLIARDS
by Mike Shamos

(hardcover, 310 pages, $30.00), Lyons & Burford, New York, 1993. A much-needed reference with two thousand alphabetized entries, many with photos and diagrams. An eight-page center section features historic billiard art in color.

WILLIE'S GAME
by Willie Mosconi and Stanley Cohen

(hardcover, 256 pages, $20.00), Macmillan Publishing Co., New York, 1993. An as-told-to autobiography recounting the life and triumphs of one of the game's greatest champions, who died shortly after the book appeared. Text alternates between Mosconi and Cohen, a freelance writer, teacher, and author of several baseball books. Eight pages of black-and-white photos, half from the files of Mosconi and half from pool historian Charlie Ursitti. (Note: Macmillan Publishing Co. is now part of Simon and Schuster.)

SECRETS OF THREE-CUSHION BILLIARDS
by Darrell Paul Martineau

(large-format softcover, 180 pages, $27.50), self-published, 5916 Bar Harbour Court, Elk Grove, California 95758, 1994. A detailed number system for three-cushion billiards worked out by a veteran tournament player after years of experimentation.

THE BILLIARD ATLAS VOL. ONE, 1991; VOL. TWO, 1993; VOL. THREE, 1996
by Walt Harris

(large-format softcover, 198 pages, $28.50 each), self-published, P.O. Box 321426, Cocoa Beach, Florida 32931. Three-cushion systems gathered from the world's top players by a true lover of the game.

THE PHYSICS OF POCKET BILLIARDS
by Wayland C. Marlow

(softcover, 292 pages, $32.45), self-published, 1794 Mokehana, Kihei, Maui, Hawaii 96753, 1994. The most complete and rigorous examination of the physics of the game since Gustave Coriolis's great work in 1835. Plenty of formulas and technical analysis, hard to follow without a math background.

POCKET BILLIARD SECRETS
by Hal Mix

(large-format softcover, 66 pages, $27.00), self-published, 517 Cedar Place, Philomath, Oregon 97370, 1994. A coach and teacher revered by the many professional players he has helped lays out his approach to the game.

WINNING ONE-POCKET (1992) AND SHOTS, MOVES, AND STRATEGIES IN ONE-POCKET (1995)
by Eddie Robin and others

(300 pages, $38.50 each), Billiard World Publishing, P.O. Box 12357, Las Vegas, Nevada 89112. Comprehensive manuals for serious students of an intriguing, chess-like game. Robin is a former U.S. three-cushion champion.

UPSCALE ONE-POCKET
by Jack Koehler

(softcover, 212 pages, $17.95), self-published, 25832 Evergreen Road, Laguna Hills, California 92653, 1995. Not as ambitious as the Robin titles, but a good place to start and full of useful insights and observations available nowhere else.

BUDDY HALL: RAGS TO RICHES
by W. W. Woody

(softcover, 358 pages, $30.00), Huckleberry Publishing, Lebanon, Tennessee, 1995. Biography of a top tournament player whose deliberate nine-ball style often approaches perfection. The small type is very hard to read, but the effort is rewarded by accounts of some memorable experiences.

PLAY YOUR BEST POOL
by Phil Capelle

(softcover, 442 pages, $29.95), self-published, Billiards Press, P.O. Box 400, Midway City, California 92655, 1995. A worthy addition to the instructional literature by a financial advisor who is also a pool instructor certified by the Billiard Congress of America. The book covers both the physical and psychological aspects of pool playing. Includes lengthy and helpful sections on position play and the tactics of eight-ball and nine-ball.

PLAYING OFF THE RAIL: A POOL HUSTLER'S JOURNEY
by David McCumber

(hardcover, 365 pages, $24.00), Random House, New York, 1995. A very well written book by a professional author who recounts his adventures with pro player Tony Annigoni as they travel the country looking for money games. The emphasis is on gambling and sleaze, but the style is evocative; a hard-to-put-down insider's look at the game's shadowy underside. For excerpts and discussion, see *Billiards Digest*, April 1996.

BYRNE'S BOOK OF GREAT POOL STORIES
edited by Robert Byrne

(softcover, 302 pages, $18.00), Harcourt Brace, San Diego, 1995. Thirty-one short stories on pool, billiards, and snooker, covering 150 years, by such legends as Leo Tolstoy, Alexander Pushkin, A. A. Milne, Stephen Leacock, John O'Hara, Wallace Stegner, Walter Tevis, and others, with brief introductions to each selection by the bashful and lovely author of the book you are holding.

Permissions and Acknowledgments

"How to Win Without Actually Cheating," by Stephen Potter. Excerpted from *Three-upmanship* by Stephen Potter. Copyright 1951, 1952 © 1962 by Stephen Potter. Copyright 1950, 1951 by Holt, Rinehart and Winston, Inc. Copyright © 1990 by Lady Heather James. Reprinted by permission of Henry Holt and Co., Inc.

"Watching Snooker on the Telly," by Oliver Pritchett. Originally appeared under the title "If only I could get a break" in the *Daily Telegraph* (London), April 22, 1987. © The Telegraph plc, London, 1987. Reprinted by permission.

"At Thurston's" by J. B. Priestley. From *Self-Selected Essays* by J. B. Priestley. Reprinted by permission of the Peters Fraser & Dunlop Group Ltd.

The pencil-sketch portraits were drawn by Cynthia Nelms-Byrne and are based in part on photographs from the following sources: Pat Fleming, 1995—photograph by Robert Byrne; Joe Davis, circa 1930—photographer unknown, courtesy of the Billiard Archive; Jay Bozeman, circa 1936—photographer unknown; Welker Cochran, 1952—photograph by Cal-Photos; Sang Lee, 1992—photograph by Joseph Ratke; "Minnesota Fats," circa 1982—photograph by Mike Panozzo.

Many of the selections in this book first appeared in *Billiards Digest*.